LOST LITERACIES

STUDIES IN COMICS AND CARTOONS
Jared Gardner, Charles Hatfield, and Rebecca Wanzo, Series Editors

LOST LITERACIES

Experiments in the Nineteenth-Century US Comic Strip

ALEX BERINGER

The Ohio State University Press

Columbus

Library of Congress Cataloging-in-Publication Data
Names: Beringer, Alex, author.
Title: Lost literacies : experiments in the nineteenth-century US comic strip / Alex Beringer.
Other titles: Studies in comics and cartoons.
Description: Columbus : The Ohio State University Press, 2024. | Series: Studies in comics and cartoons | Includes bibliographical references and index. | Summary: "The first full-length study of US comic strips from the period prior to the rise of Sunday newspaper comics. Introduces readers to artists and editors such as Frank Bellew and T. W. Strong, who experimented with the storytelling possibilities of the sequential comic strip"—Provided by publisher.
Identifiers: LCCN 2023040763 | ISBN 9780814215395 (hardback) | ISBN 0814215394 (hardback) | ISBN 9780814283257 (ebook) | ISBN 081428325X (ebook)
Subjects: LCSH: Comic books, strips, etc.—United States—History—19th century. | LCGFT: Comics criticism.
Classification: LCC PN6725 .B44 2024 | DDC 741.5/973—dc23/eng/20231011
LC record available at https://lccn.loc.gov/2023040763

Other identifiers: ISBN 9780814258965 (paperback) | ISBN 0814258964 (paperback)

Cover design by Laurence J. Nozik
Text design by Juliet Williams
Type set in Adobe Caslon Pro
Composition by Stuart Rodriguez

To my family, in memory of Arthur Beringer

CONTENTS

ILLUSTRATIONS

ACKNOWLEDGMENTS

The research for this project began over a decade ago when I started browsing the Hathitrust database in search of material for (what I assumed would be) a breezy little article on nineteenth-century comics. At the time, I had pleasant childhood memories of trips with my father and brothers to Capitol City Comics in Madison, Wisconsin; I thought that a study on comics might be a fun way to complement my research on nineteenth-century American literature and visual culture. That simple search led me in directions that I could never have imagined. A few images from an issue of *Yankee Notions* multiplied into thousands of PDFs and reference photos that opened my eyes to an expansive and unexpected culture of artists, publishers, and comic strips. The research I initially conducted from my laptop on my kitchen table turned into recurring treks to archives, to libraries, and to symposia—and for cups of coffee—where I enjoyed rich exchanges and even richer relationships with a host of brilliant scholars, archivists, and editors. In the meantime, my breezy little article grew into a yearslong undertaking that required heroic levels of patience and support from family, friends, and colleagues. I would thus like to extend my appreciation to the institutions and people who have made this book possible along the way.

The University of Montevallo has consistently come through with assistance for travel, the purchase of materials, and time off to conduct research. Grants from UM's Faculty Development Advisory Committee paid for trips to archives, image reproductions, publication subventions, editorial assistance, and summer stipends. The UM Board of Trustees and

President John W. Stewart facilitated an invaluable sabbatical that allowed me to complete an enormous amount of research and writing. I would also like to express my appreciation for the UM English Department and our chair, Paul Mahaffey, for giving me the space and creative freedom to regularly teach courses on comics. Insights from UM faculty have also been an important source of intellectual and professional support. Thanks to friends and colleagues Emma Atwood, John Bawden, Stephanie Batkie, and Stefan Forrester for lively conversations that animated my thinking on comics. Emily Gill generously answered all my questions about nine-teenth-century fashion. Special thanks are in order to Clark Hultquist for patiently listening to half-formed ideas and careful reading of my chapter on theater comics.

I consider the American Antiquarian Society to be my "home away from home" as far as research is concerned. This extraordinary institution and the community that surrounds it have had a profound influence on my book project. In 2019 I received financial support from the AAS through a Jay and Deborah Last Fellowship in graphic arts that allowed me to spend extended time at the AAS. The talented research fellows I first met during this visit—Ben Bascom, Sonia Hazard, and Elspeth Healey—have since become some of my most trusted colleagues due to our twice-weekly writing group. Staff at the AAS, including Brianne Barrett, Dan Boudreau, and Nate Fiske, ensured that I was never held in suspense when attaining materials or high-quality images. I am consistently awed and humbled by the expertise and the generosity of curators Vincent Golden, Lauren Hewes, and Laura Wasowicz—they are leading authorities on this subject matter, thoughtful educators, and wonderful advocates for their collections. One could not ask for a better ambassador than AAS's vice president for programs, Nan Wolverton. I am forever grateful to Nan for insisting that I visit Richard Samuel West, whose depth of knowledge and sage advice has been crucial to my understanding of the lives, histories, and culture of the cartoonists described in this book.

The National Endowment for the Humanities provided a fellowship that allowed me to attend the "City of Print" project in 2015, organized by Mark Noonan. My approach to periodical studies has been enlivened by Mark's walking tours of New York City and by ongoing discussions with City of Print's accomplished faculty and participants, including Adam McKible, Karen Roggenkamp, Sarah Salter, Janice Simon, Daniel Worden, and particularly Jean Lee Cole, who has become an indispensable mentor on periodicals, comics, and scholarship in general.

Colleagues at The Ohio State University—both the press and the institution—have been vital contributors and collaborators. Jared Gardner's 2021 symposium "Caricature, Cartooning, and Comics" offered an unparalleled opportunity to converse with people from around the world in our little subfield of early comics amid the global pandemic. Here, I would like to extend a special thanks to Guy Lawley for sharing his deep knowledge of nineteenth-century print history. Susan Liberator, Caitlin McGurk, and Jenny Robb at OSU's Billy Ireland Cartoon Library and Museum offered important guidance and support in this unique archive. At The Ohio State University Press, I would like to thank acquisitions editor Ana Jimenez-Moreno for her careful reading of drafts and expert help with navigating the publication process. I would also like to express my gratitude to series editors Jared Gardner (again), Charles Hatfield, and Rebecca Wanzo as well as the two anonymous peer reviewers for advocating for my book's publication.

Thanks also to my editorial consultant, Vijay Shah, whose laser-like attention to detail and thoughtful advice helped me find my writer's voice. Archivists Jaime Bourassa at the Missouri Historical Society, Clayton Lewis at the University of Michigan, and Jane Parr at Boston University all provided capable guidance and timely delivery of materials. Gregg Crane, June Howard, and Erik Rabkin all gave important early encouragement and insights.

Portions of chapter 1 were first published by The Ohio State University Press as "Spectacular Failures: Comics in Nineteenth-Century Humor Magazines," *American Periodicals* 32, no. 2 (Fall 2022). Portions of the introduction were previously published by Duke University Press under the title "Transatlantic Picture Stories: Experiments in the Antebellum Comic Strip," *American Literature* 87, no. 3 (September 2015): 455–88.

Finally, a few words on those closest to me: Donald R. Beringer is my first and best reader; Mary K. Burke, the first phone call I make at moments of uncertainty. Heartfelt appreciation to John Burke and to Tim and Dana Beringer. Ashley Wurzbacher is my dear confidante and the keeper of my prose. Matt and Sara Beringer have always given safe harbor when I needed it most. I cannot thank you all enough.

Transatlantic Picture Stories

When asked about the origins of American comic strips during an 1895 interview, Frank Beard—a famous cartoonist at the time—identified a quartet of mid-nineteenth-century humor magazines as the site of their inception. Beard reflected, "The first paper that published cartoons was the *Yankee Notions*. . . . Then *Nicknacks* [*sic*] appeared, which was followed by the *Comic Monthly* and Frank Leslie's *Budget of Fun*. Then we had *Vanity Fair* and then *Mrs. Grundy*." The well-known turn-of-the century publications *Puck* and *Judge*, Beard said, "were later creations . . . and now the daily newspapers are publishing their cartoons."[1] Beard went on to link these earlier works to storytelling and especially the genre of the picture story. "Pictures," Beard explained, "tell a story so much quicker than anything else that they will always be in demand."[2] With this, Beard referred to a seminal, yet widely overlooked, moment in the history of graphic narrative in the United States.

Beginning in the late 1840s and early 1850s, comic artists in the United States began a robust period of experimentation, appropriating the format of the multipanel picture story that they had encountered in French and Swiss comics. Unlike US comics of that period, which typically relied on single-panel caricatures and cartoons, French and Swiss artists commonly divided their comics into sequential panels, allowing for extended stories

---

1. Carpenter, "American Cartoons," 18. Another version of the interview appeared in Carpenter, "Taught by Pictures," 14. Beard elaborates on mid-nineteenth-century American comics in Beard, "Old Time Art and Artists," 85–91.

2. Carpenter, "American Cartoons, 18.

and elaborate sequences of actions and movements. These sequential European comics emphasized storytelling, characters, wordplay, and light entertainment over caricature and politics. For US artists, this new sequential approach to comics was crucial. As Beard brought up, mid-nineteenth-century artists' experimentation with this style of visual storytelling laid the foundation for the explosion of comics creativity in the color humor magazines and newspaper supplements of the 1890s and thus modern comics.

This story of a robust culture of multipanel comic strips prior to the Sunday newspaper comics contradicts widely accepted versions of US comics history. Most histories trace the beginnings of comic strips in the United States to the appearance of Richard F. Outcault's famous Yellow Kid character in newspapers in 1895. The so-called "Yellow Kid thesis" holds that comic strips emerged in the United States after Outcault's humorous cartoons of tenement children gained a following among readers of the *New York World* and the publisher responded by turning the cartoons into an ongoing series entitled *Hogan's Alley.* The extraordinary popularity of *Hogan's Alley* in turn led to bidding wars for Outcault's services, drove demand for other comic strips, and eventually solidified the Sunday comics supplement as a fixture of all major US newspapers, which in turn laid the basis for the superhero comic books, underground comix, and graphic novels of the twentieth century.[3]

The belief that US comic strips originated with Outcault appears to have its roots in Coulton Waugh's 1947 history *The Comics,* which begins by describing Outcault's Yellow Kid character as standing "right on the spot when the volcano shot off."[4] Although Waugh himself alluded to the existence of earlier US comic strips, the assumption that the medium first came to the United States in the 1890s has persisted in scholarly histories and the popular imagination. As the field of comics studies emerged, Waugh's periodization was used as the starting point for influential histories like Pierre Couperie and Maurice Horn's *A History of the Comic Strip* (1968), Robert C. Harvey's *The Art of the Funnies* (1994), and Ian Gordon's *Comic Strips and Consumer Culture* (1998). Since then, a crush of distinguished monographs, articles, anthologies, and popular histories on the turn-of-the-twentieth-century comic strip have followed a similar course. While these later works occasionally make passing reference to earlier US

---

3. Pedri, *Concise Dictionary of Comics,* 108.
4. Waugh, *The Comics,* 6.

comic strips, they ultimately land on the 1890s as the starting point for any substantive discussion.[5]

For studies of European comics, the story has been quite different. Historians have argued for a continuous tradition of European comic strips, dating back at least to the early nineteenth century and in some cases even earlier. In a 1956 lecture, the preeminent art historian Ernst Gombrich asserted that the nineteenth-century Swiss artist Rodolphe Töpffer had "invented, propagated the picture story, the comic strip."[6] Gombrich's student David Kunzle expanded on this claim with his groundbreaking two-volume set, *The History of the Comic Strip.* Published nearly twenty years apart, *The Early Comic Strip: Narrative Strips and Picture Stories in the European Broadsheet c.1450 to 1825* (vol. 1, 1973) and *The Nineteenth Century* (vol. 2, 1990) collected and described an exhaustive survey of mass distributed "pictorial sequences" from fifteenth-century England, France, Germany, and the Netherlands to the end of the nineteenth century. Later volumes by Kunzle provided thorough accounts and anthologies of the work of major nineteenth-century European comic strip artists like Töpffer, Cham (Amédée de Noé), Gustave Doré, and Marie Duval.[7] Such efforts created a foundation for vigorous historical criticism and surveys of earlier European comic strips by scholars like Thierry Groensteen, Simon Grennan, Benoît Peeters, and Thierry Smolderen.[8]

These diverging approaches to US and European contexts have often resulted in a misperception of nineteenth-century US graphic humor as a tradition confined to single-panel illustrations of grotesque caricatures or political cartoons. Works like E. W. Clay's racist illustrations of T. D. Rice as Jim Crow or Thomas Nast's famous editorial cartoons of Boss Tweed are what most commonly preoccupy discussions of US comics prior to the 1890s. The elaborate narratives of multipanel picture stories have, in the meantime, remained associated with an established canon of European publications and artists. The United States, readers are frequently told, would have to wait at least until the 1890s for the more sophisticated comic

---

5. Recent examples of distinguished scholarship and anthologies on the US comic strip from the turn of the twentieth century include: Cole, *How the Other Half Laughs*; Dauber, *American Comics*; Maresca, *Society Is Nix*; Meyer, *Producing Mass Entertainment*; and Saguisag, *Incorrigibles and Innocents*.

6. Gombrich, *Art and Illusion*, 336.

7. Kunzle, *Cham*; Kunzle, *Gustave Doré*; and Kunzle, *Rebirth*.

8. For example, Groensteen, *M. Töpffer invente*; Peeters, *La bande dessinée*; Smolderen, *Origins of Comics*; and Grennan, Sabin, and Waite, *Marie Duval*.

strips that signaled a robust engagement with sequential comic art as a form of storytelling.

Lost Literacies tells a new story of US comics history by introducing readers to a vibrant culture of comic strips that appeared in the mid-nineteenth-century United States. These works were neither caricatures nor political cartoons but emphatically *stories* with distinctive characters, settings, plots, and situational humor. While it is difficult to identify any single moment as the "first" instance of a comic strip in the United States, this earlier period was clearly a breakthrough. Starting in the 1840s, publishers in the United States began releasing original sequential comics in high volume. Long-form picture stories first appeared in book-length precursors to graphic novels known as "graphic albums."[9] These oblong volumes (6" × 4") featured illustrations with captions on each page that follow a single protagonist through a series of humorous picaresque adventures. Soon after, serialized picture stories and short illustrated skits also began running in humor magazines with regularity, starting with a few works in the semiannual pictorial supplements to *Brother Jonathan* (1842) and in weeklies like *Yankee Doodle* (1846) and *The John Donkey* (1848). The trend then expanded into later humor publications, including *Yankee Notions* (1852), *The Picayune* (1852), *Phunny Phellow* (1853), *Nick Nax* (1856), *Comic Monthly* (1859), *Leslie's Budget of Fun* (1859), *Vanity Fair* (1859), *Funniest of Phun* (1860), *Jolly Joker* (1862), *Merryman's Monthly* (1863), and *Wild Oats* (1870). Even the venerable *Harper's Monthly* (1850) and *Harper's Weekly* (1857) underwent short stints in the 1850s and '60s where picture stories were featured in each issue.

A cursory glance through these graphic albums and humor magazines quickly dispels any misunderstandings about their purported backwardness or obscurity. Over the course of their runs, these publications featured inventive and often elaborate comic strips and picture stories. They boasted circulations in the tens of thousands and employed a who's-who of major US illustrators, including Frank Bellew, George Carleton, Felix Darley, Livingston Hopkins, August Hoppin, Justin H. Howard, John McLenan, Henry Louis Stephens, Thomas Worth, and others.[10] Works with titles like "Obadiah Oldpot," "Mr. Slim," "Young Fitznoodle," "Master Charley,"

---

9. On the relationship between the graphic album and the graphic novel, see Mellier, "Origins of Adult Graphic Narratives," 21–38.

10. For instance, *Yankee Notions* sold thirty-three thousand copies per month in the first year and at least ten thousand monthly issues toward the end of its run. Nickels, "Yankee Notions," 324.

and "Jonathan Abroad" were serialized through multiple issues, in some cases lasting as long as twelve months. And far from mere derivations, US publishers and editors were adamant in their policies of charting a distinctively "American" style of visual storytelling. Just as Ralph Waldo Emerson hoped for the end of "our long apprenticeship" to Europe, comic artists insisted that graphic narratives should, as one editor wrote, "fix on the honest, home-writ page."[11]

The tone, audience, and approach of these comics could range along a spectrum of ideologies and sensibilities, often lining up with the ethos of the publication or publisher. Among magazines, *Leslie's Budget of Fun* was explicitly family friendly with its rejection of "even the mildest kind of profanity," while the bohemian-tinged *Vanity Fair* reveled in imagery and jokes about men in saloons smoking hashish and experimenting with queer forms of gender expression and sexuality.[12] Graphic albums could vary widely too. Some, like *The Adventures of Mr. Tom Plump,* were explicitly designed with children in mind; other albums could be bawdy and adult-oriented like *The Adventures of Slyfox Wikoff*; still others could be genteel and reflective like Augustus Hoppin's semi-autobiographical travel albums.[13] The artists and their comics were hardly peripheral to US literary and artistic culture but rather were engaged with many of the major undercurrents of their time. As this book demonstrates, the social and intellectual milieu of nineteenth century US comics extended to influences ranging from Walt Whitman's transcendentalist poetry to Benjamin Baker's bawdy stage comedies to the travel writings of Mark Twain.

While the mere existence of these playful nineteenth-century comic strips should prompt one to rethink some basic assumptions about US comics history, their significance extends beyond filling an important historical gap. They also point to a reconsideration—or perhaps a rediscovery—of forgotten ways of thinking about comics as a form of storytelling. During this period when the medium of comics was so new and unsettled, artists were not confined to established norms for visual language or genre. Basic conventions of the modern comic strip like speech balloons, panels arranged as grids, and methods for transitioning between panels could not be taken for granted. Amid this formal and ideological instability, what emerged was less a unified "American" approach to comics than

11. "Preface to Volume I," iii–iv.

12. Leslie, "Frank Leslie to His Readers," 1; and Bohan, "Vanity Fair," 57–69.

13. Hoppin, *Ups and Downs*; McLenan, *Sad Tale*; and *Adventures of Mr. Tom Plump*.

an environment in which competing practices produced multiple ways of experiencing the relationship between image and text. As this book suggests, the comics that appeared on the pages of graphic albums and periodicals were characterized by a wildly experimental quality and a taste for novelty. Artists pursued deliberately novel and idiosyncratic approaches to caricature, movement, and depiction of time. Some lacked definite plots; others merely delivered a series of puns; still others organized the passage of time and progression through space in ways that will feel unfamiliar to the modern viewer.

The audience for this first wave of US comic strips was strikingly sophisticated in its reception of this material. The sense of flux—the idea that the visual language could turn on a dime—was often precisely the appeal. Rather than becoming attuned to a single format or reading style, readers of nineteenth-century American comics took pleasure in novelty. They were alert to the fact that they might need to train themselves to absorb new visual languages each time they opened the pages of their favorite illustrated periodical. Here, an important similarity can be observed between the history of cinema and the history of the comic strip. Film historians have long admired the sophistication of audiences of precinematic technologies. Nineteenth-century advertisers of the magic lantern and the zoetrope termed these devices "philosophical toys" because they were understood as forms of training in new, modern approaches to visual perception. To be modern was to know how to acquaint oneself with the diverse forms of visual perception created by different visual illusions and to understand the science behind how those illusions worked.[14] Nineteenth-century audiences were well attuned to the diverse forms of visual perception created by the magic lantern's projected images, the zoetrope's simulations of movement, and the stereoscope's striking illusion of a three-dimensional plane. Parallel observations can be made about those same audiences' first encounters with comic strips.[15] Nineteenth-century audiences cultivated literacy in their comic strips' diverse approaches to the interaction between image and text. Even more importantly, they understood that a comic artist might not simply offer an amusing skit or bit of social commentary but could issue a challenge to the reader to imagine visual and verbal experience in new and different ways.

---

14. Gunning, "Hand and Eye."
15. Gunning, "Hand and Eye."

As innovative as they may be, many of the inventions of the early American comic strip signal neither a record of "winners" nor the "founders" of modern comics. Instead, it is frequently a record of lost visual literacies: ideas that fell by the wayside and did not become widely accepted as conventional elements of graphic storytelling. The stakes of exploring this multiplicity of visual literacies are greater than just the recovery of practical techniques; it is also an epistemological project. As the philosopher Martin Heidegger contends, drawing is itself "a mode of knowing," and so the act of rendering a character or depicting timing in a new way is to come up with distinctive conceptions of character and time.[16] With this in mind, revisiting these sources means reconvening with historically situated ways of thinking about human experience within nineteenth-century American culture.

At a moment when scholars in art history, literature, cultural studies, and comics studies are rushing to embrace the history of graphic narrative as an object of study, it seems essential to grapple with the diversity of comics *histories* in the archive. Much of the recent scholarly attention paid to comics stems from interest in what the medium can reveal about the broader project of narrative representation. As critics Hilary Chute and Patrick Jagoda observe, comics "enable an intense focus on how complexly woven stories unfold across time and space and, particularly, how these involve the reader . . . to generate meaning through interacting with, or themselves shaping, spatiotemporal form."[17] And indeed, scholars have begun charting the complex narrative work transpiring within comics and graphic novels. The last few years have seen insightful research on subjects ranging from Alison Bechdel's important output on memory to critical reassessments of modern classics like George Herriman's *Krazy Kat* to the radical undertones of Silver Age superheroes. But this discussion of the diversity of narrative styles within comics has largely extended to twentieth- and twenty-first-century comics. Meanwhile, earlier works have been overlooked or subsumed into a one-dimensional progress narrative that divides between "comics" and "proto-comics."[18]

These limitations are partly due to the unorthodox origins of graphic narratives as a subfield. One of the primary weaknesses of the initial scholarship on graphic narratives was that it relied so heavily on the observation of

16. Heidegger, "Origin of the Work of Art," 184.

17. Chute and Jagoda, *Comics & Media*, 1.

18. Inge, "Origins of Early Comics," 25–31; and Ndalianis, "Why Comics Studies?," 113–14.

artists from within the contemporary comics industry, like Scott McCloud and Will Eisner, who tend to describe current industry practices as transcendent rules for graphic narrative.[19] As Thierry Smolderen explains, the practices of a few artists from the late twentieth century have been naturalized as "a seamless craft that integrates all the tactful, rational choices one has to make to accomplish the job in a realistic and convincing fashion." For Smolderen, "appreciat[ing] the nuances between different idioms of progressive action" necessarily involves understanding the ongoing negotiation between "existing visual languages" and "new ways of seeing."[20] Critiques like Smolderen's underscore the need for a historiography that traces the diversity of context-specific styles of creating graphic narrative and the extent to which the language of comics is a volatile, changing entity. Such insights help avoid the pitfall of treating current industry methods as the idealist model to which so-called "proto-comics" were progressing and in turn the realist standard from which all postmodern "experimental" comics diverge.

Highlighting the fundamental pastness of earlier graphic narratives promises to undermine the perception that conventions like the modern comics grid and the dominance of linear action-to-action sequences (and the ways of thinking inherent in these forms) are somehow inevitable. The goal is to move from a historiography that looks not toward the telos of a singular, unified approach to one that emphasizes how the past signified a moment of possibility and diversity—a family tree where some branches lead to later genealogies and others stop, suggesting potential that never materialized. To view the history of the comic strip in this way is not to discount the approaches that *did* persist. After all, many of the innovations of the mid-nineteenth-century comic strip exerted significant direct and indirect influence over future artists. Yet, it should also be noted that these nascent elements of the modern comic strip coexisted alongside other equally promising modes and methods for making comics. Hence, in examining the US comic strip's points of continuity and its lost literacies, this book at once seeks to recover a forgotten chapter in the history of comics and catch an indirect glance at the histories that could have been.[21]

---

19. McCloud, *Understanding Comics*; and Eisner, *Comics and Sequential Art*.

20. Smolderen, *Origins of Comics*, 129.

21. For a discussion of this approach to historiography, see Marvin, *When Old Technologies Were New*, 232–35.

Francophone Appropriations, American Innovations

It is vital to understand the context around the early American comic strip. No publication more clearly exemplified the new realities of the illustrated press and its approach to comic art than Thomas W. Strong's *Yankee Notions* in 1852. *Yankee Notions* was the first of several monthly, folio-sized, illustrated humor magazines to imitate the apolitical leanings and dynamic multipanel sequences of French periodicals. In the 1830s and '40s, French illustrated periodicals like *Le Charivari* and *L'Illustration* turned away from explicitly political cartooning in the wake of Honoré Daumier's and Charles Phillipon's imprisonment over caricatures of King Louis-Philippe. Wary of scrutiny and censorship, French publishers increasingly emphasized light apolitical satire and serialized picture stories as a means of maintaining broad commercial appeal and staying out of trouble.[22] While Strong would have had little reason to fear censorship like that of 1830s France, he evidently saw the light humor and lively imagery of the French publications as filling a gap in the US market.

Strong's new monthly folio constituted a significant break from earlier US humor magazines, which were primarily weekly publications modeled after the British magazine *Punch*. Indeed, the editorial pages of earlier humor publications from the 1840s warred over which magazine would be the American counterpart to *Punch*. For instance, *Yankee Doodle* was not atypical in featuring illustrations of their magazine's character "Yankee Doodle" shaking hands with Mr. Punch. When the rival publication *Judy* folded, *Yankee Doodle* published a sarcastic obituary, attributing the failure to her "extravagant imposture" of pretending to be the wife of Mr. Punch while giving "coarse libels on the origina[l]."[23]

In contrast to the *Punch* imitations, *Yankee Notions* echoed the apolitical leanings of the Francophone picture stories and their dynamic imagery while avoiding "the acids" perceived to emanate from the politically charged pages of *Punch*.[24] Strong proclaimed that *Yankee Notions* "will embody all the good things that are constantly floating about society." He identified his writers and artists as "preservers of jokes" who would draw out those rarely noticed "facetiae" that "sometimes find their way into the

---

22. See Childs, "Big Trouble," 26–37; and Wechsler, *Human Comedy*, 66–82.
23. "Fatal Case of Destitution and Infatuation," 252.
24. Strong, "Preface to Volume 13," 2.

corners of newspapers, or serve to eke out a scanty column."[25] And yet, in delivering this light brand of humor, Strong hinted that *Yankee Notions'* blustery writings and lively engravings would become a source of spectacle. He thus advised readers that his magazine contained "manifold wonders and unique 'astonishers,'" capable of "flabbergasting the reflective apparatus" of the intelligent reader.[26] Hence, the suggestion from the moment readers picked up the magazine would at once encounter a playful look at the details—the "notions"—of American life and a visually impressive publication designed to grab hold of the reader's senses.[27] The multipanel comic strip was an essential element of these ambitions.

Comics from France and Switzerland are often viewed as the basis for the twentieth-century comic strip because they featured elaborate stories with closely linked sequential frames.[28] The francophone "picture story" broke from the widely known eighteenth-century British tradition of satirical prints, which exerted significant influence in the US and Europe throughout the nineteenth century. Pillars of this eighteenth-century tradition, like William Hogarth and James Gillray, created large single-panel cartoons that used the conventions of history painting to communicate narratives about moralistic or political themes. A print by Hogarth or Gillray typically crowded a single scene with an assortment of allegorical figures and allusions that a reader might ponder as the eye roved around the image searching for layers of meaning. With visual information confined to one scene, grotesque racial and ethnic caricature became central to the storytelling of cartoons in the mold of Hogarth and Gillray because these techniques offered an efficient means of communicating ideas about character and behavior to readers who were adept at recognizing stereotypes about the perceived physical features of certain racial and ethnic types.[29] By contrast, the francophone tradition of the picture story relied far less on allegory or caricature and steered away from overt political commentary. These works preferred a spare visual style that chronicled the happenings of everyday life by pulling the reader's eye across multiple frames. While picture stories were not entirely free of caricature, they deemphasized it in favor of successions

---

25. Strong, "Beloved and Honored Reader," 2.

26. Strong "Preface to Volume 10," 2.

27. On the use of print as spectacle, see Lehuu, *Carnival on the Page.*

28. Kunzle, *History of the Comic Strip, Volume 2*; and Smolderen, *Origins of Comics.*

29. Bricker, *Libel and Lampoon*, 209–33; Smolderen, *Origins of Comics*, 3–23; and Taylor, *Politics of Parody*, 3–5.

of frames that conveyed ideas about character and behavior by showing the progression of an individual's movements or thoughts over time. Sequences focused on physical movement, subtle mannerisms, and situational comedy took center stage in this newer approach to graphic narrative.

Starting with the works of Rodolphe Töpffer in the late 1830s and gaining further popular appeal with volumes by Cham (Amédéé de Noé) and Gustave Doré, the picture story was, as Smolderen notes, regarded as a "novel in prints," in which "the relationship between the illustrator and the writer would be inverted."[30] After their initial popularity as book-length graphic albums, they began appearing in French magazines of the 1840s like *Le Charivari* and *L'Illustration*. In adapting these works to fit this format, images were generally shrunk down and stacked next to each other, shifting what had originally been one or two pictures per page into a grid pattern that resembles the modern comic strip (though, as Smolderen points out, the *Charivari* grid is not a direct forerunner to the modern comic grid, but instead, a comparable solution that evolved independently).[31]

Töpffer's picture stories were especially influential for the development of this strand of graphic narrative. Sometimes described as "The Father of the Comic Strip," Töpffer is widely acknowledged as the first artist to popularize the practice of dividing his panels into distinct, sequential events.[32] This practice of presenting images in series proved an important breakthrough because it meant that Töpffer could tell extended stories and portray sequences of distinct actions. From a narrative standpoint, his work had as much in common with theater as it did with the satirical prints of Hogarth and Gillray. Töpffer's frames were presented in the proscenium view, reproducing the perspective of an audience member looking at a stage, and they borrowed extensively from the classic conventions of restoration comedy and slapstick pantomime.[33] Paired with Töpffer's spontaneous and whimsical visual style, this theatrical presentation enabled his work to enjoy a fast-paced sensibility that could play upon comic timing and repetition. His thematic sophistication should also be noted: Töpffer's brand of picaresque seemed reminiscent of Laurence Sterne's *Tristram Shandy*. Upstart characters such as Monsieur Vieux Bois, Jabot, and Cryptogame disrupted the order of polite society, wreaking satirical havoc on subjects as diverse

---

30. Smolderen, *Origins of Comics*, 52.
31. Smolderen, *Origins of Comics*, 53.
32. Kunzle, *Father of the Comic Strip*.
33. Willems, "This Strangest of Narrative Forms," 127–38.

The gallopade arrives, knocks over the chair, and Jabot suffers the misfortune of being caught on the hook.

Mr. Jabot is unhooked by the return of the gallopade.

FIGURE 0.1. Selection from *Histoire de Monsieur Jabot*, reproduced in David Kunzle, *Rodolphe Töpffer: The Complete Comic Strips* (Jackson: University Press of Mississippi, 2007), 21.

as social climbing bourgeois, the Catholic Church, and nineteenth-century science (fig. 0.1).

The inspiration provided by French magazines and picture stories was apparent in the first issue of *Yankee Notions* with the serialized comic *The Adventures of Jeremiah Oldpot*. The series took its name from Töpffer's *Les Amours de Monsieur Vieux Bois* (which, in its English translation, was entitled *The Adventures of Obadiah Oldbuck*). In adapting the medium for an American audience, *Yankee Notions* came up with a comic that was equal parts homage and theft. The creator of *Jeremiah Oldpot* lifted artwork from several picture stories in *L'Illustration*, doctored the images, and added original captions to create a picture story, infusing the structure and style of the Töpfferian picture story with a self-consciously "Yankee" flavor.[34] *Jeremiah Oldpot* is less a scene-by-scene adaptation of any existing story by Töpffer or Cham than it is a new work that freely samples images and

---

34. For examples of plagiarized artwork, see frame #5 in Rodolphe Töpffer, "Histoire de M. Cryptogame," 380; frame #6 in Cham, "Aventures Anciennes," September 13, 1845, 28–29; and frame #1 in Cham, "Aventures Anciennes," September 20, 1845, 44.

Et il leur applique de tels coups de fouet, qu'au risque de s'enrhumer, ils s'échappent par l'incision cruciale, laissant leur peau à M. le baron de Crac.

By the combined aid of his dog, whip, and physical energy, Mr. Oldpot achieves his purpose in the most triumphant manner.

Après avoir longtemps promene en vain ses rèveries, M. le baron de Crac rentre chez lui. — En franchissant le seuil de sa cuisine, il trouve une idée.

Mr. Oldpot hits upon a subtle expedient, and the wherewithal to carry it out, at one and the same time.

His faithful dog being attached to his master, is at once attached to the diminutive trunk. *Touching solicitations follow,* and taking immediate advantage of the extension which his idea had effected in the trunk, Mr. Oldpot, with infinite satisfaction, stows away the entire number of the articles designed for his use and comfort in that land of gold whither his aspirations led.

FIGURE 0.2. Excerpts showing *Yankee Notions*' repurposing of illustrations from the French periodical *L'Illustration*. Cham's original "Aventures Anciennes et Nouvelles d'un Chasseur Connu" appears at left, *Yankee Notions*' "Jeremiah Oldpot" at right. *L'Illustration* images courtesy of the Internet Archive; *Yankee Notions* images courtesy of the American Antiquarian Society.

situations from those artists. Coonskin caps and buckskin jackets are drawn over the top of European clothing; images are reordered; the French captions are replaced by an entirely different English-language story (fig. 0.2). The resulting concoction offers a surprisingly original take on the genre of the picture story tailored to a US audience.

Where the comics of Töpffer satirized the bourgeois classes in Europe, *Oldpot* skewered the entrepreneurial spirit of the American self-made man. *Oldpot*'s protagonist is a New York tin merchant who abandons his wife and children to pan for gold in California. Where Monsieur Vieux Bois's ambitions lead him into parlors, picturesque meadows, and other scenes of bourgeois European life, Oldpot's adventures take him on a continent-spanning journey across America, where he encounters a veritable cross-section of landscapes and social types as he meets tinkering inventors, immigrant miners, and racist caricatures of Native Americans.

Among the strip's highlights is its wickedly funny send-up of US consumerism. In an early installment, Oldpot visits the emporium of the unscrupulous salesman "Hoax'em Mac Scratchit" who cons him into purchasing a host of unnecessary gadgets (fig. 0.3). The premise was partially borrowed from a brief Cham sequence in which a hunter purchases a bear suit, but *Oldpot*'s creator expanded Cham's simple premise into a far more elaborate satire.[35] Mystified by Scratchit's claims of "Electro-Galvanic-Vulcanized-India-Rubber," Oldpot equips himself with a slew of ridiculous costumes for survival in the wilderness.[36] Much of the satire hinges on the contradiction between Oldpot's romantic view of himself as a rugged frontiersman and his attachment to consumer goods. The interplay between the captions and images captures the back and forth between these dueling tendencies. In one frame, the captions highlight Mr. Oldpot's inflated sense of self as a "hero . . . duly sensible of the perils which, in all probably, he will have to encounter."[37] In the next, they reveal Scratchit's ability to exploit Oldpot's meek urban tendencies with a snake-oil pitch that plays to his insecurities. Scratchit offers products such as the "Never-sinking, self-inflating, and everlasting diving apparatus" and the "Life-protecting, bone-defending, heat-securing, Indian-exterminating hunting dress for all nations" and in doing so simultaneously strokes Oldpot's ego and reminds him of the dangers he is supposed to be facing.[38] Oldpot's frontiersman self-concept becomes further deflated for the audience by the illustrations, which show how he has become made to look like an elephant or snowman underneath his accumulated goods and costumes. The whole sequence takes a further madcap turn with the embarrassed reaction of Mr. Oldpot's children. Shocked at their father's foolish appearance, the children's

---

35. See Cham, "Aventures Anciennes," 44.
36. "Adventures of Jeremiah Oldpot," March 1852, 93.
37. "Adventures of Jeremiah Oldpot," March 1852, 93.
38. "Adventures of Jeremiah Oldpot," March 1852, 93.

" A bird in the hand is worth two in the bush ! "

OR,

THE ADVENTURES OF JEREMIAH OLDPOT.

Mr. Oldpot resolves to go prepared for the most terrible adventures.

Duly sensible of the perils which, in all probability, he will have to encounter in his voyage to the land of gold, Mr. Oldpot makes his way to the emporium of Mr. Hoax'em Mac Scratchit, patentee of nine hundred and ninety-nine articles, indispensible to emigrants, and entirely composed of Electro-Galvanic-Vulcanized India-rubber.

Mr. Oldpot tries on the Never-Sinking, Self-Inflating, and Everlasting Diving Apparatus.

He tries the aquatic costume first, which will enable him to remain, with ease, at the depth of 47¼ fathoms beneath the surface of the sea, for 15 days and ten minutes.

Mr. Oldpot is courteously received by Mr. Mac Scratchit.

There, being waited upon with the utmost politeness by the illustrious patentee himself, with him Mr. Oldpot takes counsel. Having reviewed the entire stock of inventions, two in particular excite our hero's attention, both of which he incontinently purchases. Then, selecting upwards of fifty minor articles, including a patent magnetic-India-rubber warming pan, and a wheel-barrow of similar material, Mr. Oldpot hastens homewards, impatient to try on his two more important purchases.

Mr. Oldpot arrays himself in the Patent Life-Protecting, Bone-Defending, Heat-Securing, Indian-Exterminating, Hunting Dress for all Nations.

Having done so, he is delighted at the prospect of achieving a world-wide reputation for courage and prowess. While exultingly striding up and down, he creates a terrible consternation in the minds of Mrs. Oldpot and the seven children, who, peeping in at the door, which had been left open, are perfectly appalled at the singular appearance of the head of the family.

FIGURE 0.3. "The Adventures of Jeremiah Oldpot," *Yankee Notions,* March 1852, 93. Courtesy of the American Antiquarian Society.

"eyes start out of their head," flying around like small butterflies, to be caught and retrieved by a horrified Mrs. Oldpot and (in a savage twist) the dog.[39] The trajectory from mild vanity to madcap anarchy encapsulates the sequence's basic operation of taking the manners and customs of Americans and throwing them into sharp relief through comedic timing and humorous storytelling.

Yankee Notions' adaptation of Töpffer and Cham serves as an example of the broader project that Strong and his fellow publishers undertook in bringing the medium of graphic narratives to US audiences. Jeremiah's farce and journey through the American landscape is at once a panoramic survey of American social life, an exercise in sheer silliness, and a frenzied visual spectacle. And it is here—at the intersection of the social, the silly, and the spectacular—that the humorous illustrated press focused their energies. The comic paper and the graphic album provided a new national form of entertainment where the average reader could recognize their own experiences, enjoy a release from the difficulties of their lives and work, and maybe even find themselves astonished by the new ways of experiencing the printed image.

There were potentially radical undertones in the combination of an expansive cast of American characters, praise of idle fun, and visual innovations that recurred throughout the media where comics appeared. As we'll see in the next section, the publishers and creators of comics were themselves part of an insurgent cultural movement that was pushing American art, literature, and entertainment in an increasingly egalitarian direction. Let us examine the cultural milieu that inspired these playful early comics.

New Printscapes

The distinctive "printscape" of New York's illustrated publishing industry through the 1840s and '50s was essential to the creative and commercial process that produced graphic albums and humor magazines like *Obadiah Oldbuck* and *Yankee Notions*.[40] New York's importance to the growth of the

---

39. "Adventures of Jeremiah Oldpot," April 1852, 117.

40. The critic and historian Mark Noonan uses the term "printscape" to describe the interplay between "geographical and imaginative space" in the "production, circulation, and reception of printed documents." For Noonan, a "printscape" describes the historical circumstances of a "locatable space" (such as the actual publishing houses, laborers, literacy rates, and emerging technologies) *and* the ways "page and place are suffused by social and cultural practices, imbued with symbolic meaning and memory." See Noonan, "Printscape," 9–11.

comics market in the US was due to a convergence of historical circumstances. During this time period, New York became a hotbed of innovation not only for creating comics but mass-produced illustrated publications of all sorts. The area along Nassau and Fulton Streets that would become known as "Newspaper Row" was dotted with upstart publishing houses that catered to working- and middle-class demand for the spectacle provided by inexpensive printed images. These publishers enjoyed the editorial freedom that came with the loosened restrictions on free speech in the 1850s. Close proximity to the Nassau theater district and the city's many bars and restaurants also meant that New York publishers saw a steady supply of creative laborers who were eager to enjoy New York's social life while taking inspiration from the city's cultural scene. And thanks to new technologies, the mass production of illustrated publications cost a fraction of what it had only a decade earlier.

The comics boomlet of the 1850s was hardly the first US-based attempt to publish sequential visual narrative. Efforts to combine sequences of images with text had been a longstanding project of the US illustrated publishing industry in New York and elsewhere. At least as early as the 1820s, publishers were regularly incorporating elaborate sequences of images with puns and wordplay into materials like comic almanacs, broadside prints, and the short-lived medium of the "comic scrapbook."

D. C. Johnston, a Boston-based artist and printer known the "Cruikshank of the New World," was probably the most successful of these early US-based experimenters. In his broadsides and comic scrapbooks, Johnston spun his reader through ornate sequences of illustration and verbal wit (fig. 0.4). Johnston understood the enormous potential of comics as a new artistic and literary form, and he saw himself as pioneering a new approach that yoked imagery and verbal wit. Never one for modesty, Johnston once claimed (only half-jokingly) that the "odd combinations of language" and "fantastical linear representations" of his sketchbooks were "emphatically the same" as those witticisms "once conjured up by John Milton."[41] The early efforts of Johnston (and a few others) occasionally met with commercial success. Starting in 1828, each annual volume of Johnston's comic sketchbook, *Scraps*, boasted a then-impressive circulation of about three thousand subscribers and was distributed in every major city on the East Coast until its demise in 1837.[42] As significant as Johnston's commercial and artistic accomplishments were, they were largely the exception. High

41. Johnston, "Johnstonian System."
42. Larkin, "What He Did for Love," 5–6.

printing costs and a lack of audience familiarity with comics generally prevented other publishers from following Johnston's lead with extended print runs of multipanel comics.

The circumstances that had limited the reach of Johnston and his contemporaries in the 1820s and '30s changed signficantly in the decades that followed as new technologies and audiences created new opportunities. Driven by technological advancements and middle-class demand for illustrations, publishers offered an array of illustrated publications that were directly involved with new ways of thinking about combining image and text. Comics were in this regard only one small part of a larger wave of products emerging from New York's illustrated presses. Publishers produced a stunning variety of almanacs, pictorial newspapers and magazines, comic valentines, children's books, and moveable toy books. All these works deployed varying levels of sequential images and combinations of image with text. Artists, editors, and engravers worked in multiple capacities, experimenting with new ways of combining image and text and using sequences of images to animate movement and create rudimentary visual illusions on paper.[43]

New York's status as a hub for a commercialized periodicals industry was significant in producing the conditions necessary for this innovation to happen. As a publishing scene, New York was known for catering to middle- and working-class audiences, thus distinguishing itself from acknowledged centers of high culture like Boston and Philadelphia.[44] For instance, Boston hosted important publishers like J. P. Jewett and Ticknor & Fields, prestige periodicals like *The Atlantic,* as well as cultural institutions like the Handel and Haydn societies. Indeed, such concentrations of distinguished writers once prompted author Bret Harte to joke that one could scarcely "fire a revolver without bringing down the author of a two-volume work."[45] New York's publishing industry was known for cheap publications such as the penny press papers of Benjamin Day, the richly illustrated magazines and books from the House of Harper, and various illustrated presses that produced everything from crudely illustrated comic almanacs and valentines to photorealistic illustrated newspapers and broadsides.

---

43. See Lehuu, *Carnival on the Page.*

44. Boston and Philadelphia both sported popular presses, but these cities enjoyed neither the quantity nor reputation of New York. Reynolds, *Beneath the American Renaissance,* 174.

45. Qtd. in Martin, *Rebel Souls,* 80.

FIGURE 0.4. David Claypool Johnston, "Trollopania," *Scraps*, vol. 4. (Boston: D. C. Johnston, 1833), 4. Courtesy of the American Antiquarian Society.

The emergence of the electrotype as a commercially viable printing technology in the late 1840s marked an especially important development for US-produced comics because it made it easier and more practical to incorporate multipanel sequences of images. An electrotype was produced by coating a mold of wax in black lead and then using a lead-acid battery bath to apply even layers of copper to the surface. This process proved an important advancement over the earlier stereotype method in which the form was coated with a soft metal such as lead, causing it to create distorted images or break apart under the pressure of the steam press after only a few hundred impressions. A single electrotype easily outperformed the older technologies with its ability to produce thousands of high-quality impressions in sharper detail and at a lower cost than the earlier process.[46] The economies of scale were stunning. For comparison, Johnston's *Scraps*, which was only four oversized pages, retailed at the steep price of $1.00 per issue in 1840 (or about $30.00–$40.00 in today's money). Illustrated monthly magazines of the 1850s cost about 10–15 cents per issue and featured 30–40 pages per issue with engravings on each page.[47] In other words, in 1850, a printed page with illustrations cost 1/100th of what it did only a decade earlier.

Strong's own career trajectory represents a microcosm of the rapid development taking place across the New York illustrated press in the middle of the nineteenth century. Strong, a savvy businessman, was among the first to recognize the enormous commercial potential of cheap, mass-produced illustrations. Between the early 1840s and mid-1860s, he built a thriving publishing firm, known for its diverse variety of illustrated print material. The financial potency of Strong's endeavor was physically embodied by the massive building that he constructed in Manhattan in 1852, which at once served as a New York landmark and a monument to the lucrativeness of illustrated publishing. The commercial and spectacular appeal of illustration pops out in a striking advertisement for Strong's publishing house (fig. 0.5). The promotion displays a crowd gathered around Strong's emporium, marveling at the printed matter in the storefront, touting "wood engraving in all its various branches, neatly executed on the most moderate terms," listing everything from "Primers . . . Child's A.B.C." and "Valentines of a thousand kinds" to "envelopes, and Fancy laced and embroidery paper in endless variety."[48]

Early on in his career, Strong helped with experiments in combining image with text. A teenage Strong apprenticed as an engraver under Robert Ellton, creating comic almanacs and comic anthologies where he and others were already working through the familiar comic strip elements of text, frames, and boxes. For instance, a Strong-engraved piece for *Ellton's Comic All-My-Nack 1839*, titled "He Licks Her (Elixir) of Life" (fig. 0.6), features a series of illustrations arranged in sequential boxes showing a woman's progression through an illness from "very ill" to "worse" to "worser" to "worserer." As he developed his own publishing firm, Strong would pursue increasingly ambitious ventures that combined illustrations

46. Michelson, *Printer's Devil*, 36–37.

47. "Nick-Nax," May 1857, 2; "Scraps, No. 6, for 1835"; and "Here Is a Curious Thing!!"

48. Strong, "Strong's Publishing Warehouse"; see also West, *T. W. Strong*.

FIGURE 0.5. Advertisement for Strong's Wood Engraving and Publication Office appearing in *Troubles of Harry Careless* (New York: T. W. Strong, 1848). Courtesy of the American Antiquarian Society.

with text as forms of spectacle. His early publications ranged from sensational periodicals like *The Tragic Almanac* (1843), which featured lurid illustrations and accounts of murders and natural disasters, to the more subdued *Art of Landscape Painting* (1850), which offered realistic pencil sketches and vibrant colors to be imitated by amateur painters. In addition to creating humor magazines and pictorials, Strong's periodical business produced works like *The Illustrated American News* (1851) and *Strong's*

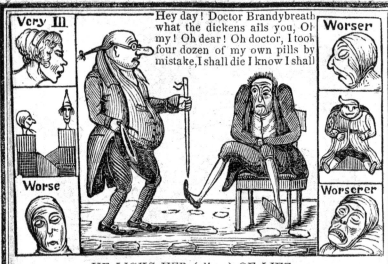

FIGURE 0.6. "He Licks Her (Elixir) of Life," *Ellton's Comic All-My-Nack 1839* (New York: Ellton, 1838). Courtesy of the American Antiquarian Society.

Campaign Pictorial (1852–60), where news events were presented through sequences of images.[49]

The interest in creating new forms of interaction between image and text was particularly evident in the many "toy books" that Strong and others developed for the US market both before and after the emergence of sequential comics. These lush items adopted animation as a rudimentary form of visual illusion that bears important similarities to many of the period's comics. An early example from Strong, *My Own ABC of Quadrupeds* (1842) was an accordion-style book that served as both an optical toy and a book. Readers would animate a succession of images by pulling the end of the book, revealing a succession of different animals, potentially flipping back and forth by releasing the pressure on the first page. Basic animations like *ABC of Quadrupeds* became precursors to the more ambitious moveable toy and magic transformation books from Strong's and, later on, the famous McLoughlin Brothers' publishing house.[50]

When it came to the comics themselves, Strong's employed a gimmicky approach in keeping with the illustrated press's broader ethos of using illustrations as a form of spectacle. Even the covers for the first year of *Yankee Notions* formed a sequence in Augustus Hoppin's cover illustrations. Each month, Jonathan (the publication's mascot) engaged in a different activity; these illustrations were then republished as a full-page grid in the annual pictorial to reveal the ongoing progression of Jonathan's life over the course of the year. In a not-so-surprising move, Strong issued the collected covers as a print to be sold on its own.[51] Strong's use of comics as novelty and spectacle was the norm. As we'll see throughout this book, publishers and artists embraced a dazzling array of tactics in their search for new, surprising ways to grab readers' attention.

Apart from these commercial and technological developments, early US comic strips were bolstered by New York's artistic and literary scene from the 1850s through the 1870s. At this time, an unprecedented number of cultural workers migrated to lower Manhattan, attracted by the economic opportunities presented by the publishing industry and the adjacent Nassau theater district. The resulting concentration of creative types led to a cosmopolitan atmosphere unparalleled in the United States. Unlike previous generations of US writers and artists, the figures who gathered in

---

49. West, *T. W. Strong*, 8.

50. For example, Howard, *Naughty Girl's & Boy's Magic Transformations*.

51. West, *T. W. Strong*, 6.

mid-nineteenth-century New York dwelled at the fringes of polite society and pursued social mobility through cultural labor. Writers, artists, actors, and editors regularly met at restaurants, bars, and cafes such as Crook & Duff and Pfaff's cellar, where they drank beer, ate German pancakes, and discussed their creative endeavors. They lived together in boarding houses and loafed about the streets in search of entertainment, even as they maintained punishing publication schedules just to make ends meet.[52] Out of this milieu emerged new approaches to American literature and art, shaped by urban life and dedicated to a broad, egalitarian version of republicanism.

Outside the world of comics, this newer brand of urban literature and art was best conveyed by Walt Whitman's innovative verse and bold assertion that the "roughs and beards . . . the vast masses" were really what gave the United States its "fullest poetical nature."[53] Whitman not only frequented many of the same restaurants and bars as the period's comic artists but also traced his artistic origins to his work as a journalist, supporting himself financially with his writings by recording the city's happenings. The egalitarian ethos and journalistic sensibility echoed in the works of countless other figures who, like Whitman, were influenced by the social and intellectual milieu of New York's print culture: Artemus Ward (also known as Charles Farrar Browne), whose folksy performances of Yankee humor popularized the form that would later become known as stand-up comedy; the painter Winslow Homer, who expanded his subjects beyond the well-born and wealthy; actor Frank Chanfrau, who achieved fame playing the working-class Bowery B'hoy, Mose; Thomas Bailey Aldrich, who celebrated juvenile naughtiness in his "Bad Boy" stories; Fanny Fern, who gained a national following through conversational acerbic newspaper columns, commenting on the lives of middle-class women; and the fiction of Mark Twain, whose breakthrough story "The Celebrated Jumping Frog of Calaveras County" was first published in the *Saturday Evening Press.*

While firsthand accounts of nineteenth-century US cartoonists are scarce, the writings of British-born author and artist Thomas Butler Gunn offer a rare window into their world. Gunn, best known for his book of urban sketches, *The Physiology of New York Boarding Houses,* remained a tireless chronicler of mid-nineteenth-century New York. Throughout his writings, Gunn describes comic artists as integral figures in the array of

---

52. On the role of boarding houses in New York's popular and illustrated press, see Faflik, *Boarding Out,* 3–9.

53. Whitman, "Preface 1855," 616.

personal, professional, and artistic relationships that sustained New York's publishing scene. For instance, Gunn characterized the prolific artist Frank Bellew as a fixture among New York's cultural luminaries. Regularly spotted in Howell's tavern alongside the likes of the poet Whitman, bohemian editor Henry Clapp, and actor John Brougham, Bellew was said "to recognize and be recognized by everybody." According to Gunn's fanciful account, Bellew carried a "black valise that contain[ed] box wood, not shirts" and, when the evening was over, could sketch any of the tavern-goers with his "eyes shut and one of his hands tied behind him" (fig. 0.7).[54]

FIGURE 0.7. Thomas Butler Gunn, "The Restaurants of New York: House of Lords," *New York Picayune*, March 26, 1859, 101. Courtesy of the American Antiquarian Society.

Gunn's diaries also feature important clues about how comic illustrators signaled their status as members of New York's artistic and intellectual community. In the illustrations that Gunn collected and composed, artists are often seen wearing elaborate facial hair, foreign clothing, deliberately gaudy accessories, and other elements that identify them with romantic subcultures. A striking page from his notebook contains an illustration that depicts artists John McLenan and Thomas Nast loafing about New York dressed in attire that would likely cause a stir among polite company (fig. 0.8).[55] McLenan, to the left, with his walrus moustache, loose-fitting frock coat, and fishing hat (McLenan was an avid fisherman) sports a combination that signals both his identification with the working-class "roughs" and an affinity for nature.[56] Meanwhile, Nast wears a "Calabrian" hat and facial hair trimmed to look like the Sicilian troops that he encountered during his recent tour through Italy.

54. Gunn, "Restaurants of New York," 100–101.

55. Illustration in Gunn's diary is clipped from Solomon Eytinge, "Recruiting for the War," 392–93. In the article, McLenan and Nast were depicted at a recruitment meeting for the Union Army in City Hall Park in New York, loafing and conversing.

56. On McLenan's fishing hobby, see Doesticks, "Doesticks Goes Trout-Fishing," 83.

FIGURE 0.8. John McLenan (*left*) with Thomas Nast (*center*) in Thomas Butler Gunn, *Thomas Butler Gunn Diaries Volume 18*. Courtesy of the Missouri Historical Society.

The urban origins of Bellew, McLenan, and others emerged in their comics' free-wheeling and expansive sensibility. This spirit could take many forms. In some cases, it meant shifting the kinds of subjects deemed appropriate for comic drawing. Like the social world of Whitman's poetry, comics engaged with a large, inclusive version of American culture. They developed rich situational comedy arising from chance encounters in public spaces where urban toughs, drunks, and newsboys cohabitated with Yankee rustics, effeminate swells, and fashionable women wearing hoop dresses. They presented readers with a parade of outcasts, drunks, artists, and other interrupters of polite social order who did not conform to the stultifying conventions of haute bourgeois society. It could also mean exposing a scandalous side of American society with scenes of free love, secret identities, and gender-play. This ethos is even there in the odd mixture of cosmopolitan refinement and thievery that had led uncredited European comics to appear in US magazines. But most of all, the fingerprint of New York's exuberant creative atmosphere pervaded the improvisational and experimental qualities of the US comics of this period. To live and work in New York's print industry was to be inured to a culture of innovation and novelty—of exciting new ways of thinking about the project of what literature and art could look like and who could compose it.

The ferment between comics and New York's print culture scene during the 1850s and '60s thus bears a significant resemblance to the lauded underground "comix" movement of the 1960s and '70s. As scholar Charles

Hatfield notes, late twentieth-century underground artists like Alison Bechdel, R. Crumb, and Art Spiegelman offered an entirely new model that "departed from the familiar, anodyne conventions of commercial comics . . . [and] gave rise to the idea of comics as an acutely personal means of artistic exploration and self-expression."[57] In the twentieth and twenty-first centuries, these kinds of innovations would lead to a boom in ambitious alternative comics and graphic novels. During the nineteenth century, there exists a parallel development through which outward gestures toward nonsense and fun became integral to innovations in comic art and storytelling.

An Overlooked Archive?

While it may seem odd that such a rich archive has been so understudied, its omission can be explained by looking to the kinds of obstacles faced by previous scholars. The graphic albums and magazines themselves are extremely rare, fragile, and dispersed across dozens of archives and unwieldy microfiche collections. For a long period of time, research was conducted by individual scholars visiting archives, locating partial runs, then comparing their findings. This kind of collaboration produced the important annotated guide *American Humor Magazines and Comic Periodicals* (1987), edited by David E. E. Sloane. Sloane's book features nearly fifty distinct contributors, providing a series of bibliographic overviews of each magazine. It is rightfully considered the most comprehensive overview of the genre and thus foundational to the study of periodical humor in the United States. However, its limitations are acute when it comes to examining visual material. Where the humorous stories and jokes in the magazines could be easily transcribed and reproduced, the illustrations were broadly available only to the researcher looking at the magazines or in fragmentary selections. Sloane's contributors thus spoke in broad encyclopedic terms, for instance, referring to cartoons being "important to the character" of a magazine or to a publication featuring a "captioned cartoon that often appeared through several pages."[58] The bibliographic work of Sloane and others was made even more difficult by the fact that, due to their unusual format, many of the comic strips that appeared in graphic albums and magazines might not strike a modern reader as a "comic strip" at all. In many cases, comics are not formatted in the familiar comics grid, with

---

57. Hatfield, *Alternative Comics*, ix.
58. Nickels, "Yankee Notions," 324–25.

illustrations and captions appearing wherever editors could fit them, sometimes stretched over multiple pages, and often blending in with the prose stories, jokes, and caricatures that also appeared in illustrated magazines.[59]

Digital humanities initiatives are rapidly offering avenues for scholars to build on the foundation created by Sloane and others. Projects like Hathitrust, Google Books, the Billy Ireland digital collection, and the American Antiquarian Society Historical Periodicals Series have made the visual material available in ways that would have been unimaginable even ten years ago. Collections that would have taken decades to assemble can now be prepared in a matter of hours. Additionally, the technology enables rapid broad-based comparisons of materials stretched across the archive. From the standpoint of visual humor, this facility is particularly important. A researcher can scan through and survey the breadth of different types of illustrations, observing patterns in the artwork and composition of these materials. What emerges is a newly coherent picture of recurring forms, conventions, and themes with which comic artists were experimenting.

The robust use of databases does not do away with the need for conventional archival work or interpretation as much as it offers a powerful addition to the critic/historian's repertoire. In this sense, digitization projects represent a good example of the "computer-assisted literary criticism" that scholars such as David Ramsay regard as a more pragmatic, if less flashy, version of the digital humanities than more highly publicized efforts. As Ramsay emphasizes, the digital revolution is here, but it has been a quieter revolution than expected. Instead of drawing splashy conclusions about life expectancies of genres or the scope of national literatures as promised by early digital studies, contemporary digital humanities scholarship uses "tools—practical, instrumental, verifiable mechanisms—that enable critical engagement, interpretation, conversation, and contemplation."[60] The hard work of sifting through, reading, viewing, and interpreting materials remains vitally important and still needs to be supplemented with work in the physical archive.

This kind of digital scholarship does not lack pitfalls. There can be risks of privileging certain types of publications and materials over others. The reasons that materials can be overlooked are various. In some cases, a publication might be less accessible because it is rare, fragile, or partially intact. It might be held by a private owner rather than a public archive or is cataloged in a way that does not identify it as containing comics or graphic

59. For example, "Wonderful Hunting Tour of Mr. Borridge," 9.
60. Ramsay, *Reading Machines*, x.

humor. Data storage costs may hinder image quality or the quantity of images that can appear publicly. Certain archives may prioritize what they deem to be high-demand materials. Additionally, the physical experience of handling a periodical can differ quite substantially from that of scanning through on a screen. For example, there are vast differences between the experience of reading comics that appear in an oblong graphic album with a trim size of 6" × 8", a folio-size monthly at 11" × 17", and a standard-size magazine at 5" × 8". Distinctions like trim size or paper quality can be lost if a scan is cropped too closely or reproduced at a lower resolution.

A handy rule of thumb for addressing these issues is that researchers should cultivate an awareness of the processes and institutions behind each digitization project. Attention to elements such as cataloging methods, principles of selection, and overall goals of a digitization project are hence essential information. Indeed, one of the most important and most underestimated differences between the physical and the digital archive is that it is often much easier for a researcher working in a digital archive to detach the sources from a physical archiving process. With no librarian hauling out a stack of materials on a special collections truck, it can be easy to forget that the process of making material accessible involves human labor and human error.

The American Antiquarian Society's (AAS) collaboration with the Gale company on the American Historical Periodicals database stands as a central resource in my own research. This utility results from the fact that the underlying principles of the project so closely resemble those adopted by the AAS's physical archive, which is itself respected as a premiere destination for research on US print matter. They have catalogued material according to the AAS's standard practices, and the goal of the project is to form a comprehensive and objective record of the AAS's periodical holdings. Material is scanned and released based on its date (earliest publications scanned first) rather than prioritizing high-demand or high-volume publications. Even scraps of individual pages are often preserved, and similar to a physical archive, catalogers must occasionally improvise, grouping scraps with material that is potentially related, leaving a so-called "gravestone." In some cases, new acquisitions or especially fragile materials skip to the front of the queue, but these exceptions are far and few between.[61]

Another way to answer the question of why this important archive has gone understudied is that it has *not* been overlooked but has merely been studied in ways that tend not to garner attention from academic

---

61. Stoeffel, interview.

departments at universities. My experience in researching this book has shown me that many of the most knowledgeable people about nineteenth-century American comics are not high-profile literary critics or art historians but archivists, private collectors, and periodicals dealers. Figures like John Adcock, Robert Beerbohm, Richard Samuel West, and others have, over the course of many years, published extensive, distinguished writings about nineteenth-century comics; however, their work often escapes the notice of university-based scholars because it is aimed at an audience of collectors, dealers, and enthusiasts. For example, Beerbohm, West, and Richard Olson's introduction to "Victorian Age" comics in the *Overstreet Price Guide* qualifies among the most important scholarly discussions of pre-1900 comics and graphic humor in the United States.[62] Similarly, rich resources for Victorian-era cartooning are available through Adcock's blog, *Yesterday's Papers*; Beerbohm's online discussion thread, "Platinum Era Comics"; and West's writings, which stretch across a variety of scholarly, popular, and trade publications.[63] Needless to say, the accomplishments in this area should give any university-based scholar pause about their process of seeking out useful insights, bibliographic or otherwise.

Apart from giving just due to the scholarship outside of academia, there is also an important discussion to be had about how individual collections shape (or fail to shape) readers' understanding of a historical period's print matter. Within comics studies, the most famous example of this is Bill Blackbeard's prominent collection of turn-of-the-century Sunday supplement comics. Blackbeard's collection became instrumental in establishing a popular and scholarly awareness of early Sunday newspaper comics like Outcault's *Hogan's Alley* and Rudolph Dirks' *Katzenjammer Kids*. Blackbeard is legendary among collectors for his efforts to procure and preserve early Sunday newspaper comics at a time when few scholars or archivists

---

62. With some embarrassment, I must admit that this invaluable source eluded my view until relatively late in my own research process. Initially, I had considered the *Overstreet Guide* as a collector's source that might be used to assess the value of the superhero comic books sitting in my long box at home, but not much else.

63. Adcock's *Yesterday's Papers* is notable for its extensive coverage of Victorian-era woodcuts, as the majority of early comics blogs focus on the lush, color illustrations of the early twentieth century. It is, to my knowledge, the longest extant online discussion of Victorian-era comics, having begun in 2005 and continuing to the present day. Beerbohm's "Platinum Era Comic Books" began as a Listserv in 1991, before migrating to Yahoo and, most recently, to Facebook. A significant portion of these discussions are no longer available to the public due the deletion of the listserv and Yahoo threads from their original servers. Writings of West most pertinent to the present study include West, "Britisher among the B'Hoys"; West and Kahn, *Puck*; West, *T. W. Strong*; and Brown and West, *William Newman*.

were interested in the material. In the middle of the twentieth century, libraries began destroying their vast archives of physical newspapers under the misguided impression that black-and-white microfilm would save physical space while offering a long-lasting record of the content appearing in newspapers. In 1967 Blackbeard learned that the San Francisco Public Library (SFPL) was preparing to destroy their newspaper collection. In response, he and his wife formed a nonprofit organization called the San Francisco Academy of Comic Art, which salvaged and stored comics from all over the United States, amassing over seventy-five tons of print matter. The comics in Blackbeard's collection would eventually form the primary source material for both the seminal book *The Smithsonian Collection of Newspaper Comics* and the important Sunday newspaper holdings at The Ohio State University's Billy Ireland Cartoon Library.[64]

Blackbeard's story serves as a vital lesson in the power of individual collections to define narratives about culture. Blackbeard has occasionally been criticized for feeding into a nationalist narrative that Americans somehow "invented" comics at the turn of the twentieth century, given that his *Smithsonian Collection* anthology focuses entirely on US newspaper comics after 1896.[65] While there is some truth to the idea that Blackbeard's collection and writings established a rigid Amero-centric definition of comic strips, some of the fault surely lies with an uncritical reception of his work. Like virtually all collectors, Blackbeard curated his collection based on personal areas of interest. And yet, scholarly and popular writers alike often treated Blackbeard's anthology and collection as if they were a final and comprehensive archive rather than a partial view or a suggestion that more materials may be in the offing.

The major privately held collections of nineteenth-century American comics have yet to produce a publicized effort analogous to Blackbeard's. Some collections have been lost or dispersed, while others have yet to make their way to a wider audience. Consider the cautionary tale of Gabriel Laderman, a periodicals dealer, professor, and artist based in New York from the 1950s to the early 2000s. Laderman reputedly possessed a deep knowledge of nineteenth-century American graphic humor and amassed one of the world's most impressive collections of early American comics. However, he never produced a manuscript and, upon his death, his collection was auctioned off, dispersed among multiple private and

---

64. Robb, "Bill Blackbeard." See also Thomas, "Renaissance for Comics Studies," 255–66; and Blackbeard and Williams, *Smithsonian Collection of Newspaper Comics*.

65. See Lefevre and Dierick, *Forging a New Medium*, 12.

public archives. One can only wonder how a Blackbeard-style publication of Laderman's collection might have shifted the discussion of American comics had it emerged in the 1970s or 1980s—and how it might compare to other publicly available collections and collections yet to become available.[66] Clearly, this kind of a loss must be prevented from happening again.

Lost Literacies

The importance of this first wave of US comic strips was not lost on all nineteenth-century observers. At least some were aware that figures like Frank Bellew, John McLenan, Augustus Hoppin, and T. W. Strong had forged something new and special with these early experiments in comic strips. Such observers were also aware that this body of work was at risk of being forgotten in ways that held significant ramifications for how US comics history would be understood by future generations.

The author of an 1885 retrospective from the magazine *Art Union* reflected on the "boisterously Bohemian" spirit of comics prior to the Sunday Funnies. The author characterized the period of the 1850s and '60s as a time of vibrant accomplishment for comic strips, even if the artists themselves received few of the accolades accorded to the artists whose work appeared in newspapers and color magazines. "The geniuses of McLenan's day," the author wrote, "drank nothing weaker than whiskey, scorned the tailor, and abhorred the barber." Although cartoonists of the 1890s were better dressed and more widely respected, their work, according to *Art Union*, actually marked a regression from the previous generation. "In the past," the author writes, "the idea was everything." The newer works tended either toward the "unpolished skits" of Frederick Opper in *Puck* or the "inanities of humor, illustrated with the politest care" that would be seen in *Life* magazine's famous Gibson Girl.[67]

The author's characterization of the comics of the 1850s underscores a larger point that turns the common wisdom of comics history on its head: namely, the generation immediately following Bellew and McLenan could view the historical trajectory as one of devolution. Actually, for the *Art Union* writer, the 1850s seemed like an Edenic moment, while the 1880s—a time now regarded as the "beginning" of modern comics—is the beginning of a regression toward frivolity and "unpolished skits." This inversion

---

66. Carbonell email to the author; Adcock email to the author.

67. "Caricature in America," 109.

prompts questions about the current scholarly tendency to characterize pre-twentieth-century comics as stepping stones in a larger progress narrative. Perhaps what is often thought of as the beginning of modern comics in the 1890s was also the end of something else.

Of course, this history need not be premised on the notion that comics somehow devolved or regressed. To do so would merely substitute one fallacy for another. Instead, the possibility of a sort of cultural relativity when it comes to comparisons between past and present comics should be taken seriously. Indeed, much of the acclaim for contemporary graphic novelists is premised on these works' ability to represent human experience in new and interesting ways by rethinking the storytelling techniques of their comics. Avant-garde experiments and visual puzzles of twenty-first-century artists like Lynda Barry, Warren Pleece, Marjane Satrapi, and Chris Ware have been credited with reframing the activity of reading comics as a heady exercise in instructing readers in new ways of thinking about perception—or, as Michael Chaney puts it, "seeing in the metaphysical sense."[68] Likewise, Alison Bechdel's comics are often regarded as some of the most important contributions to LGBT literature—graphic or otherwise—thanks largely to her innovative "archival mode of reading," which incorporates found objects and photographs into the medium of graphic narrative.[69] Are these breakthroughs really so different from the innovations of the mid-nineteenth century? Surely parallel developments can be located, whether they be in the experiments with animation and layout, the fine characterization and complex allegories of the multipanel character study, or the spatial negotiations of the travelogue strip. If drawing is indeed "a mode of knowing," then one can say that the work of Bellew, McLenan, Hoppin, Strong, and other artists and editors of the early US comic strip represented a multitude of rich intellectual traditions.

In tracing these varied nineteenth-century traditions of US comics, this book includes a critical introduction, four chapters, and an epilogue. Each of the main chapters situates a distinct "literacy" in nineteenth-century comics in the context of US print culture and literary history. By organizing the book in this manner, I aim less to offer a comprehensive history than an approach to this rich archive. Following this introduction, I delve into the different styles of visual animation that comic artists deployed during this crucial period after the arrival of the Töpffer bootleg, *Obadiah*

---

68. Chaney, *Reading Lessons in Seeing*, 15. On comics as instructing readers in new approaches to visual and metaphysical experience, see also Sousanis, "Shape of Our Thoughts."

69. Cvetkovich, "Drawing the Archive," 111.

Oldbuck. While many artists imitated Töpffer's approach, even more treated it as a point of departure for experimenting with new, original innovations in organizing and arranging multipanel sequences. As will be seen, this process of experimentation was fueled not only by the creativity of individual artists but a broader constellation of influences ranging from existing forms of print culture to precinematic visual technologies to the vagaries of a publishing scene where space could be limited and editorial decisions mercurial.

The second chapter will discuss the important subgenre of the multipanel character study. As magazines became the primary media for sequential comics, the content of the comics turned increasingly toward short skits and character studies. These brief skits focused on the simplest of subject matter, emphasizing the mundane happenings and mannerisms of everyday life. For all of their simplicity, they could be surprisingly rich both in their comedic possibilities and efforts to envision American social life. Much of this chapter focuses on the contrasting approaches of Frank Bellew and John McLenan, whose character studies were among the most accomplished of the period. For Bellew, the character study provided an apt vessel for a style of observational humor tinged with transcendentalist philosophy that Bellew termed "merrymaking." To rove about the street, observing the silly things happening in everyday life offered Bellew more than just a cheap punchline; it was a means of gaining a broader sympathy with one's fellow humans and thus reconnecting with human nature. Meanwhile, McLenan engaged in a more pessimistic, circumspect project. McLenan's recurring scenes of zany protagonists initially seem like humorous improvisations, but they register profound insecurities about the pressure to conform to bourgeois and heteronormative values.

The third chapter explores the mutual influence between comic strips and theater. The publishing houses that pioneered the comic strip in the United States typically dwelled just blocks from urban theater districts, facilitating a rich circuit of exchange. Comic artists adopted the gestures, recurring characters, and dialogue that appeared in productions of Shakespearean travesties, prevaudevillian burlesques like Benjamin Baker's *A Glance at New York* (1837), and sophisticated social comedies like Anna Mowatt's *Fashion* (1849). Just as importantly, they strived to reproduce the modes of communal spectatorship attached to the volatile social world of urban theater. By highlighting these place-specific conventions, chapter 3 emphasizes the role of the "local" in the evolution of visual language in sequential comic art.

Chapter 4 examines the robust subgenre of travel comics as they emerged in magazines and long-form picture albums. Artists were responding to a widespread interest in travel literature, driven by the sense that travel could lead to personal transformation. For many nineteenth-century Americans, to read or write about travel was to draw comparisons with other regions and thus come to a better sense of one's own regional and national identity. These travelogue strips thus rarely feature much in the way of scenery. Instead, they are organized around the evolution of the individual subject. This chapter focuses on the trajectory of one the subgenre's most ambitious practitioners, August Hoppin. Over the course of thirty years, Hoppin developed an approach to travel comics that foreshadowed and responded to the sophisticated blend of satire and self-reflection at work in the writings of literary travel writers like Margaret Fuller and Mark Twain. Hoppin's genteel and introspective sequences suggest a tantalizing counterfactual—a moment in time when US comics seemed poised to become a serious form of literary and artistic expression.

Chapter 4's invitation to ponder the unrealized potential of the travel comics genre is emblematic of the broader goals of this book. Apart from digging an overlooked culture of American comic strips out of the archives, this study aims to recover a sense of possibility that was also lost when these works fell out of fashion. Unruly and unstable in their methods, early US comic strip artists innovated a wealth of approaches for communicating nineteenth-century experience while challenging their audiences to develop sophisticated literacies in comics conventions. In their time, these artists were understood as modern and forward-looking as they charted a course that could have taken the medium of the comic strip in countless directions.

CHAPTER 1

"Giotto's Magic Circle"
Breakthroughs in Sequential Comics

The multipanel comic strips that began appearing in the United States in the late 1840s must have seemed like a major departure to audiences of the time. These new comics involved a transformation in how the reader/viewer experienced images. Instead of treating pictures as static objects of contemplation or reflection, the creator of the multipanel comic treated successions of images as an apparatus for instigating sensations of movement and of the passage of time. As critic Tom Gunning notes, multipanel comics were one among several emerging forms of media like the moving panorama and the zoetrope that naturalized "a visual vocabulary of motion that not only depicted movement, but constructed a reader/viewer who could follow action through a series of images. The reading of a comic thus came to resemble the viewing of precinematic technologies and animation insofar as the reader/viewer was encouraged to sit back and allow a succession of images guide them through the experience of the story.

Sequential comic strips were not unheard of in the 1840s, but most graphic humor of that time relied on styles of cartooning where the image was locked in place and the viewer moved their eye around a single frame. This earlier approach to graphic humor had its roots in the satirical broadsides of eighteenth-century England. This earlier model is at work in "The Celebrated Racer de Meyer," an 1846 cartoon that lampooned Austrian pianist Leopold de Meyer's tour through the United States (fig. 1.1).[1] The image features a single scene with a complex system of allegorical figures;

---

1. "Celebrated Racer de Meyer," 18.

FIGURE 1.1. "The Celebrated Racer de Meyer," *Yankee Doodle*, September 1846, 18. Courtesy of the American Antiquarian Society.

below runs a long series of humorous explanations that diagram the intricate details of the illustration. The image itself did not change as much as the viewer picked out details from the byzantine illustration and used the elaborate text as crib notes for decoding the various elements of the allegory. The artist of the satirical print in this style assumed a level of familiarity with an existing vocabulary of allusions and intertextual references. In this manner, the implied reader/viewer could read the print at a glance by pulling from their knowledge of cultural cues that include likenesses of public figures, references to political events, or imagery evoking other forms of media like theatrical performances and newspapers.[2]

---

2. On the eighteenth-century satirical broadside, see Taylor, *Politics of Parody*, 3–5.

In contrast to poring over the complicated details of an image like "Racer de Meyer," the multipanel comic seemed to spring to life with ease. In an 1865 *Atlantic Monthly* essay, the writer H. M. Fletcher compared the transition from the older satirical print to the picture story to the drawing of "Giotto's magic circle," a quasi-mythical episode where a single stroke of a pencil initiated the Renaissance's approach to perspective. Fletcher wrote that, unlike the older satirical prints, which encouraged viewers to gaze at the illustrations "as we would at some half-civilized creatures," the new approach featured a "rollicking freedom" that prompted viewers to "recognize ourselves" in the subjects and to "laugh with them as we would with friends or acquaintances."[3] Arranging pictures in "series" allowed an artist's characters "to leap into the very existence he wishes them to assume."[4] In short, the simple act of putting illustrations into sequence seemed like a revolutionary transformation in how comics could tell stories because it introduced the possibility of animation.

As this chapter demonstrates, the sequential breakthrough signaled by the arrival of picture stories from France and Switzerland was really only the beginning of a larger revolution in the use of comic drawing for visual animation. Early on, US artists imitated the methods of figures like Töpffer and Cham for organizing comic strips, but they were eager to strike out in new directions. The distinctive use of montage that appeared in the pirated European albums that first made their way to American shores thus gave way to countless methods for suggesting relationships between images and text: artists organized strips around wordplay, puns, and musical notation; they encouraged readers to flip physical pages to suggest movement between scenes; and they experimented with elaborate panel layouts to simulate the visual illusions created by precursors to cinematic technology such as the zoetrope and stereoscope. Such examples only capture a small portion of the expansive and diverse repertoire that was fast developing among US comic artists. The works produced in the United States starting in the 1850s and through the 1870s thus exemplify scholar Thierry Groensteen's theory of "braiding" (*tressage*) as a means of understanding the basic visual language of multipanel comics. Groensteen resists the idea that there are finite or stable types of sequences or transitions between panels in favor of a model that emphasizes relationships between panels as the basis of meaning making. He indicates that within multipanel comics "every panel exists, potentially if not actually in relation with each other." Hence, the

---

3. Fletcher, "Rodolphe Töpffer," 564.
4. Fletcher, "Rodolphe Töpffer," 564–65.

question of how these relationships are constructed is perpetually in flux as images can be combined and recombined in novel ways.[5]

Multiple factors stimulated the vibrant culture of novelty and improvisation that played out in magazines and graphic albums. Sometimes the invention of a new braiding technique was a conscious artistic choice. Sometimes it was accidental, driven by things like space limitations or pressure from publishers to produce something innovative. In either case, the new styles of animation in multipanel comics were valued not only as vehicles for narrative or humor but as entirely new kinds of visual spectacles.

The Töpfferian Picture Story
Comes to America

Picture stories in the Swiss and French style first appeared in the United States in 1842 when the Brother Jonathan Company offered a pirated edition of Töpffer's album *Monsieur Vieux Bois* under the English-language title *The Mishaps and Adventures of Obadiah Oldbuck*.[6] In the decade that followed the publication of *Obadiah Oldbuck*, American publishers released about a dozen original albums. Works like the gold rush–themed *Journey to the Gold Diggins* (1848) and *The Wonderful! And Soul Thrilling Adventures of Oscar Shanghai by Land and Sea* (ca. 1855) all closely imitated the Töpfferian model.[7] US-produced bootlegs of albums by British artist-writers also gained significant footholds with successful releases, including *Peter Piper in Bengal*; Richard Doyle's *Adventures of Messrs. Brown, Jones, and Robinson*; and Cruikshank's *Bachelor's Own Book* and *The Toothache*.[8] With advertisements for these works often featuring the all-important endorsement of having been composed "after the fashion of Obadiah Oldbuck," the trend was assured.[9]

Despite the outsized influence that Töpffer's work exerted on the illustrated press, few Americans at the time knew the artist's name, much less

---

5. Groensteen, *System of Comics*, 146.

6. Töpffer, "Adventures of Mr. Obadiah Oldbuck," *Brother Jonathan Extra*.

7. A.L.C. (pseud.), *Wonderful! And Soul Thrilling Adventures*; and Read and Read, *Journey to the Gold Diggins*.

8. Cruikshank, "The Toothache"; Cruikshank, *Bachelor's Own Book*; *Hunting Adventures*; and Schmitz, *Sure Water Cure*.

9. "New Publications"; and "Strange and Wonderful Adventures."

identified him with the picture story or the comic strip. Töpffer, however, was by then already being credited in Europe as the inventor of a radically new approach to graphic narrative. A schoolmaster, author, painter, and cartoonist in the cosmopolitan center of Geneva, Töpffer began creating what he termed "*histoire en estampes*" (story in prints or picture story) in 1827 as a hobby to amuse his pupils and friends. He remained reluctant to publish his picture stories until 1832 when one of his albums made its way into the hands of no less a figure than Johann Goethe who marveled at the way the "strange" and "witty" albums were able to "draw multiple motifs out of a few figures."[10] After Goethe's remarks were printed posthumously, Töpffer began self-publishing albums such as *Histoire de Monsieur Jabot* (1833), *Les Amours de Mr. Vieux Bois* (1839), and *Histoire de Monsieur Cryptogame* (1845), among others. Through the 1830s and '40s, Töpffer's albums gained recognition in the German and French literary scenes. Parisian journals serialized versions of his work, and the popularity of his comics spawned well-regarded imitators including Cham and Gustave Doré, who created their own innovative variations on the picture stories.[11]

Obadiah Oldbuck, the pirated album that had introduced Töpffer's work to the US market, first appeared in the United States as a supplement to the humorous newspaper *Brother Jonathan.* The publisher Brother Jonathan had used plates from a British bootleg that had originally been cofinanced by British caricaturist George Cruikshank. For the supplement, Brother Jonathan reformatted the album to match the quarto size of their newspaper, resulting in a publication that coincidentally resembled the size and shape of modern superhero comic books. Brother Jonathan's printer, Wilson and Company, published it again in 1844 as a standalone album, this time restoring it to its original oblong format.[12] Unauthorized copies of the English version of another Töpffer picture story, *Monsieur Cryptogame,* also achieved significant distribution as an oblong album with the Wilson and Company's publication of *The Strange Adventures of Bachelor Butterfly* in 1843.

Brother Jonathan was at the forefront of the fast-growing market for selling inexpensive books and periodicals to middle-class families. By 1842, when *Oldbuck* was released, the company was functioning as a partnership

---

10. Qtd. in Kunzle, *Father of the Comic Strip,* 52.

11. Kunzle, *Father of the Comic Strip,* 49–56, 74–76; and Kunzle, *Rodolphe Töpffer,* xliii.

12. Kunzle, *Father of the Comic Strip,* 162, 175; and Rodolphe Töpffer, *Adventures of Mr. Obadiah Oldbuck* (1844).

between Wilson and Benjamin Day Sr.[13] Today, Day is best known for launching the first successful "penny press" papers in the United States. He had revolutionized the industry by selling newspapers at below cost and then recouping the losses by relying on advertising revenue instead of subscriptions. His sensational newspaper stories generated unprecedented circulation and profits for his newspapers, most famously in the case of the *New York Sun*'s "The Great Moon Hoax," a series of articles that made the unbelievable (and untrue) claim that a race of humanoid bat people had been discovered on the lunar surface. The Brother Jonathan Company's approach to the book and periodical market featured a similar blend of price-consciousness and sensationalist flair.

Obadiah Oldbuck contained a combination of qualities that were attractive to the new class of readers that Day and Wilson pursued. In plotting and sensibility, Töpffer's picture stories bore a closer resemblance to novelistic fiction than the raunchy cartoons of the humor almanacs or the caustic images of political broadsides. Brother Jonathan could thus confidently advertise them alongside other offerings of the "Brother Jonathan Cheap Book Establishment," which included pirated British and European classics, wholesome humor collections like *Mrs. Partington's Carpet-bag of Fun*, and educational texts about science and nature.[14] On the other hand, *Oldbuck* and *Bachelor Butterfly*, with their generous number of illustrations and dynamic sense of movement, fit nicely into Brother Jonathan's larger strategy of translating new print technologies into forms of visual spectacle. *Oldbuck*'s production was inseparable from a larger media ecology. Amid what Isabel Lehuu terms the antebellum "Carnival on the Page," publishers engaged in intense competition to create increasingly lavish and eye-catching publications as they tried to grab readers' attention.[15] For the Brother Jonathan Company, engaging in this meant producing everything from visual gimmicks like enormous "mammoth editions" to its illustrated

---

13. The Brother Jonathan Company and publication of the same name had apparently been founded by Park Benjamin and Rufus Griswold in 1839 with printer James G. Wilson. By 1842 Benjamin and Griswold had left for the rival publication *The New World*. Thanks to Guy Lawley for calling my attention to Benjamin Day Sr.'s involvement with Brother Jonathan. See Barnes, *Authors, Publishers, and Politicians*, 27; Lossing, *History of New York*, 275; "Sketches of the Publishers," 234; and Gardner, "Antebellum Popular Serialities," 41.

14. An ad typical for the time lists *Bachelor Butterfly* alongside Dickens's last novel, *Collet's French Dialogues and Phrases*, and *Colburn's Arithmetic*. "Books Just Rec'd," 2.

15. Lehuu, *Carnival on the Page*, 59–68.

weekly, which could sport an impressive one hundred engravings in an issue.[16]

In introducing Töpffer's albums to readers, Wilson, Day, and others emphasized its status as an exotic new form of storytelling and spectacle, distinct from earlier styles of illustration and graphic humor. The tone and approach of one of the first advertisements to appear in *Brother Jonathan* was reminiscent of promotions for Barnumesque curiosities. The blustery ad announced "HERE IS A CURIOUS THING!!" and suggested that *Oldbuck* would "challenge comparison."[17] Paralleling Barnum's winking references to mythical creatures in promotions such as the Feejee Mermaid, the ad asserted that readers had "undoubtedly heard graphic narrations spoken of and will be compelled to acknowledge that this work comes entirely under that description." It then went on to spell out exactly what made *Oldbuck* so different: *Oldbuck* was "not a 'story and picters [*sic*] to match'" like a reader might find in a conventional illustrated book, but instead "a story told entirely with the graver."[18] Other ads and notices described this new medium of "graphic narration" as offering narrative possibilities unavailable in conventional text-based expression. An article in the *Bedford Street Budget* went so far as to describe Töpffer's style as an improvement on the novel, asking, "Who in plain prose can describe his wonderful adventures?—his author saw it was impossible, and had recourse to painting—why should we then essay what the mighty mind of the author despaired of?"[19] Still others suggested that this new medium might be understood as an immersive new style of visual spectacle. For example, an advertisement in the *New York Sun* described *Oldbuck* as "a pictorial extravaganza that out sancho's Sancho Panza."[20] In at least one case, images from *Obadiah Oldbuck* were converted into a magic lantern show or "dissolving views" and exhibited as part of an evening's entertainment, which also included views of American and European landscapes, microscopic views of the "water devil," and "Pyramic Fires of Dazzling brilliance."[21]

---

16. Gardner, "Antebellum Popular Serialities," 41.
17. "Here Is a Curious Thing!!"
18. "Here Is a Curious Thing!!"
19. "Budget's Review," 14–15.
20. "Brother Jonathan."
21. "Local Matters—Whipple's Dissolving Views."

With these types of promotion efforts leading the way, Töpffer's works achieved consistent and substantial readership. Printings of *Oldbuck* and *Bachelor Butterfly* rolled out in distribution for nearly the entire second half of the nineteenth century with booksellers promoting the work from its initial release in 1842 through the late 1860s. In 1845 Wilson and Company claimed that their first two editions of *Oldbuck* had each sold twenty thousand copies within their first three months.[22] Advertisements and notices spread in every major city in the Northeast, as far south as New Orleans and South Carolina, and as far west as Minnesota and Milwaukee, with notices appearing in California slightly later.[23] Characters and phrases from the books made their way into everyday conversation. For instance, the names "Oldbuck" and "Bachelor Butterfly" served as shorthand for romantic and pastoral figures throughout the second half of the nineteenth century in works such as Toler Wolfe's *Book of Odds and Ends* and Hart Merriam's *Birds of Connecticut*.[24] In the press, someone was commonly described as "like Obadiah Oldbuck" if they "turned over a new leaf" and then failed to follow through on their promised reforms.[25] References to Töpffer even appeared in Thomas Wentworth Higginson's journals with the abolitionist describing how his contentment at taking agricultural lands from secessionist troops paralleled that of "Mr. Obadiah Oldbuck, when he decided to adopt a pastoral life, and assume the provisional name of Thyrsis."[26]

At the heart of *Obadiah Oldbuck*'s appeal was a distinctive new visual language that Töpffer had more or less invented himself. While Töpffer's tactic of arranging frames in sequence may at first seem like the boxy patterns of later newspaper comics, the similarity only skims the surface. Töpffer and his American imitators typically rely on what scholar David Kunzle describes as a "Töpfferian montage," a style of animation characterized by alternation between continuous scene-to-scene transitions and abrupt transitions or "jump cuts" that interrupt the action, creating

---

22. "Obadiah Oldbuck Again on Horseback."

23. "Daily Bulletin"; "'Rage' of the Day"; and Agassiz, "Letter from Professor Agassiz."

24. *Birds of Connecticut* described how an amusing bird-watching episode "reminds one forcibly" of "Bachelor Butterfly, on page 14th, where he jumped overboard, and, in order to save the life of the Naturalist." Hart, *Review of the Birds of Connecticut*, 71. Toler Wolfe writes, "Mr. Oldbuck adored his fair lady" alongside reference to Davey Crockett's Bravery and Samson's strength. Wolfe, *Book of Odds and Ends*, 53.

25. "Local Items"; "Little Too Much"; "Those Who Have Read"; and "It Is so Easy."

26. Higginson, *Writings of Thomas Wentworth Higginson*, 130.

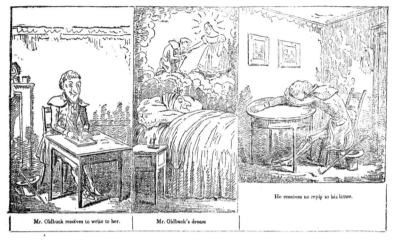

FIGURE 1.2. Rodolphe Töpffer, "The Adventures of Mr. Obadiah Oldbuck," *Brother Jonathan Extra*, January 1, 1842, 4. Courtesy of the American Antiquarian Society.

a "haphazard flow."[27] Where twentieth-century comics typically look to evoke a sense of fluidity between frames, Töpffer's comics hinge on a deliberate tension between continuity and discontinuity. Forces of action and reaction are set against one another in alternation, leading critics to compare his sequences to "a mechanism that flies off the handle."[28]

The herky-jerky rhythm of a Töpfferian montage is evident in the example shown in figure 1.2. Here, the protagonist Oldbuck writes to his "ladye

27. Kunzle, *History of the Comic Strip, Volume 2*, 349.

28. Smolderen, *Origins of Comics*, 45. See also Gunning, "Art of Succession," 42.

love," dreams of her response, and then falls into suicidal melancholy when she does not respond. The sequence hinges on the back-and-forth between a pendulum-like vacillation of moods and gestures. The starry-eyed dreams of love precipitate a jump cut to despair, which in turn prompts the suicide attempt and then a jump cut to a disjunctive moment in which Oldbuck is unexpectedly dropped (figuratively *and* literally) into his old life, thinking of lunch. In the meantime, the captions remain essential to the peculiar rhythm and humor of the Töpfferian picture story. Typical of Töpffer, the captions supply dry, comedic understatements and overstatements whose humor resides in how they *fail* to convey the scale of the action. For example, the simple caption noting that Oldbuck "receives no reply to his letter" in frame #3 dramatically undersells the melodramatic image of Oldbuck prostrating himself on the table, just as the reference to Oldbuck's "life dying of hunger" dramatically oversells the image of the bemused figure on the floor. In this manner, Töpffer produces a lively back and forth between caption and image that amplifies the larger pattern of action and reaction that plays out in the panel transitions.[29]

US-produced imitations of Töpffer's picture stories are interesting largely for how they reveal the diverse ways that Töpffer's visual language and stories were received. Virtually all of the Töpffer copycats imitated the plotlines, rhythms, and boxcar-shaped panels of a Töpfferian montage. But here was where the similarities ended. As we'll see, the format was adapted to a wide variety of subjects and approaches.

Most commonly, the Töpffer copycats refashioned the trope of the roving, picaresque heroes of European imports like *Obadiah Oldbuck* and *Bachelor Butterfly* into stock characters associated with the regionalist humor of the Old Southwest. Such works turned to disruptive Yankee and Southwestern characters like the rugged frontiersmen of the *Crockett Almanacs*, James Kirke Paulding's Yankee rustics, or the puckish urban rascals of Doesticks's humor. The medium of the picture story offered a vital new dimension in how this distinctively American brand of humor could be presented to audiences. Artists were not bound by the long verbal yarn that writers like Paulding and Doesticks depended upon. Instead, the picture story could bring these plotlines into the realm of visual spectacle. Slapstick action and wild swings in plot and character could be depicted instantaneously in a kinetic frenzy.

---

29. Töpffer, "Adventures of Mr. Obadiah Oldbuck" (1842), 4.

This kinetic reimagining of regionalist humor was certainly a main attraction of *The Wonderful! And Soul Thrilling Adventures by Land and Sea of Oscar Shanghai* (ca. 1855), an anonymously penned picture story that was advertised as a work "after the fashion of *Obadiah Oldbuck*."[30] Appearing first as a serial and then an album, *Oscar Shanghai* replaced the Töpfferian picaresque hero with a carousing New York businessman.[31] Reminiscent of Töpffer's characters, Oscar's impulsive tendencies lead him into roving adventures that create headaches for the characters he encounters and correspond to similarly unpredictable plot turns and tonal shifts. For example, the opening scene clearly takes inspiration from Vieux Bois's disruptive pursuit of "the beloved object" as Oscar sends his bookkeeper into an apoplectic fit when he suddenly resolves "that business becomes very stupid" and spontaneously "decides to travel." The obsessions and impulsivity, the halting panel transitions, and the caption play are all vintage Töpffer.

Where Töpffer's albums maintained the delicate irony of the picaresque novel, *Oscar Shanghai* had far more in common with the exaggeration and slapstick of the American tall tale. Nowhere is this contrast more apparent than in *Oscar Shanghai*'s climax in which Oscar travels to Turkey and unwittingly starts a revolution. In the sequence, Oscar meets the Sultan, is named grand vizier, goes mad with power, and is then run out of the country when he begins decapitating people and starts a revolution among the populace. The author/artist of *Oscar Shanghai* condenses this whole chain of events down to a lean six frames, emphasizing the breakneck pace of events (fig. 1.3). Shifts from the puzzled expression of the decapitated head to Oscar on a soapbox fomenting revolution to his hasty retreat make for a breakneck pace that condenses the elaborate sequence of events down to several quick shocks. Other sequences in *Oscar Shanghai* rely on hyperbolic slapstick as Oscar is variously swallowed by a whale, has his body contorted by a fall from a hot air balloon, does battle with a lion, and is

30. "New Publications."

31. *Oscar Shanghai* appeared in a variety of forms, including a serial in the *New York Picayune* and *Pictorial Picayune*, a fifty-page album from Dick & Fitzgerald, and a second printing with a new title that foregrounded the travel themes: "New Publications—The Wonderful and Amusing Doings by Sea and Land, of Oscar Shanghai" (*Richmond Whig*, 1855); "Untitled Comic about Mr. Brown's Travels" (*New York Picayune*, 1853, 3); "The Wonderful! and Soul Thrilling Adventures of Anarcharsis H. Brown ESQ" (Part I) (*New York Picayune*, August 13, 1853, 1); "The Wonderful! and Soul Thrilling Adventures of Anarcharsis H. Brown ESQ" (Part II) (*New York Picayune*, October 22, 1853, 1); and A.L.C. (pseud.), *Wonderful! And Soul Thrilling Adventures by Land and Sea of Oscar Shanghai*.

FIGURE 1.3. A.L.C. (pseud.), *The Wonderful! And Soul Thrilling Adventures by Land and Sea of Oscar Shanghai* (New York: Dick & Fitzgerald, ca. 1855), 16.

shot out of a giant crossbow by African natives. In each case, scene-to-scene frame transitions are used to initiate sequences that, while inspired by Töpffer, deliberately align its tone and sensibility with the rough and tumble sensibility of American regionalist humor.

Other efforts to rethink the narrative possibilities offered by the Töpfferian picture revealed even greater flexibility in terms of content and approach. For example, a few Töpfferian albums were produced not for large audiences but as semiprivate commemorations. *Ichabod Academicus*

(1849), the most widely distributed of these, was published by three Yale graduates who adapted the form of the visual picaresque as a remembrance of their time in school.[32] *Ichabod* reads as a fascinating hybrid between yearbook, scrapbook, and comedic novel; the authors embroider their tale with insider references to Yale traditions such as the Skull and Bones Society and a giant wooden spoon bestowed on Yale's most popular junior.

A further variation on the format arrived with the shrewd blend of parody and gossip that *Yankee Notions* and *Harper's* artist John McLenan employed in *The Sad Tale of the Courtship of Slyfox Wikoff* (1855). McLenan's graphic album was a loose adaptation of *My Courtship and Consequences* (1855), the memoir of Henry Wikoff, a US diplomat who prompted an international scandal after the Italian government accused him of forcing an heiress into marriage. McLenan cannily recognized the picaresque elements of Wikoff's memoir and converted episodes of that book into a Töpfferesque lampoon of Wikoff's rakish tendencies and romantic pretentions.

Ironically enough, the impact of the Töpfferian visual language was probably most apparent in the period's more hackneyed albums. To that end, interest in replicating the success of the *Oldbuck* album was so great that publishers even reused plates from old cartoons and caricatures to string illustrations in a series—often from multiple artists—and then tossed captions underneath to create the semblance of a picture story.[33] *The Fortunes of Ferdinand Flipper* (1850), the most widely circulated of these collages, was Brother Jonathan's first attempt at an original follow-up (if that term can be applied here) to the success of *Oldbuck*. *Ferdinand Flipper* culled illustrations from sources ranging from the French fantasy pictures of J. J. Grandville to the ethnic caricatures of US illustrator Charles Martin and knitted them together through captions that told a bizarre, often incoherent story of Ferdinand Flipper's birth, growth, and death. The album's look and feel vacillate wildly from mischievous satire to mawkish sentimentality, frequently struggling to sustain a consistent tone within a single layout. Many times, it even becomes difficult to discern which figure Ferdinand is supposed to be because his appearance changes so much from frame to frame.

---

32. Peters et al., *College Experience of Ichabod Academicus*; and Schiff, "Ichabod's Progress." See also Attwood, *Manners and Customs*; and Hayward, *College Scenes*.

33. Avery, *My Friend Wriggles*; "Adventures of Noahdiah Nobbs"; and *Fortunes of Ferdinand Flipper*.

As strange as it may seem, *Ferdinand Flipper* was probably *not* dismissed by its audience as a mere throwaway or fraud. Instead, readers would likely have understood and enjoyed the fact that the album was a collage of unrelated woodcuts. This surprising conclusion makes sense when considering the habits of its likely readers. As discussed previously, US audiences in the late 1840s and early 1850s were accustomed to seeing pilfered and recycled woodcuts in their print matter even as they demonstrated a keen interest in any print matter that featured images (especially when those images produced the Töpfferian spectacles of animation). Cast in this light, *Ferdinand Flipper* reads less as an attempt to fool its audience than an effort to engage savvy readers in an ironic joke in which incongruous materials are juxtaposed to humorous effect.

And indeed, *Ferdinand Flipper* is remarkably successful at turning the conventions of Töpfferian montage to humorous effect. The layout pictured in figure 1.4 is one of *Ferdinand Flipper*'s most effective sequences due to its use of dizzying shifts in visual style to replicate the madcap play of action and reaction that characterized Töpffer's work. Hence, alternations between the realistic style of the action scenes (frames #1 and #3) and the grotesque caricature of the bystanders' reactions (frames #2, #4, and #5) produce an outrageous resolution to each sequence. When Flipper's coat is caught on the dock or thieves are apprehended, the slapstick becomes amplified by the bulging eyes and exaggerated features of the bystanders. In the meantime, the captions adopt a decidedly Töpfferian form of comic understatement as they wind through dizzying plot turns ("Young Flipper now resolves to go on a journey, but a strange accident prevents his starting," "The accident frightens a bystander nearly out of his wits," etc.).[34] In doing so, this sequence takes the basic structure of the Töpfferian montage to its most logical conclusion; the extreme vacillations in tone and form play not as discontinuity but as an absurdist form of hyperbole.

The surprising effectiveness of *Ferdinand Flipper*'s humor highlights an important fact about the breakthrough of multipanel comics: in post-Töpfferian US print culture, readers became primed to look for relationships between images and text, regardless of the provenance of the images themselves. Whether this effect was achieved through a new original picture story, a bootlegged European album, or a collage of pilfered woodcuts was less important than the fact that a dynamic spectacle was appearing in the first place.

---

34. *Fortunes of Ferdinand Flipper,* 54–55.

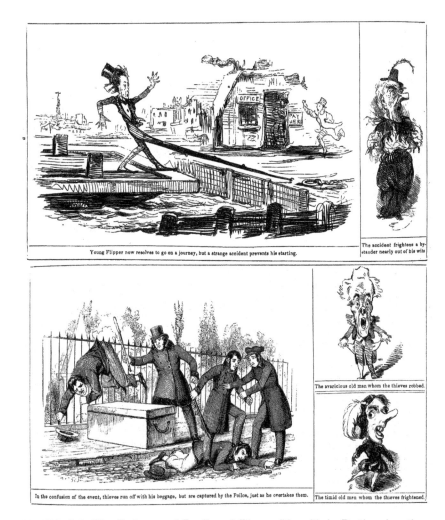

FIGURE 1.4. *The Fortunes of Ferdinand Flipper* (New York: Brother Jonathan, 1850), 54–55, showing repurposed woodcuts combined to emulate the Töpfferian method. Courtesy of Beinecke Rare Book and Manuscript Library, Yale University.

For the most part, attempts to publish album-length picture stories that replicated the appeal of *Obadiah Oldbuck* were met with limited success. As the writers of *Ichabod Academicus* noted, with "the expense of lithography" and "so limited a subscription," publishers had little to gain in terms of profit or reputation from selling album-length graphic narrations.[35] As I discuss in the next section, it was instead in the humor magazines of the early 1850s that multipanel comics began to flourish. Magazine artists, writers, and publishers in the United States applied the basic Töpfferian

---

35. Peters et al., *College Experience of Ichabod Academicus.*

formula and turned it toward a wild brand of experimentalism fitted not to the unwieldy 150-page volume but rather a shortened form that was produced for the pages of humor magazines and other periodicals. Here, the multipanel comic focused on brief vignettes in ways that foreshadowed the short skits of the Sunday Funnies, even as artists and publishers reconsidered the very terms of how sequential comic art might be composed.

The Attractions of Magazines

As sequential comics became increasingly common in the magazines of the 1850s, the definition of what constituted a "sequence" became a fluid concept that regularly fell outside the province of either the Töpfferian montage or that of the single-panel satirical prints. Plot-driven picture stories in the Töpfferian mode shared space with comics that took a seemingly improvisational approach to the different kinds of relations that images could have to one another. The ways comics panels could be braided together (that is, how they juxtaposed illustrations and combined those illustrations with captions) were seemingly endless. The medium of the magazine was itself central to this development. Magazines, and especially humor magazines, featured a unique combination of editorial policies, printing technologies, and market pressures that encouraged experimentation with the format and style of the comics.

An important factor that prevented comics from stabilizing into regular or predictable forms was the perpetual revisability of humor magazine page layouts. Humor magazines featured an ever-shifting array of content such as jokes, stories, essays, advertisements, and illustrations. With all this content competing for space, editors regularly tinkered with layouts to accommodate the different elements of their publication (an editorial practice that would lead editor and writer Cornelius Mathews to compare *Yankee Notions* to "a hasty meal when the housewife is put to her wits to pick up a dinner").[36] Amid this organizational chaos, comics were placed wherever editors could fit them. Longer sequences were sliced into smaller bits while shorter cartoons could be juxtaposed to create a "comicalities" section, displaying multiple comics on the same page. As a result, the reading experiences associated with comics could shift spontaneously

---

36. Qtd. in West, *T. W. Strong*, 8.

and unpredictably, forcing artists and readers alike to cultivate flexibility in their methods for scanning from image to image.

Another encouragement to experimentation was the ephemeral, semi-disposable quality of humor magazines. Where the graphic album was a keepsake to be displayed on the parlor table or kept for posterity, magazines appeared periodically and could be discarded after a few readings. Due to the demand for new material to fill pages each week or month, artists were under pressure to create larger amounts of comics and to do so quickly. And because these comics were relatively temporary, the penalties for turning out a bad comic were low. Put simply, artists were empowered to try new things because they were now allowed to fail.

Lastly, innovation was driven by a consistent demand for new and different approaches to visual storytelling. Throughout the 1850s and '60s, cheap printed images were still relatively new, and publishers like T. W. Strong, Jesse Haney, and indeed, Benjamin Day Sr. understood that novelty could drive sales. Within this marketplace, the braiding technique regularly served as the primary attraction of the comic strip. This period of novelty in US magazine comics can be likened to Tom Gunning's description of early film as a "cinema of attractions."[37] Like the silent spectacles of the Lumiere brothers' *Arrival of the Train* or Georges Méliès's *Voyage to the Moon,* the emphasis in these early comic "strips of attractions" lay not with the plotting or characterization or social commentary but with how the emergent medium of comic strip provided novel forms of visual and verbal experience. For audiences and publishers, the multipanel comic was no mere vessel or container but the primary attraction itself.

Many visual storytelling techniques were created solely as one-offs, invented for a single comic, only to be forgotten or discarded. For readers, the appeal of puzzling through these novelty comics seemed to lay with the epistemological adventure of testing how a change in format could produce a distinctive sensation or response. For example, "Archaeological Intelligence," an early comic in *Yankee Notions,* spins an elaborate visual puzzle out of Egyptian hieroglyphics (fig. 1.5) as readers must use a key to decode the meaning of "tiles from an ancient college in Thebes." In the upper section of each layout, illustrations resemble the pictograms appearing on the sides of Egyptian tombs, which yield few clues to the meaning of the comic when read in isolation. In the lower section, the key translates

---

37. Gunning, "Cinema of Attractions," 56–63.

FIGURE 1.5. "Archaeological Intelligence," *Yankee Notions*, April 1858, 103. Courtesy of the American Antiquarian Society.

the meaning of the cryptic illustrations for the reader. Upon reading the key, readers learn that the mysterious figures are not so mysterious after all as the pictograms depict ancient Egyptian college students who lead lives similar those of nineteenth-century college students. Like their modern counterparts, the Egyptian students obsess over stylish clothing, entertain romantic rivalries, and fantasize about impressing classmates at their thesis defenses.[38] With such a mundane "solution" to the puzzle posed by the comic, "Archaeological Intelligence" ultimately reveals itself to be a work that prioritizes the quiet pleasure of puzzle-solving over big punchlines. It

38. "Archaeological Intelligence," 102–3.

is less a satire of Egyptology than an invitation to experience the satisfaction of codebreaking.

Experiments with captions offered a rich source for novel approaches to organizing comic strips. Comics were presented as playscript dialogues, poetry, humorous aphorisms, wordplay, rebuses, and strings of literary quotations. "Study of the Stars" by John McLenan was typical of a subgenre of comics that treated the succession of images as an occasion to guide the reader through a series of related puns. Here, McLenan used a series of puns on astronomy to move the reader through slapstick vignettes about a policeman's night out on patrol. The caption "Falling Star" indicates a botched arrest of a criminal, while another caption, "Evening Star," finds our policeman shooing away a young street urchin, and still another caption, "Star of the First Magnitude," puns on the policeman's encounter with an obese mustachioed police chief."[39] An especially inventive innovation with captions was A. L. Carroll's "Four Experiences in Waltzing" (fig. 1.6), which did away with words altogether and instead used musical notation that could be played on a piano. And indeed Carroll's "Four Experiences" would have rewarded those who attempted to play the musical composition embedded in the captions. Rapid shifts in key signatures and increasingly frenetic rhythms serve as a prelude to the comic's punchline in which the male dance partner loses his footing and falls on his bum in time with a fermata (known in music parlance as "a grand pause").[40]

Within this volatile world of nineteenth-century illustrated periodicals, it was also unsafe to assume that a grid or single-page layout was the most desirable option for displaying sequential comics. The editors of the magazine *Nick Nax* were particularly fond of placing each frame of a sequence in the same position on each successive page of a single issue. As a reader flipped through the magazine, they would see a new frame of the comic revealed in the same position of successive pages within a single issue. While this tactic may at first seem like an editorial compromise based on spatial limitations, it could in fact become essential to the narrative flow of the comics because artists could achieve an effect reminiscent of the flipping between pages to reveal text and image that readers would have encountered in moveable toy books.

"The Trials of a Man with a Gold Watch," a twelve-panel comic from *Nick Nax* in 1857, seems to have been composed with this precise

---

39. McLenan, "Study of the Stars," 40–41.
40. Carroll, "Four Experiences in Waltzing," 278.

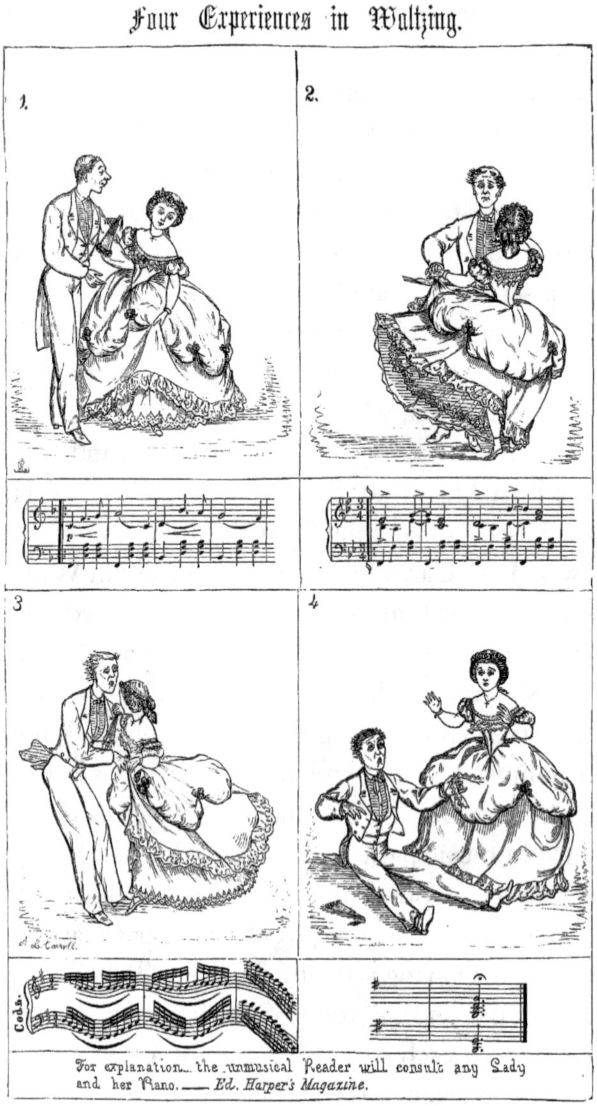

Four Experiences in Waltzing.

FIGURE 1.6. A. L. Carroll, "Four Experiences in Waltzing,"
Harper's New Monthly Magazine, July 1863, 278. Courtesy
of the American Antiquarian Society.

assumption in mind (fig. 1.7).[41] This artist makes use of this distinctive format by using the separation between the frames to generate a sense of
suspense. The frame transitions are thus organized as leaps between a series
of self-contained tableaux, each of which presents the reader with a new
punchline. Nearly every frame visits a new disaster upon the protagonist

41. "Trials of a Man with a Gold Watch" (1857), 36–37.

FIGURE 1.7. "Trials of a Man with a Gold Watch," *Nick Nax for All Creation*, June 1857, 43–46, showing installments appearing in the lower-right of each page. Courtesy of the American Antiquarian Society.

as he gets into a scrape with a new would-be antagonist who he suspects of coveting his gold watch. This creates a distinctive set of cadences, as each page flip brings a novel situation and new slapstick punchline. The protagonist's tense encounter with a stranger on the street sets off a chain of events, including an awkward conversation with his boarders, a crazed bedroom scene where he fires his shotgun at his coatrack after mistaking it for an intruder, and a final scrape with the police who arrest him and make off with his watch. In each case, the pleasure of the comic resides not with the illusion of fluid motion but with the halting rhythms and surprising incongruities that emerge each time the page is turned.

"Man with a Golden Watch" reappeared two years later as a grid-based comic when *Comic Monthly* repurposed the plates and laid them out on a single page as a 3 × 4 grid. This second version of the comic looks strikingly less effective (fig. 1.8).[42] Without the turning of pages to slow down the narrative flow, the punchlines come too quickly, resulting in a disjointed sequence that features none of the sharp comic timing of the original *Nick Nax* version.

Regardless of which version of the comic one prefers, its appearance in both formats is interesting due to what it illustrates about the larger dynamics of sequential comics in the 1850s and '60s. During this period of instability and limited resources, publishers and audiences took a flexible approach to how their comics should be read and braided together. While this flexibility occasionally led to hackneyed comics that potentially wrought havoc on an artist's intentions, it also offered a certain freedom to experiment. This creative freedom, moreover, decreased as the form of the humor magazine—and the picture stories within—matured into a more stable, predictable medium.

Setting aside instances like "Man with a Gold Watch," the use of full one- and two-page spreads was a striking source of variety and novelty. Not all publishers held the resources or inclination to devote full pages to a single multipanel comic (political caricature was consistently likelier to occupy this valuable space). However, in the instances where artists were lucky enough to receive uninterrupted pages for a multipanel comic, the results could be inspired. The flexibility of the uninterrupted layout could offer a breathtaking variety of reading experiences that extended beyond the frame-to-frame sequences of the conventional comics grid. For the

---

42. "Trials of a Man with a Gold Watch" (1859), 16.

FIGURE 1.8. "Trials of a Man with a Gold Watch," *Comic Monthly*, April 1859, 16, showing the sequence reformatted as a 3 × 4 grid. Courtesy of the American Antiquarian Society.

most accomplished artists, the visual embellishments and innovative layouts composed more than mere decorations, instead offering crucial aspects
of the thematic content and the sensations that artist was trying to produce for their reader. The result was a hybrid form that combined elements
of the older Hogarthian style (in which the reader spent time contemplating a single heteroglossic image) and this newer Töpfferian style (which
emphasized motion and sequence).

Innovative visual design in multipanel magazine comics reached a high-
water mark in the extraordinary run of comics that appeared in *Harper's
Monthly* from 1855 to 1865. During this time, *Harper's* dedicated at least two
pages per issue to the work of a single US comic artist (in 1853, *Harper's*
regularly published a column called *A Leaf from Punch*, but these were
merely copies of pages that had appeared in *Punch*). A widely read national
publication, *Harper's* offered access to audiences, credibility, and financial
opportunities that outstripped anything from the smaller niche publications, offering greater payment for drawings.[43]

A couple of years into the run, *Harper's Monthly* published a group
of comics that punctuated American artists' departure from Töpfferian montage. Where the earliest multipanel comics in *Harper's Monthly*
hewed closely to Töpffer's picaresques, later comics in the run took a hard
turn toward experiments with visual perspective. Starting in 1857, *Harper's
Monthly* editorial practices emphasized comics that prompted the viewer to
contemplate vision as the premise of the comic itself. These works exemplified the fascination in US print culture with comics that did not merely tell
stories but were themselves visual spectacles and sources of novelty. Each
month, *Harper's Monthly* offered their readers comics that foregrounded
a new visual conceit, a new way of understanding how multipanel comics
might be made to inspire a response or sensation from their viewers.

We can notice this emphasis on visual experience in "Shadows over the
Way" (fig. 1.9), a comic that places readers in the perspective of a voyeur
who peeps into a boarding house and experiences the resulting scene as

---

43. Thomas Butler Gunn's diaries suggest that the humor magazines were less profitable
for artists. For example, Gunn recounts how Frank Bellew avoided *Nick Nax* in favor of putting "time to more profitable use" at the same period of time that his publications in *Harper's*
increased. In the same entry, Thomas Nast is also described as avoiding *Nick Nax* for better-
paying work. See Gunn, *Thomas Butler Gunn Diaries Volume 14*, May 23, 1860. Later on, Gunn
describes *Harper's* as the site of rivalry between Bellew, McLenan, and William Newman.
McLenan and Newman, Gunn notes, were "equally injured" by "Bellew's return and resumption
of his inevitable position." Gunn, *Thomas Butler Gunn Diaries Volume 18*, November 18, 1861.

Shadows over the Way.

Vol. XX.—No. 116.—8*

FIGURE 1.9. "Shadows over the Way," *Harper's New Monthly Magazine*, January 1860, 295. Courtesy of the American Antiquarian Society.

an impromptu shadow puppet show. Curtained windows create a series of images in which the figures inside the building cast shadows of lightly satiric silhouettes of family life such as a child taunting a parent, a couple kissing, a boxer taking a cheap shot. "Shadows over the Way" creates play between what Andrei Molotiu terms as "iconostasis" ("the perception of the layout of a comics page as a unified composition") and "sequential dynamism" ("the formal energy [that] propel's the reader's eye from panel to panel") through a layout in which each window frame constitutes a self-enclosed vignette while the entire page suggests a single line of motion.[44] Distinct characters are shown in each window, even as repeating shapes and proportions hint at progressive motion. The proportions of the large

44. Molotiu, "List of Terms for Comics Studies."

husband and small wife in frame #1 are, for instance, repeated in the figures of the large father and small child in frame #2 in ways that create an implicit dynamism between the two frames.

An even more impressive use of visual perspective appeared in M. Davenport's "The Doleful History of an Omnibus Horse" (fig. 1.10). This surprisingly macabre comic demonstrated *Harper's* willingness to publish dark subject matter and imagery in the name of offering their readers innovative approaches to graphic narrative. "Doleful History" is drawn to resemble the walls of a mausoleum as it tells the story of a horse who is overworked, is sold to a French restaurant for meat, and returns to exact vengeance on its owner. As the comic proceeds, Davenport uses clever shifts between cartoonish and realistic visual styles in order to build tension between dark humor and gothic horror. The overall effect is reminiscent of the disquieting visual ironies that arise in Art Spiegelman's graphic novel *Maus,* in which cartoonishly rendered illustrations of mice and cats occupy the realistically rendered setting of the Holocaust. Like Spiegelman, Davenport layers irony upon irony until it becomes difficult to disentangle comedy from horror. On one hand, engravings on the side of the mausoleum render scenes of the horse's life and death in a cartoonish visual style reminiscent of what appeared in other humorous comic strips. The grisly abuse inflicted on the horse is reduced to sketchy stick figures in ways that leave readers to wonder whether the cartoonish style is meant to minimize the horror by declining to depict the full scale of the violence or to intensify it by emphasizing the horse's vulnerability. In the meantime, the finely textured images of the statues and decorations that appear on the walls of the mausoleum pull the visual style back into a gothic mode of expression. Images of realistic statues shed tears and laugh at the horse's fate. These opposing visual modes merge in the sequence's shocking final frame in which two gargoyles pull a curtain away to reveal a detailed rendering of the owner awakening from a nightmare to find the ghost of the horse perched upon his chest.

While Davenport's "Doleful History" is an especially challenging comic from both a formal and thematic standpoint, its presence in *Harper's* highlights a consistent pattern among the artists and publishers who elaborated on Töpffer's initial version of the comic strip. Artists and publishers showed evidence of ambition to push formal and thematic boundaries. Rather than settling into the comfort of a predictable format or subject matter, artists and publishers challenged their readers to cultivate a sense of openness

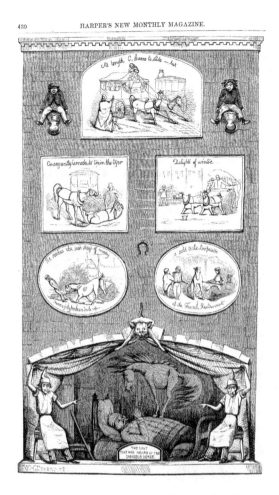

FIGURE 1.10. M. Davenport, "The Doleful History of an Omnibus Horse," *Harper's New Monthly Magazine*, August 1860, 429–30. Courtesy of the American Antiquarian Society.

about what the genre of the comic strip could do and, in doing so, suggested that the medium was only just beginning to reveal its potential.

Precinematic Experience: Three Ways

These new multipanel comics seemed so extraordinary to nineteenth-century US audiences in part because of their connection to a broader revolution in nineteenth-century visuality. New visual technologies were rapidly transforming how people in the United States and Europe experienced images and entertainment. As art historian Jonathan Crary notes, intellectuals as prominent as Goethe, Schopenhauer, and Marx all commented on an "increasing abstraction of optical experience" in which vision was understood not as a transparent window into reality but as a physiological sensation prompted by external stimuli. These theoretical conceptions found practical counterparts in the period's visual technologies. Precursors to modern film such as the moving panorama, the zoetrope, the magic lantern, and the stereoscope reframed spectatorship as a passive experience in which a viewer was confronted with a sequence of distinct images and thus experienced the sensation of motion or the passage of time. In this sense, the newer techniques of observation posited a viewer who was receptive to forms of visual training that highlighted the potential for sequences of juxtaposed images to simulate motion and gesture (even if those simulations were not necessarily "cinematic").[45]

A parallel series of experiments is evident in multipanel comic strips of the period. Like their precinematic counterparts, comics encouraged novel styles of optical experience through their own distinctive approach to juxtaposing images. While the question of whether comic artists took inspiration directly from the zoetrope or stereoscope must remain a matter of speculation, it seems clear that comics, like other technologies and art forms, participated in the broader nineteenth-century transformation of optical experience.[46]

The variations between different precinematic modes of optical experience depended heavily on the level of distance that the device physically placed between the viewer and the object itself. For instance, thaumatropes, moveable toy books, and phenakistiscopes demanded a relatively high level of involvement. With the moveable toy book, the viewer would manipulate the object, flipping back and forth between two changing images, sometimes accompanied by words and riddles. Similarly, the phenakistiscope was a spinning disk that created a basic animation when held up to a mirror as the viewer looked through a slit. Operating on the same basic principle of retinal persistence as a flipbook, it could be slowed down or even stopped by the viewer. The result was style of viewership in which the viewer, by speeding things up or slowing them down, would examine each distinct gesture in isolation. The zoetrope moved the viewer farther away by couching the animation through a spinning drum. Meanwhile, the praxinoscope moved the viewer still farther away and gave less control by creating the effect on a spinning mirror mounted in the center of

45. Crary, *Techniques of the Observer*, 105–13.
46. Crary, *Techniques of the Observer*, 42.

the drum. This mirror removed the need for the viewer to peer through a slit, thus allowing for multiple people to view the effect at the same time and to stand at a physical distance from the apparatus. In turn, the relative passivity of the zoetrope's or praxinoscope's spectator would find its logical conclusion with the modern cinema, where the spectator sits in a darkened theater with no physical relationship to the apparatus. These varying approaches can be mapped to spectatorship onto different styles of movement that comic artists looked to achieve as they experimented with different methods for juxtaposing panels.[47]

Bellew, who was by most accounts the most prolific artist in American sequential comics of the 1850s and '60s, typically embraced a style of animation reminiscent of optical instruments and toys where the observer maintained a great deal of control over the animation. Like the moveable toy book or the phenakistiscope, the primary activity resided in flipping back and forth between contrast views, playing and replaying the animation. In at least one case, Bellew created a folding metamorphic toy that could be cut out of the magazine or purchased separately to simulate Jefferson Davis's trial and execution.[48] More commonly, his animations reveled in the joy of small movements that could be mentally replayed as the viewer moved his eyes back and forth between the frames in a recursive, nonlinear fashion. For instance, "Tricks upon Canines" is a simple strip in which an unseen mischief maker has attached a balloon to a terrier's tail (fig. 1.11).[49] The sequence puts the viewer in the perspective of the practical joker. Each frame depicts a stage in a simple sequence of actions wherein the unsuspecting canine's tail drifts subtly upward, culminating in hyperbolic "unutterable disgust," a caption that Bellew attributes to the canine upon realizing that it has become the butt of the joke.

From the standpoint of depicting movement, Bellew's "The Fight for the Championship" from *The Comic Monthly* ranks as one of the most accomplished comics to appear in any of the humor magazines (fig. 1.12). Bellew's comic consists of a fusion of the snappy exchanges of the burlesque, the hucksterism of the Barnumesque public spectacle, and precinematic visual technology.[50] In this elaborate sequence, readers follow the staging of a boxing match between the British and American champions. The opening scenes play largely within the register of Barnum's promotions as Bellew

47. See Gunning, "Hand and Eye," 495.
48. Bellew, *Jeff Petticoats*; and Bellew, "Life of Jeff Davis in Five Expressive Tableaux."
49. Bellew, "Tricks Upon Canines."
50. Bellew, "Fight for the Championship," 8–9.

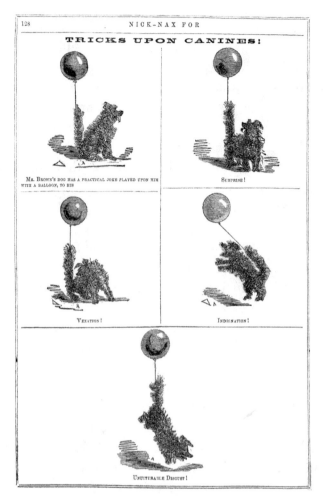

FIGURE 1.11. Frank Bellew, "Tricks upon Canines," *Nick Nax for All Creation*, August 1857, 128. Courtesy of the American Antiquarian Society.

offers a series of tableaux that make outlandish claims about the American champion's prowess. One scene features the mildly grotesque sight of the champion flexing to reveal two biceps on the same arm, accompanied by the caption stating that "his muscles are so greatly developed as to get in each other's way." He is portrayed exercising in a winter coat, consuming large amounts of ale, and lifting enormous dumbbells, all as part of his transformation from out-of-shape retiree into a Herculean figure.

From here, the comic picks up speed as Bellew presents a series of action-to-action frames, diagramming the blow-by-blow movements of the fight itself. However, the fight is not staged naturalistically but instead by selecting a tableau of the pantomime. The boxers undertake a choreographed

FIGURE 1.12. Frank Bellew, "The Fight for the Championship," *Comic Monthly*, May 1860, 8–9. Courtesy of the American Antiquarian Society.

dance that transforms the violence of prizefighting into whimsical farce. In frames #7–#10, they mirror each other's movements, leaping and twirling into synchronized gestures that are more pirouette than elbow drop. As the clumsy ballet progresses, Bellew injects spectacularly violent slapstick into the mix. At one point, the British champion punches his fist clear through his opponent's chest cavity; the American responds with a blow so fierce that it decapitates the Brit, prompting a quick break in the action so that a trainer can sew the fighter's head back onto his body.

What makes this sequence so dynamic and ultimately so successful is not its anticipation of cinematic modes of visuality, with their emphasis on a fluid and linear persistence of vision. Instead, it relies on the convention, common to apparatus such as the moveable toy book and the phenakistiscope, of pausing and holding a pose for examination. Hence, in the sequence in frames #7–#10, Bellew offers a way of reading motion that lingers on the different constituent parts of the movement, holding each gesture for comedic effect. The fact that readers are following a series of action-breaks rather than fluid cinematic motion allows Bellew to take viewers into other elements of the scene, darting off, for instance, to observe the shenanigans at ringside and within the crowd. The referent is not merely the motion of the fighters per se but the process of midcentury spectatorship, more broadly conceived. In this mode of viewing, the ability to look to one's left or right to gauge the reactions of the crowd are just as vital to anything taking place on stage. Readers could therefore contend that Bellew's cartoon actually posits a broader vision than many postcinematic comics. Instead of a unidirectional focus on a single subject, the viewer is guided toward the simultaneous movements of multiple subjects, thus simulating a 360-degree field of vision.

The recursive style of animation in "Fight for the Championship" was just one among many strategies that artists employed. In some cases, these new approaches to animation began to resemble the fluid continuity of the zoetrope or even the cinema. In others, artists drew upon the wider array of models available during this period of novelty and instability.[51]

Wild Oats, the premiere humor magazine of the 1870s, stood out as a particularly rich publication in its diversity of approaches to movement. In many ways, *Wild Oats* was a transitional sort of publication when it came to animating movement in picture stories. At once, it forged links to the approach to graphic narrative of the older folio monthlies while also anticipating the models that would be seen in the Sunday newspapers and glossy color magazines like *Puck* and *Judge.* During his time at *Wild Oats* (1871–80), George Small (who went by the pseudonym "Bricktop") employed a mix of familiar names from the 1850s and '60s such as Bellew and Thomas Worth, as well as younger cartoonists, including Livingston Hopkins, C. J. Howard, Frederick Burr Opper, Joseph Keppler, and Palmer Cox, many of whom would go on to become major names in subsequent decades.[52] Many of the comics in *Wild Oats* unfurled a fluid, linear sense of movement of the type that would come to dominate twentieth-century comics' approaches to movement.

Hopkins, who would later enjoy great popularity in Australia, stood among the most accomplished at creating this sort of effect. Many of Hopkins's pages are entirely wordless, dispensing with captions in favor of sequences that narrate plot and create punchlines entirely through pantomime. "A Romance As Is a Romance, or a Story without Words" is one of Hopkins's most impressive displays of fluid, linear movement (fig. 1.13).[53]

---

51. West, "Wild Oats."
52. On Hopkins's Australian career, see Graeme, "Little Boy from Manly."
53. Hopkins, "Romance As Is a Romance," 13.

FIGURE 1.13. Livingston Hopkins, "A Romance As Is a Romance, or a Story without Words," *Wild Oats*, March 14, 1872, 13. Courtesy of the American Antiquarian Society.

Unlike the recursive movements of Bellew's animations, "A Romance" orchestrates a rigidly structured viewing experience in which the viewer's eye is tightly controlled in its movement across the page. In the strip itself, the male suitor approaches his intended bride three different times. First, he steals a kiss and is sent away; next, the suitor approaches her and is shoed away with a broom; finally, he reappears with a sack of money, which she accepts before proceeding to the chapel for a quick marriage. The sequence looks simple enough, as it applies that most basic comedic formula "the rule of three" in which the same action is repeated three times with a humorous variation providing the punchline on the third repetition. However, Hopkins's ability to create this effect depends entirely on his tight management of a whip-smart pattern of repetition and variation. If the eye moves recursively or is invited to revisit frames for contemplation as in Bellew's "Fight for Championship," Hopkins loses his ability to manage the flow of the strip and the effect is lost.

Hopkins accomplishes this outcome by using a 4 × 4 grid and incremental movements in his illustrated subjects to pull the viewer's line of vision from left to right across each row in a rigid, linear fashion. He even numbers frames to ensure that readers follow this intended path. The result is an effect in which the movement of the eye across the page comes to implicitly depict the passage of time with each frame representing a clear and finite period within the sequence of movements. Within the structure of the comic, the blank frame (frame #11) appears especially significant because Hopkins uses it to indicate that time continues to pass as the eye is still moving across the space of the page while visual action and sound do not. In this sense, frame #11 functions much like a rest or silence in a piece of written music. In the meantime, the tableaux at frames #15 and #16 serve a far different function. These frames momentarily pause the passage of time, inviting the viewer's eye to linger on the individual frame for a few extra beats (in contrast to frame #11, where the movement of the eye continues even in the absence of any activity).

While the animation style of "A Romance" most closely resembles the fluid cinematic motion that came to dominate the comic strip throughout the twentieth century, it by no means led to the inevitable conclusion for how one might coordinate imagery with sensation. Another possibility was the sense of spatial immersion that viewers experienced with the stereoscope. Stereoscopes and stereograph cards created a three-dimensional scene whereby the viewer peers through lenses at a card with two slightly different images. The stereoscope provides its viewer with sensations of spatial immersion by creating a layering effect, with some items appearing in the foreground of the image while others appear toward the background. Stereoscopes were described by nineteenth-century observers as facilitating virtual forms of travel from the safety of their own homes. Stereographic cards thus commonly featured scenes of popular tourist destinations, exhibitions and sporting events, natural disasters, military battles, and voyeuristic scenes of urban tenement life as well as "exotic" cultures outside of Europe and the United States.

A range of nineteenth-century paintings experimented with depth in ways that parallel the stereoscope's use of layered planes of vision to produce a sense of spatial proximity to the objects therein. As Crary suggests, the stereoscope's distinctive combination of "depth and cutout flatness" shares a common spatial logic with works including Gustave Courbet's *Ladies of the Village* (1851), Edouard Manet's *View of the International Exhibition* (1867), and George Seurat's *Sunday Afternoon on the Island of La Grande Jatte* (1884–86). Such attempts to create sensations of proximity to the object also dazzled in the illusionistic effects of the trompe l'oeil paintings that enjoyed popularity with nineteenth-century middlebrow audiences in America.[54]

Worth's comics in *Wild Oats* (which appeared alongside Hopkins's comics) were particularly notable as an attempt to achieve an immersive effect, similar to that of the stereoscope. In organizing his layouts, Worth usually presents different aspects of a single scene and features multilayered perspectives, reminiscent of the three-dimensional scenes produced by the stereoscope. His subject matter emphasizes precisely the kinds of public spectacles and scenes of visual interest that were common to stereographic cards. He composed comics about horse racing, boating, bumpy rides in omnibus cars, urban baseball, and even the hazing rituals of Freemasons.[55] In sharp contrast to Hopkins's linear sequences, Worth's layouts show little interest in depicting the passage of time. They instead invite a roving viewing experience in which the eye wanders around the page at will.

Worth's affinities with stereoscopic immersion are particularly apparent in his 1872 cartoon "The Great National Game of Baseball," an elaborate two-page spread depicting scenes taking place over the course of an entire baseball game (fig. 1.14).[56] Early urban baseball in the United States was an extraordinarily dangerous, often violent sport, with players regularly suffering injury for lack of proper equipment and entering into fights. Worth revels in the violent, dynamic quality of the game. Scenes from "The Great National Game" play with repetitive scenes of players beaned in the head, a bunch contorting their bodies and taking pratfalls to pursue loose balls, and a host of figures on crutches and peg legs fashioned from old baseball bats. The center of the spread features a large splash panel, providing the

---

54. Crary, *Techniques of the Observer*, 126.

55. Worth, "Horse Racing"; Worth, "Scenes and Incidents"; Worth, "Boating Mania"; Worth, "Mr. and Mrs. Thumper's Experience"; Worth, "Great National Game of Baseball"; and Worth, "Female Freemasons."

56. Worth, "Great National Game of Baseball," 8–9.

FIGURE 1.14. Thomas Worth, "The Great National Game of Baseball," *Wild Oats*, August 1, 1872, 8–9. Courtesy of the American Antiquarian Society.

viewer with a wide-angle perspective on the entire baseball field, with a visual perspective that cascades upward, which suggests three-dimensional viewing. Through all of this spectacle, Worth offers no indication of continuous motion or even a clear chronological progression. Instead, there is a collection of motions—flashes of action—that, when they are taken together, depict the violent sights that might take place over the course of nine innings.

Although Worth's approach to sports comics did not carry the fluid sense of motion of Livingston's or even Bellew's comics, it is important to resist perceiving them as unsophisticated by comparison. Instead, Worth's sports comics might be understood as an advancement along an entirely different trajectory: toward the representation of three-dimensional physical space. And indeed, when considering the comic's apparent intent to simulate a baseball game, Worth's prioritization of three-dimensional space over fluid motion makes perfect sense. For many spectators, the appeal of baseball—a notoriously slow game—resides not in dynamic, real-time action but in its sense of spatial immersion. Baseball fans tend to savor the details of the physical space as it surrounds them. The "friendly confines" of the field, details of uniforms and equipment, and mannerisms of players and umpires are common objects of preoccupation. When action does occur in a baseball game, it often comes and goes with a glance. Worth's approach ingeniously attends to both elements of baseball spectatorship by allowing for a roving gaze around the field while freezing the crucial moments of action in place so that they can be inspected and pondered.

The roving gaze and spatial emphasis of Worth's "The Great National Game of Baseball" brings us full circle. At first glance, Worth might seem like a throwback. Similar to readers of single-panel cartoons like "The Celebrated Racer de Meyer" (1846) and earlier satirical prints, Worth's implied reader pores over the image in search of details and visual ironies that gradually bring the action and the humor into focus. But Worth was no throwback. He had not missed the sequential breakthrough and new forms of visual animation that H. M. Fletcher had celebrated as allowing comics to "leap into existence." On the contrary, Worth's experiment with stereoscopic vision was a sign of just how far comic strips had come since the 1842 arrival of the Töpffer bootlegs. Like other artists of the 1860s and '70s, Worth did not feel moored to Töpffer's approach to sequential comics. In fact, the herky-jerky rhythms of Töpfferian montage would have felt antiquated to most readers by 1872. Instead, Worth and his contemporaries seemed far more preoccupied with the question of what forms of animation might come *after* that initial sequential breakthrough. Comics readers and audiences of the 1870s were, in other words, interested in how the future might bring an assortment of approaches to arranging images and text in sequence and how those approaches could produce new and surprising forms of perception.

CHAPTER 2

Everyday Adventures

Character Studies and Skits

As magazines became the primary media for comics through the mid-nineteenth century, their content turned increasingly toward the happenings of everyday life. A large proportion of the comics that appeared are indeed striking for their mundane qualities. Names were mere indicators of social types or tendencies while the premises were simple occasions to observe and poke light fun at everyday human behavior. The title or the first line typically gave away the entire premise in works such as "Tale of an Umbrella," "Mr. Meek Concludes to Go to a Camp Meeting," and "An Everyday Adventure."[1] These works are neither the vice-ridden cautionary tales of Hogarth nor the anarchic improvisations of later comic artists like George Herriman and Lyonel Feininger. Instead, artists and writers created situational comedy based on close observation of the quirks and absurdities of people's daily goings-on. Whether it was a simple act of navigating cold weather, going on an excursion, or riding an omnibus, artists treated manners less as a means to an end than an end in itself.

Despite the apparently modest aspirations of character studies and skits, these works were central to the broader project pursued by the magazines that published comics. Similar to the humorous commentary that appeared throughout US magazines, comics were often understood as a form of observational realism, capturing an underlying mood and rhythms of American life. The interest in the mundane was not devoid of its

---

1. Carleton, "Tale of an Umbrella," 6; "Mr. Meek Concludes," 24–25; and "Every-Day Adventure," 5.

allegorizing tendencies. American fiction's preoccupation with observation often legitimized American nationhood by locating an underlying sense of coherence within the nation's diverse people and regions.

Such an approach paralleled the literary tradition that ran through Washington Irving's fiction and much of the period's regionalist humor. This strand of thinking favored close attention to folkways, speech patterns, and customs, as Irving wrote, not "with the eye of the philosopher" but rather the "sauntering gaze with which humble lovers of the picturesque stroll from the window of one print-shop to another; caught sometimes by the delineations of beauty, sometimes by the distortions of caricature, and sometimes by the loveliness of landscape."[2] The artistic eye is a mediating link between the audience and an artist's observation of manners, customs, and ways of speaking and acting. In this casual style of flânerie, no object of interest is too subtle or insignificant to capture the notice of the writer (or the cartoonist) because each detail provides an occasion to experience and reflect upon the broader patterns that characterized American society.

As we'll see, the flexibility of these simple character studies is apparent in the contrast between the work of two of the period's most well-known and prolific artists, Frank Bellew and John McLenan. If the object of these sketches and skits was to provide an ongoing exploration of every nook and cranny of city life, these two figures—two of the most prolific cartoonists of the period—took very different approaches to what comics could mean within that context. Bellew, a figure shaped by romantic and transcendentalist philosophies, rendered the American social landscape as a space rich with possibilities for encounters with eccentric individuals and surprising absurdities buried just beneath the surface of everyday life. This may at first seem trivial, but triviality was precisely the point. Many of Bellew's strips embrace a quality that he once described as "merrymaking," where unpredictable acts of silliness offer occasions to gain relief from the pressures of modern life and to reconnect with nature. McLenan, in the meantime, engaged in a more pessimistic, circumspect project. Like many artists and writers in the US, McLenan felt the brunt of economic hardship, and he embedded his humorous comics with subtle allegories and reflections on social and economic class. McLenan's recurring scenes of zany protagonists initially seem like humorous improvisations only to register insecurity and frustration over the impossibility of conforming to

---

2. Irving, *Sketch Book of Geoffrey Crayon*, 13.

bourgeois values. In both cases, the innovations of these artists foreshadow elements that would become synonymous with comics into the early twentieth century and beyond.

Manners and Magazines

The simple sequences of activities and social types that appeared throughout US comics can be explained in part through their connection to the then-popular genre known either as the "sketch" or the "physiology." Sketches were prominently featured in books of light humor like Irving's *Sketchbook of Geoffrey Crayon* (1819), Joseph C. Neal's, *Charcoal Sketches* (1838), Cornelius Mathews's *A Pen and Ink Panorama of New York* (1853), Q. K. Philander Doesticks's (Mortimer Thomson) *Doesticks' What He Says* (1855), and Thomas Butler Gunn's *Physiology of New York Boarding Houses* (1857). They were also central to the productions of the early illustrated press, including humor anthologies, illustrated almanacs, collector cards, broadsides, comic valentines, jestbooks, and comic sketchbooks. The sketch was typically understood as a quasi-journalistic form that acquainted the reader or viewer with imagined social types that one might imagine encountering on a walk through the city or the countryside.

Nineteenth-century American sketches were themselves part of a longer European tradition that stretched across prose and illustration. As early as the sixteenth century, the famed caricaturist Annibale Carracci took to the streets of Bologna to capture the likenesses of everyday people, plying their trades. In Carracci's book, *Diverse Figure al Numero di Ottanta* (1646), the gruff illustration of the butcher or the vendor on the street displaced images of nobility and idealized visions of perfectly symmetrical human bodies. By emphasizing a physical feature or playing to a stereotype, Carracci and other caricaturists purported to reveal an essential quality of the social types who inhabited the city, even as they expanded the scope of possible artistic subjects beyond the nobility or the wealthy. Versions of Carracci's practice of roving about the city, making humorous sketches of everyday social types was a near constant practice in European drawings and prose from the early modern period into the nineteenth century. Sketches of representative urban types were, for instance, central to the lighter brand of satire that emerged in the French illustrated press during the period when artists were subject to censorship from the French crown. As Judith Wechsler points out, French artists deployed a "pungent and rapid communicative vocabulary" to create simple illustrations of representative types to be "consumed casually" by the French public "along with the news and the morning coffee."[3] Authors ranging from Honore de Balzac to George Cruikshank to Charles Dickens also participated in a robust culture of producing these semi-humorous portraits of social types engaged in everyday activities.[4]

Sketches and humorous prose were presented as part of a larger effort to position humor magazines as quasi-journalistic publications that chronicled the funny side of American social life. Artists and writers were identified as "correspondent[s]" and "preservers of jokes" whose roles paralleled that of a newspaper reporter or the pictorial correspondents. This conception of the comic artist as a communicator of national character was crucial to how the comic sketch was understood in its context. The individual sketches operated less as isolated vignettes than as part of a larger patchwork of diverse social and ethnic types coming together to form a single nation.[5] Juxtaposition or collection of multiple sketches are thus what ultimately gave the form coherence. By collecting and comparing isolated glimpses of individual social types, the viewer might extrapolate out to imagine a broader social landscape where ethnic types clashed and combined to form a unified national whole.[6]

The publication *Leslie's Budget of Fun* was perhaps the illustrated press's most enthusiastic promoter of the viewpoint that comic art constituted its own peculiar form of journalistic commentary. At the outset of each issue, the editor's column (probably written by Thomas Powell) gave breathless accounts of how his comic artists had been following notable events such as the Prince of Wales's visit as well as the daily churn of people and sights on the street.[7] An early editor's column went so far as to deliver a mock

---

3. Wechsler, *Human Comedy*, 15, 82.

4. See Lauster, *Sketches of the Nineteenth Century*; and Teukolsky, *Picture World*, 21–61.

5. See "View on the Sixth Avenue," 7; "From the Seat of War," 4; and Bellew, "Hot!: A Letter from Our Artist," 1. On this tactic in French publications, see Wechsler, *Human Comedy*, 15, 26–27.

6. The conception of the US nation as a collection of ethnicities resembles the forms of "ethnic nationalism" that Sandra Tomc has observed in nineteenth-century ethnographies and fashion illustrations, which conceived of US nationhood as a "patchwork of cultures and ethnicities, each with its own ancient past, locales, and forms of the dress." Tomc, *Fashion Nation*, 73.

7. "Frank Leslie to the Budgetonians," May 1, 1859, 1; and "Frank Leslie to the Budgetonians," June 1, 1860, 1.

oath vowing that *Leslie's* cartoonists would illustrate every conceivable detail of city life:

> Whereas Barnum's Museum, fast horses and the big meteor are as yet discussed. Whereas poetry is far from being a drug—particularly when fresh. Whereas the endless cullud pusson continues to agitate, rack, disturb, disquiet, annoy and otherwise bore the community. Whereas candidates and politicians of forty-five stripes, excluding the Harmonious Democracy, are dancing their hoedowns and cornshucks over the face of this delightful conn'ry. Whereas the fashionable world continues to revel in all fling-diddle fancies and elegant brocatelleries at watering and other places, giving themselves, as of old, to strange luxuries and Babylonian devices of merriment. Therefore it has seemed fit that we, in this our Budget, should do up, and pictorially, or typographically, illustrate all these subjects, *secundem arlem*.[8]

The persistent suggestion that humorists and artists were roaming the streets in search of material in turn offered the tantalizing implication that the character studies appearing in the magazines provided meaningful social information. Just as the journalistic activities of monitoring of local news, gallery openings, and theater reviews offered the sensation of a connection to the ongoing happenings of an imagined community, humorous prose sketches and comics could be interpreted as an ongoing record of the funny characters, situations, and quirks to be puzzled over and examined as evidence of everyday life in America.

The particulars of the social world depicted in mid-nineteenth-century magazines most closely resembled the subjects of what critic David Sloane terms the "Humor of the Old Northeast." This style of humor was typified by the vignettes and character sketches of humorists like Neale and Doesticks, who depicted the comic absurdities of an increasingly diverse social landscape, centered around the social types and sites of the urban-industrial Northeast. As Sloane notes, "Various American characters appear in the new urban setting, where classes mingle freely on the streets

---

8. "Frank Leslie to His Beloved Budgeteers," September 1, 1860, 1. *Leslie's Budget of Fun* was the companion publication to the highly successful *Leslie's Illustrated Newspaper,* a publication famous for pictorial reporters who drew realistic illustrations alongside news stories. Leslie's interest in framing his comic artists in this manner probably speaks to the parallel that he saw between the earnest activity of pictorial reporting and the commentary-focused approach of the humorous comic sketch.

and in the democracy of the omnibus; the deal and the speculator, small or large, have a universal presence (180)."[9] For Sloane, the "panorama of lower-caste American types" provided a crucial template that explains the prominence of middle-and working-class in later US humor and media. "Structural descendants" such as Peter Finley Dunne's Mr. Dooley, Chaplin's Little Tramp, and the multicultural sitcom ensembles of *Cheers* and *Brooklyn Nine-Nine* all inhabited a similar urban terrain where encounters between diverse social types were plumbed for their comedic potential.[10]

Even as humorous magazine sketches were proffered as tracking with the daily rhythms of readers' lives, the social world itself was remarkably static. The vagaries of publication schedules and tastes of readers meant that any ongoing report could never truly constitute a live, evolving record. Instead, this comedic tradition found comfort and reassurance in characters who did not change. The spare portraits thus implied that everyday life could be reduced to a series of repeating interactions. The newsboy always had a snide quip ready for the banker; the lady's hoop dress always concealed something surprising. Despite its apparent simplicity, this static, repetitive model was incredibly effective at familiarizing readers with an enduring set of social types and social scripts that could be puzzled over and examined. This perhaps accounts for the general paucity of recurring characters in early periodical comics. Where readers of the early Sunday newspaper funnies checked in every week with the ongoing developments of a "mass mediated personality" like the Yellow Kid or Happy Hooligan, the readers of humor magazines were so acclimated to recognizing recurring social types, settings, and situations that they hardly needed the particularities associated with a named character to feel a sense of continuity.[11]

In the magazines themselves, illustrated sketches and sequences often sat side-by-side with little association to the surrounding material apart from their general thrust of conveying funny scenes from American life. Many comics were simple one- or two-panel cartoons with a witty caption or pun below. These were similar to what had appeared in humor almanacs and comic sketchbooks throughout the 1830s and were generally understood as a "modern" form by artists and audiences, often combining the illustration of a social type with sophisticated vocabulary of visual and verbal cues that allowed quick and efficient identification of each social

9. Sloane, "Study in the Humor," 180.
10. Sloane, "Study in the Humor," 201.
11. Gardner, *Projections,* 13.

type. A quick glance at a character's physiognomy, clothing, posture, and dialect provided immediate recognition.[12] Single panel sketches were regularly grouped on a page or arranged over a series of pages in ways that did not necessarily create a linear narrative so much as loosely related groupings of puns and jokes.

A page from an 1857 issue of the *Brother Jonathan* pictorial supplement is typical of this approach. In the middle of the page, a pictorial layout titled "In and Out-door Sightings about New York" features work from several artists, depicting unrelated scenes from around the city. The resulting sequence offers a kaleidoscopic perspective in which the viewer observes city life from multiple, distinct vantage points: elegant couples waltz in a frame captioned "Christmas Night at Old Tammany"; two men on the street gawk at a woman's elaborate dress, wondering "ain't that a Swell" [i.e., finely dressed man]; an adult dressed as a newsboy warns a real newsboy "Don't call me 'Swabs' [worthless] again! If you do, I'll lam you!"; a bickering couple fight over literal pieces of toasted bread in service of a pun on the word "toast." One might fancifully speculate that the editor who compiled "In and Out-door Sightings" hoped to imply a sense of omniscience—a comprehensive view of the simultaneous events and people that compose the character of the city itself. Such grand ambitions are, however, never explicitly stated, and the reader is instead left to place their own individual construction on the layout's overall meaning. This open-ended approach was wholly in keeping with the informal editorial norms of the period. Indeed, to page through a magazine of this sort was to cultivate an openness to disorganized and fleeting impressions of social types, sights, jokes, and happenings.[13]

The emergence of multipanel comics constituted a significant development for humorous sketches. Multipanel comics offered a dynamic visual and verbal grammar that allowed artists to exert tighter narrative control than was available in the collages of single-panel cartoons. In the multipanel comic strip, information did not need to be so tightly bound up in a single image or caption.[14] Gestures, changes in locale, elements of a

---

12. Tomc, *Fashion Nation*, 86.

13. "In and Out-Door Sights," 3.

14. By repeating a single design across multiple panels, artists could create an effect that Thierry Groensteen refers to as "iconic solidarity" in which the characters and scenes in different panels are understood as part of a unified narrative world rather than distinct stories or settings. Groensteen, *System of Comics*, 18.

character's personality, and patterns of cause and effect could be tracked from frame to frame, adding literal dimensions of time and space to the project of rendering a character. Even so, this did not necessarily translate to extensive plot or character development as much as it provided new tools for accomplishing the same old goal of offering a reliable set of stereotypes that could be used to identify and examine the various social types imagined to be circulating in American society.

Many multipanel character studies combined comedic premises with a microanalysis of the physical gestures involved in the simplest of activities. Sequences in this vein presented the reader with a series of illustrations that depicted the distinct components of everyday movements. In doing so, artists could effectively slow down the fast pace of modern life, breaking a given social type's gestures into a series of easily observed tableaux.[15] The humorous thing that happened on the street was no longer a fleeting gesture or momentary encounter but instead an anatomy of movement that could be lingered over and pondered. The tracing of "cause and effect" was a common subtext in these microanalyses. By incorporating wording that framed the premise as "consequences" of an action or the "surprising effects" of an activity in public life, artists further implied that their comics depicted a mechanistic logic to American social life that could be observed and learned.

The fascination with mannerisms is evident in "Omnibus Gymnastics," an unsigned strip from *Leslie's Budget of Fun*, which reimagines the activity of boarding a streetcar as a gymnastic routine (fig. 2.1). Over the course of the strip's seven illustrations, the man contorts his limbs and tumbles about as he first stretches to hail an omnibus and then crunches down into the cabin before diving headfirst into the street when the car takes a sharp turn. Just as the spectator of a gymnastics routine is invited to ponder and admire each body position of a gymnast's routine, so too is the viewer of "Omnibus Gymnastics" invited to examine the simple act of boarding a streetcar. This strip is especially notable for its muted approach to the premise. The artist, by and large, avoids exaggerated or burlesqued gestures in favor of unadorned, naturalistic depictions of movement. As a result, the sequence tends to imply everyday movements are themselves inherently interesting and worthy of close observation. Not all comic studies of gesture were as restrained as "Omnibus Gymnastics"; even so, artists still

15. Representative examples include: "Every-Day Adventure," 5. "Courting," 210; "Heart-Rending Calamity," 102; and "Advertising for a Wife," 220.

OMNIBUS GYMNASTICS

First movement.   *Second.*   *Third.*   *Fourth.*   *Fifth.*   *Sixth.*   *Finale.*

FIGURE 2.1. "Omnibus Gymnastics," *Leslie's Budget of Fun,* October 1, 1859, 16. Courtesy of the American Antiquarian Society.

maintained close attention to the nuances of everyday movements when depicting crude or violent slapstick.

Among the most significant areas of experimentation for artists of character studies were their innovations with caricature. The ethnic and class caricature of Cruikshank and Nast are well known as dominant influences in Victorian cartooning. Cruikshank and Nast relied heavily on single-panel caricatures that conveyed information primarily through physiognomic data. The racial and ethnic clichés of the hooked nose, exaggerated lips, or prominent forehead were primary devices for making social standing and interior character visible to audiences. Such stereotypes were in turn bolstered by pseudoscientific writing and photography, claiming to use measurements of heads and facial features to confirm racial and gendered hierarchies.

The multipanel character studies that appeared in US humor magazines frequently turned away from this physiognomic sensibility. Instead, they favored styles of constructing social identity based on the passage of time and on physical movement. Character and social information were thus conveyed using multiple panels, guiding the reader through various aspects of a character's life or taking a reader behind the scenes in a subject's life to show how outward appearances could be deceiving. In doing so, they added layers of complexity to the social world that comics could communicate. This is not to say that US magazine comics avoided physiognomic caricatures or ethnic and gendered stereotypes. Artists and editors were, after all, almost exclusively white men who held the assumptions common to their time. However, conventional caricature was often paired with styles that

250   YANKEE NOTIONS.

MISS WIGGINS' PHYSIOGNOMICAL EXPERIMENTS.

I.   II.

BEFORE SHE STUDIED LAVATER, AND BELOVED BY EVERY-   SHE ATTEMPTS THE YOUNG AND ARTLESS, TO CAPTIVATE
ONE.   THE BOOK-KEEPER OVER THE WAY.

FIGURE 2.2. Justin H. Howard, "Miss Wiggins' Physiognomic Experiments," *Yankee Notions,* August 1865, 50. Courtesy of the American Antiquarian Society.

used movement and negotiation of space as devices for conveying information about character. If caricature was fundamentally about finding some essential character in the physiognomy in a static, essentializing image, the multipanel comic allowed for exploration of the gaps and fissures in those assumptions because it emphasized progressive action and examination of multiple perspectives.[16]

Justin H. Howard's "Miss Wiggins' Physiognomic Experiments" conveys a sense of skepticism about the Cruikshankian attempt to discern inner character from facial features (fig. 2.2). In the sequence, Miss Wiggins studies Johan Kasper Lavater's writings on physiognomy and then attempts to contort her face to suggest personal traits that will make her attractive to male suitors. Each frame shows Miss Wiggins contorting her

16. As Jared Gardner notes, the use of sequences in early twentieth-century comics like *Happy Hooligan* leveled similar challenges to the racializing logic of caricature by setting in motion "experiments with mass-mediated personality—a personality that emerges through serial repetition," demonstrating "the ways in which stereotype fails to capture the individual." Gardner, *Projections*, 14.

face, along with a caption describing how her poses are meant to woo each distinct lover. She strikes "the young and artless to captivate the book-keeper" and "the tragic to win the lawyer" with little success. Only when she exposes her cleavage to a banker "past the age of her father" does the physiognomic experiment work. For Howard, the underlying gag—and message—is that physiognomy can reveal much less about character than ongoing observations of actions. The comic is thus at once a dismissal of facial features as accurate predictors of social types and a demonstration of an alternative means of reading for typicality.[17]

These explorations of the distinction between surface appearances and internal character responded to a broader crisis in visuality in nineteenth-century America. Modernization of American society created striking and often bewildering discrepancies between the public and the private self. While the egalitarian class relations of American society allowed one to remake and reimagine one's class position, it also presented the danger of misrepresenting the self. This was, in many ways, the darker side of the self-made man, featured in Ben Franklin's *Autobiography*. If a figure like Franklin could reinvent himself, climbing from printer's apprentice to a vaunted diplomat, inventor, and architect of US government, it also left open the possibility that appearances could be manipulated for illicit purposes. Middle-class writings of this period are deeply preoccupied with the human eye's relative inadequacy in perceiving the nuances of American social identity. Conduct manuals warned the public of the constant danger of confidence men or other social climbers who would misrepresent their status and intentions. As Karen Halttunen notes, these warnings were symbolic of a broader perceived crisis: "In what was believed to be a fluid social world where no one occupied a fixed social position, the question 'Who am I?' loomed large; and in an urban social world where many of the people who met face-to-face each day were strangers, the question 'Who are you really?' assumed even greater significance."[18] Fears of criminal fraud notwithstanding, nineteenth-century audiences approached the specter of the confidence man with equal parts anxiety and fascination. In warning of these social chameleons, the conduct manuals described by Halttunen just as frequently betray an undercurrent of wonder and admiration at their process of transformation. In the meantime, works such as Herman Melville's *The Confidence Man* compared the dizzying nature of

17. Howard, "Miss Wiggins' Physiognomic Experiments," 50–52.
18. Halttunen, *Confidence Men and Painted Women*, xv.

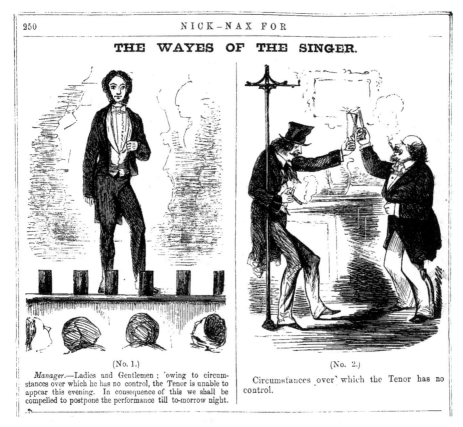

250   NICK-NAX FOR

THE WAYES OF THE SINGER.

(No. 1.)

Manager.—Ladies and Gentlemen ; 'owing to circumstances over which he has no control, the Tenor is unable to appear this evening. In consequence of this we shall be compelled to postpone the performance till to-morrow night.

(No. 2.)

Circumstances over which the Tenor has no control.

FIGURE 2.3. "The Wayes of the Singer," *Nick Nax for All Creation,* December 1856, 250. Courtesy of the American Antiquarian Society.

nineteenth-century class relations to an elaborate masquerade or theatrical spectacle.[19]

In this vein, a common pattern in the multipanel character study is its use of disguise as an organizing motif. Regular readers of humor magazines would have become accustomed to sequences that diagrammed the distinction between the disguised public self and a more authentic private self. From a visual standpoint, these cartoons posit a physical move from outward appearances to internal workings. The cartoon "The Wayes of the Singer" demonstrates this type of move with a simple peek-a-boo sequence in which a theater manager apologizes to an audience that an operatic tenor will be absent for "circumstances over which [the tenor] has no control," only to reveal the tenor as a drunkard in the next (fig. 2.3).

---

19. See Salazar, *Bodies of Reform*; Browder, *Slippery Characters.*

"The Wayes of the Singer" offers a metaphor for a larger sense that many in American life were staging an elaborate impersonation.[20] Like the tenor, people in polite society played theatrical roles, offering up a respectable façade in order to cover for unseemly realities. But, as the cartoon also suggests, multipanel comics could provide a way of putting these types of hypocrisy on full display.

A favorite source of subject matter for these "disguise" sequences was the fashionable craze for large steel hoop dresses. Artists produced dozens of cartoons showing the outlandish lengths that modern women pursued in order to project a respectable public appearance. Hoop dress cartoons could be presented as condescending satires of women's tendency to deceive innocent men or as playful celebrations of women evading patriarchal control. Regardless of whether they were oppressive or uplifting, hoop dress cartoons almost always purported to reveal elements of women's lives that were hidden from public view. Women are shown hiding articles such as groceries or even inappropriate gentleman callers underneath their skirts. A comic by Howard depicts an African American woman using her dress to conceal her facial features, resulting in an unpleasant surprise for a would-be white suitor. The skirts are shown blocking traffic on Broadway and creating problems on narrow bridges.[21] Each of these cartoons use the techniques of the comic strip—either in the form of jokes, puns, or behind-the-scenes revelations—to allow viewers to cut through the façade of feminine decorum. Rather than a tool for meticulous self-presentation, the hoop skirt becomes the very means through which the viewer is encouraged to visualize women engaging in social mischief.

"The Steel Hoops" is a notable instance because it turns the narrative flexibility of the ephemeral character study toward a searing critique of gender and class relations in the United States (fig. 2.4).[22] In this surprising sequence, the progress of a steel hoop is traced from a dreary factory floor to a cozy middle-class parlor to a young woman's dressing room. In doing so, the piece creates a dark analogy between the labor of the iron workers and the labor of fashionable women, as the first and final frames bookend a continuum of various types of labor associated with the fashion craze. The most striking image in the sequence is the final frame in which

---

20. "Wayes of the Singer," 250.

21. Some examples include "Hoops Convenient Sometimes," 248; Howard, "Dark Suspicion," 374; Bellew, "Skirt Movement," 9; and McLenan, "Hint to Ladies," 16.

22. "Steel Hoops," 234–36.

FIGURE 2.4. Scenes from "The Steel Hoops," *Nick Nax for All Creation,* December 1856, 234–36. Courtesy of the American Antiquarian Society.

a thin, plain woman stands in a dingy room, looking at the mirror, wearing only a slip and the steel hoop. Evocative of the sentimental illustrations that protested child labor, the cartoon is hardly the misogynistic farce one might expect in a satire on women's dresses. Instead, it invites contemplation about broader capitalistic forces driving the fashion and hence the expectations placed on women. Implicit here is the notion that industrial production is not limited to the factory floor but resides in multiple, unexpected places, including the rooms of the working-class woman who must arrange the dress as well as the upper-class woman who shoulders the physical labor of carrying the cumbersome apparatus.

As the examples of "The Steel Hoops" and others show, the narrative flexibility of the multipanel comic simultaneously offered a means of allegorizing a national sense of coherence *and* probing the gaps and fissures in that national consciousness. The idea of movement was crucial because it allowed for a reading of character that incorporated prolonged readings that delved through time and space. The reader was no longer bound to the momentary impression, but instead could discern character from multiple angles and explore its ins and outs with a more sophisticated point of view.

Frank Bellew and the Profound Implications of "Merrymaking"

If one aim of the simple skits that appeared in the comics was to sate readers' curiosity about the rhythms of everyday life, another was to distract from those very routines. In addition to focusing on the minutia of American life, publishers made disarmingly sincere claims that their magazines would simply provide diversions from the daily difficulties faced by their readers. Publishers promised "Fun for the million!," pages "redolent with fun and jollility," and content that would "dispel the gloom [and] chase away your cares."[23] This approach finds many of its most accomplished examples in the skits and vignettes that were produced by Frank Bellew. In a breathtakingly large number of comics, Bellew offered an array of subjects across socioeconomic groups, ages, and even species, ranging in tone from sweet and sentimental to riotously anarchic.

Bellew's approach could hardly be characterized as idle or thoughtless. It was instead influenced by strands of romantic philosophy that flourished in the middle of the nineteenth century. Bellew was known both as a key figure in New York's bohemian community of artists and writers and an acquaintance of several of the major transcendentalists, including Emerson, Thoreau, and Whitman.[24] While these influences may at first seem like a far cry from the humorous sketches of American life that appear in Bellew's comics, he shares with them a romantic preference for connecting with nature as a pathway to self-discovery. However, Bellew's version of romanticism was not necessarily the idealized "state of nature" that Emerson or Thoreau imagined as a harmonious return to natural lifestyles and landscapes (indeed, Bellew's artwork and writings regularly deal with the pleasures of city life) but instead a broader conception of "nature" as obedience to one's desires and intuitions and thus freedom from the artificial conventions of modern society.[25] Bellew's romanticism played out through comic strips that emphasized the unruly and the unpredictable in everyday subjects of American life. He used madcap subjects and situations ranging from exploding pigs to adventurous scientists to children staging indoor snowball fights to create humorous disruptions to the humdrum rhythms of everyday life. These elements of Bellew's comics feel strikingly modern in retrospect. Like the Sunday newspaper funnies that came to prominence at the turn of the twentieth century, they embody a madcap turn toward the absurd and unruly.

---

23. "Fun for the Million"; and Leslie, "Frank Leslie to His Readers," 1. Strong, "Introduction," 2.

24. "Death of Frank Bellew," 2.

25. Levin, *Bohemia in America*, 29.

Although Bellew rarely commented directly on his comics, his writings about humor and entertainment in other contexts offer clues to the philosophy behind his approach. In his most extensive commentary, *Art of Amusing*, an 1866 book on parlor entertainments, Bellew wrote "one of the great social faults of the American is, that he does not amuse himself enough . . . in a cheerful, innocent manner." For Bellew, this sentiment was wrapped up in a larger critique of a competitive and materialist mindset that had left many Americans physically and mentally "bankrupt." Americans, he said are "terribly troubled about our dignity," and a "political or prayer meeting is the most hilarious affair in which we ever indulge."[26] Echoing Thoreau's suggestion that "the mass of men lead lives of quiet desperation," Bellew wrote that Americans had generally fallen out of touch with nature, noting, "we perpetually strive to 'gouge' nature," either by racing to accumulate material wealth or chasing status symbols. "We overtax [nature] in every way," Bellew continued, "until we drive the willing horse to death, and then our journey ends; all the load of fine goods we have been to market for, must be dumped into the mud for the next traveler coming along with a fresh horse."[27] But where Thoreau emphasized a singular relationship with the natural landscape as the solution to Americans' "quiet desperation," Bellew favored what he described as "merry making" as the proper remedy, imploring his readers "to let up on nature," noting, "We should all be so much healthier, so much kinder, so much better Christians, if we would only amuse ourselves and each other a good deal more."[28]

The fact that Bellew's comics featured hints of romantic philosophy should come as no surprise given what is known about his life. Bellew was by most accounts a cosmopolitan figure, engaged with many of the major intellectual and artistic currents of the mid-nineteenth-century United States. He was born in India, the son of an Irish captain in the British army, received his education in France, and later worked for a time in London.[29] He is repeatedly cited by his contemporaries as a mainstay of the conversation clubs and salons that became common in mid-nineteenth-century New York. Bellew was a cofounder of the playfully named "Ornithorhyncus Club," which included Charles Gayler, William North, Sol

26. Bellew, *Art of Amusing*, 7.

27. Bellew, *Art of Amusing*, 84.

28. Bellew, *Art of Amusing*, 81.

29. Gunn, *Thomas Butler Gunn Diaries Volume 13*, August 18, 1860. Weitenkampf, "Frank Henry Temple Bellew," 165–66.

Eytinge, Charles G. Rosenberg, and Charles B. Seymour, among others.[30] He also carved out a career as a commentator on the artistic and social life of the Northeastern United States. Particularly during his years coediting the *Picayune*, Bellew wrote theater and art reviews, shared gossip about various public figures in New York, reflected on the vagaries of work as an artist and editor, and mused on peculiarities of daily life in the US. During his years producing comic strips, Bellew also spent time in Concord, Massachusetts, where he happened into friendly relations with Emerson and Thoreau. He debated the merits of Fourierism with Thoreau and even claimed to have inadvertently informed Emerson of Whitman's unauthorized quotation of Emerson's congratulatory note upon the publication of *Leaves of Grass*.[31]

When it came to Bellew's contributions to the early US comic strip, the prolific artist left a body of work that was simply unparalleled in its range or depth. Fellow expatriate Thomas Butler Gunn was unequivocal in his conviction that Bellew was the most significant American comic artist of his time: "As a comic artist," Gunn wrote, Bellew's "talents are extraordinary; certainly on this side of the Atlantic unrivaled. . . . Bellew has done more comic drawing and of a higher quality than all of the rest of us; we are all bunglers compared to him." Gunn went so far as to assert that Bellew even exceeded John Leech, the famous *Punch* artist, "in imagination and fancy."[32] As extraordinary as Gunn's claims may seem, they were hardly exaggerations. From 1850 until his death in 1888, Bellew drew sequential comic art and political caricatures for virtually every New York humor publication and was involved on an editorial level with many others. Bellew's political cartoons of Lincoln, Jefferson Davis, and Uncle Sam earned him a reputation as the main American rival to Thomas Nast among political cartoonists. These successes notwithstanding, Bellew's political cartoons rarely follow a consistent ideological perspective and often seem half-hearted when set alongside his apparent enthusiasm for the humor of everyday life. Indeed, in turning to comic strips and sketches, Bellew appears to have been an artist finding relief from the undercurrent of combativeness that characterized so much of US cartooning and news coverage at midcentury.

---

30. Winter, *Old Friends*, 308–9.

31. Thoreau, "Journal"; and Bellew, "Recollections of Ralph Waldo Emerson," 45.

32. Gunn, *Thomas Butler Gunn Diaries Volume 13*, August 18, 1860.

Subjects and situations that embodied Bellew's ethos of "merrymaking" appeared in his comics through the antics of characters who were in touch with nature primarily in the sense that they were authentically themselves. Self-possessed and indifferent to social convention, Bellew's merrymakers instigate the "cheerful" and "innocent" sense of play that Bellew endorsed as the basis for reconvening with nature. Precisely because of their indifference to social convention, these characters also tended to be misfits who wreaked havoc on the established social order. The presence of the unruly pet or child, eccentric individual, or unanticipated catastrophe creates momentary relief from the world of work and conformity by allowing desires and intuitions to take over. The philosophical and political undertones of his humor thus rarely arrive in the form of explicit protest against social authority as much as a spontaneous disruption of the façade of middle-class respectability.

Bellew's many comics featuring animals are among the best examples of his approach to the aesthetic and the philosophy that he called "merrymaking." For Bellew, animals carried this special status because they could be depicted as subjects who were wholly in touch with nature in ways that their human counterparts could never hope to achieve. Ignorant of human concerns for status or money, Bellew's animals are deliberately uncomplicated figures that spontaneously react to their surroundings. In depicting animals after this fashion, Bellew implied that any return to "nature" was hardly the idealized portrait so frequently celebrated by nineteenth-century American and European romantics but rather a vision of nature as thrillingly anarchic and unpredictable. Where Whitman the romantic poet might look for idealism and beauty in the "kosmos" of everyday life, Bellew emphasized the surprising ways that everyday life could reveal itself to be impulsive and eccentric.

Bellew made clear his distance from the Whitmanesque approach in "Pictures by Our Dog Worryin' Artist," an illustrated satire of Whitman's idealized view of nature. In the sequence, Bellew plays the part of a Whitmanesque transcendentalist whose plans during an afternoon communing with nature go sideways when he encounters a pack of twenty-seven domesticated dogs who roam the country roads of Madison, New Jersey. Bellew describes himself sitting in a field in Whitmanesque repose, "munching the tender ends of young grass" and thinking "all man was as good as any other atom in creation, and after all, it was very grand to be a man, and so on." Such illusions of harmony between man and nature are quickly dispelled with the dogs' arrival. What follows is an illustrated catalogue of Bellew's run-ins with the offending canines. Bellew slips nervously past the butcher's dog who "walks out very slowly and looks mad at you"; he throws rocks Deacon's Brown's shaggy dog who he believes "it would offer sincere gratification to measure my ankle"; and he contemplates "the dog of tender years who after barking and wagging his tail at you through the fence, follows you down the road with apparently, the fixed determination of accompanying you home and living with you ever afterwards."[33]

The significance of "Dog Worryin' Artist" lies with its implication that the rowdy behavior of the dogs may reflect a more authentic return to nature than the abstract mysticism of the transcendentalists. Where Whitman suggested that lying in the grass, contemplating the cosmos was the path to self-discovery, Bellew's satire concludes that this approach was naïve. The dogs, on the other hand, emerge as the heroes of the anecdote precisely because they so readily obey their instinct (which in this case involves tormenting Bellew). Bellew's animals are firmly characterized as *animals*. They are not the anthropomorphic projections of human emotions found in much of romantic literature but entities that are merely themselves. They react however the moment strikes them, and the authenticity of these reactions is precisely what puts them into conflict with social convention.

At their madcap extremes, Bellew's comics casted his animal subjects as agents of chaos who came into scandalously violent conflict with the human world of conventions and concerns. For example, through the 1850s and '60s, Bellew pursued multiple variations of the "exploding pig" sequence (fig. 2.5). In each case, the premise was simple: a pig obeys its instincts in ways that result in an obscene disruption of the order daily life. A pig eats Master Johnny's firecracker and explodes, scattering disembodied pig parts across an idyllic pastoral scene; pigs at the county fair eat corn until they swell up like balloons; crazed pigs chase gentlemen farmers off their land; and, in what is perhaps Bellew's most vulgar cartoon, pigs make a mockery of chamber music when their tails are played like piano strings, causing them to squeal at various pitches.[34] Bellew's comics read as deliberately obscene disruptions of everyday life. And this notion of obscenity

33. Bellew, "Pictures by Our Dog Worryin' Artist," 245.

34. Bellew, "Fourth of July," 12; Bellew, "Master Charley's Fourth of July," 429–30; Bellew, "Samson Shanghai's Three Days," 141–42; and Bellew, "Master Peter's Pranks," 4, 12–13.

THE "FOURTH" AND THE PIG.

No. 1. Master Johnny's father's favorite porker is struck with curiosity at seeing Johnny's fireworks.

No. 2. Not knowing the precise nature of the article, tastes it.

No. 3. It doesn't agree with him.

No. 4. The result.

FIGURE 2.5. Frank Bellew, "The 'Fourth' and the Pig," *Nick Nax for All Creation*, July 1856, 90. Courtesy of the American Antiquarian Society.

is precisely the point. Rather than fulfilling its usual role as a domesticated animal—whether it be producer of meat or scenery for a barnyard pastoral—the pig's underlying wild instincts upend any pretenses to polite decorum. As a form of what Bellew described as "merrymaking," the exploding pig satisfies an impulse to opt out of the artificial expectation to work or conform, instead embracing an elemental impulse to act out.

There was also a gentler side to Bellew's animal comics. Many of Bellew's animals invite affection and even admiration, especially when contrasted with the anxieties and absurdities of humans. In comic after comic, dogs, cats, and horses serve as bemused bystanders to human neuroses and as models of the "cheerful" and "innocent" sense of play that Bellew saw as the basis for a close relationship to nature. The three-frame sequence "More about Dog Days" (fig. 2.6) nicely captures the implicit contrast that Bellew created between admirably spontaneous animals and anxious humans.[35] In this simple sequence, the "Timid Mr. Snipkins" encounters

---

35. Bellew, "More about Dog Days," 1.

MORE ABOUT DOG DAYS.

1. THE TIMID MR. SNIPKINS SEES A DOG.   2. THE DOG WINKS AT A FLY—SNIPKINS ALARMED.   3. THE DOG YAWNS.

FIGURE 2.6. Frank Bellew, "More about Dog Days," *The Picayune*, August 2, 1856, 1. Courtesy of the American Antiquarian Society.

a tiny dog on the street and recoils in horror when the diminutive canine merely bats a fly away and yawns. With his limbs flailing and hat popping off his head, Simpkins is the very portrait of the downtrodden human figures that Bellew had described in *Art of Amusing*. So deeply entrenched in the concern of modern society, he is rendered apoplectic when encountering even the most diminutive manifestations of nature. In the meantime, the tiny dog's placid demeanor serves as droll counterpoint to Snipkins's modern neuroses. The dog's subtly rendered expressions—a small grimace followed by a widened mouth—highlight the absurdity of Snipkins's reaction while creating the sly implication that happiness and inner peace are perhaps best achieved through an uncomplicated relationship to nature.

The urban landscape of human social types was also fertile ground for Bellew's efforts to infuse his comics with the sense of play that he described in a merrymaker. In these types of works, eccentric, oddball characters and surprising situations offered premises in which the humdrum rhythms of everyday life were momentarily interrupted in ways that could at once be terrifying and exhilarating.

A notable example of Bellew's engagement with the unruliness of the urban landscape is *Mr. Bulbear's Dream,* an early Bellew series from *The Lantern,* which closely parallels the premise and structure of Winsor McCay's famous dream strips *The Dream of the Rarebit Fiend* and *Little Nemo in Slumberland.* Many of the similarities between Bellew's "Mr.

Bulbear" and McCay's work fifty years later are striking. The plot for "Mr. Bulbear" echoes *The Dream of Rarebit Fiend* almost beat for beat. Like McCay's rarebit fiend, Bellew's protagonist, a stockbroker, eats a sumptuous dinner and implicitly imbibes various illicit substances, causing him to suffer nightmares in which his urban environs transform into surrealist visions. In Bellew's sequence, Bulbear transforms into a giant penguin and proceeds through a series of misadventures such as meeting the king of Japan and waltzing with an elegant socialite. The closing frame in which Bulbear falls out of bed is nearly identical in both content and composition to the iconic recurring finale of *Little Nemo* where Nemo wakes up on the floor with a quizzical expression (fig. 2.7).[36]

While McCay was unlikely to have encountered Bellew's "Mr. Bulbear," the similarities between the two works highlight the common preoccupations of the two artists. Bellew, like McCay fifty years later, turned to the device of the dream-hallucination as an occasion to reframe everyday life as an extraordinary—even psychedelic—experience. In doing so, Bellew's "Bulbear" sequences feature a frenetic, improvisational quality that corresponds closely to McCay's strongest work. The fanciful improvisation of Bellew's comic is evident in the sequence wherein he runs his reader through a train of vacillating and sometimes self-contradictory improvisations. At each turn, the whims of the artist-narrator propel a series of free associations that lurch the protagonist from one absurd predicament to another. Bulbear's dim realization, "It never struck him that his grandmother was a penguin," gives way to "No! 'tis he that is the Penguin," which in turn leads to a horrific Freudian scenario in which Bulbear's childhood bullies harass him for his penguin-like appearance.[37] While terrifying, these scenes nevertheless offer affirmation that the experiences to be found in the everyday life of the city could be far stranger and far more interesting than a passing glance might suggest. A drunken bender or night out with friends might tend toward the extraordinary rather than the ordinary.

Another site where Bellew seems to have anticipated the Sunday Funnies and early animated cartoons was in his images of naughty children. According to Bellew's contemporaries, children were among his favorite subjects for cartooning.[38] Images of children running amok, pulling pranks, and playing pretend suffuse Bellew's comics. Bellew's child subjects seem

---

36. Bellew, "Mr. Bulbear's Dream—Continued," 186.

37. Bellew, "Mr. Bulbear's Dream," 156.

38. "Frank Bellew, the Artist Who Died," 5.

MR. BULBEAR'S DREAM---Continued.

After being introduced to Mrs. Perry, he takes a turn in the Polka with her.

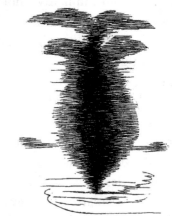

And they spin round with the most wonderful rapidity,

For which he is kicked down stairs by some one who seems to have sledge hammers for feet.

And, falling with fearful violence, awakes on the floor of his own bed-room.

STREET LYRICS.

THE CROSSING SWEEPER.

A child, scarce thirteen summers old,
   Stood sadly in the crowded street;
While by her swept the hurrying throng
   Of callous hearts and busy feet.
She had been there since earliest dawn,
   Working her slender arms a weary—
And half the city passed her by
   All heedless of a fate so dreary.

There came a merchant, rich and sleek,
   His purse was warm, his heart was cold ;
The wrinkles on his narrow brow
   Seemed furrowed there by weight of gold.
" One penny, Sir," the poor girl cried,
   " A penny, Sir, to get my dinner !"
But onwards strode, with careless ear,
   The wealthy and respected sinner.

A parson next, with face of woe,
   That masked a ribald sensual soul,
Thin lips, that seemed worn out with lies,
   An eye that sneered behind control.

Here !" thought the child, " comes one whose breast,
   Religion must have taught to pity"—
But no ! the hypocrite went by,
   The coldest heart in all the city.

And as the poor child sadly leaned
   Upon her broom, and sorely sighed—
A ragged woman, weak and poor,
   Came tottering midst the scornful tide.
And as her wandering glances fell
   Upon that shape, so full of sorrow,
She dropped a coin into her hand,
   Though half her pittance for the morrow.

Oh ! Poverty, 'twas sweet to see
   Thee help a sister on the way,
While icy wealth strode by, nor dreamed
   Of such a thing as want that day.
And if the weak would help the weak,
   Uniting in the dangerous hour—
They'd crush the cruel kings of gold,
   And burst the chains of monied power.

HEIR APPARENT.—Why is *a cross* father easily seen through ?—Because he is *trans*parent.

FIGURE 2.7. Frank Bellew, "Mr. Bulbear's Dream—Continued," *The Lantern*, May 15, 1852, 186. Courtesy of the American Antiquarian Society.

to inhabit a distinct social and imaginative world, organized around play and mischief. In this respect, Bellew's work serves as a notable forerunner to the Progressive-era comics about children, which flourished through a similar alchemy of cuteness, slapstick, and multiculturalism. As critic Lara Saguisag has shown, comics such as Outcault's *Buster Brown* and Leslie Feininger's *The Kinder-Kids* became a commercial and cultural phenomenon thanks in large part to their ability to define a distinctive childlike world that served as a forum for explorations of ideas about childhood and citizenship.[39]

Images of naughty children were by no means anything new to US graphic humor. Genre painting was a particularly rich source for this type of imagery. Works such as William Sidney Mount's *Farmer's Nooning* (1836) and James Goodwyn Clonney's *Mother's Watch* (c. 1852–56) idealized the naughty child's trespasses against adult rules. As Jadviga Da Costa Nunes observes, this affection for naughty children in American art was the result of the convergence of more permissive attitudes toward child-rearing with discourses that celebrated rebellion as the epitome of the American character. In the realm of child-rearing, post-enlightenment ideals increasingly framed childhood as a unique time of life that warranted protection. Child-rearing experts rejected the old Calvinist assumption that the child was inherently sinful in favor of an attitude that saw the child as being inherently good and possessed of a unique perspective as the disciplinarian approach of "breaking the child's will" increasingly gave way to encouragements to "bend the child's will," emphasizing tolerance, restraint, and tenderness as ideal parenting techniques. Meanwhile, sources ranging from Andrew Jackson's populist political rhetoric to Davey Crockett's frontierism to children's books celebrated "red-bloodness and vigorousness" as the defining elements of moral success for American children.[40]

The subversiveness of most prewar naughty American children was relatively limited. Although works like Mount and Clonney's genre paintings portrayed juvenile naughtiness as a break in the order and establishment, they ultimately fed into a broader nationalist story about conquest and triumph. The child subjects, while naughty, are ultimately domesticated in a way that asks viewers to envision the moment when unruly children will reform themselves and join the polite middle-class establishment. This seems particularly true of a work like *Farmer's Nooning* with its

39. Saguisag, *Incorrigibles and Innocents.*
40. Nunes, "Naughty Child," 225–28, 232.

depiction of a child playing a prank on a napping Black slave by tickling him with a piece of straw. The soft, sentimental appearance of the painting frames the prank as good-natured horseplay rather than genuine subversion. The child's trespasses, as far as readers are guided to believe, never extend beyond a momentary surprise. Even more tellingly, this prank is itself a precursor to the authoritarian position that the white child will one day hold over the enslaved. By asserting his will over the enslaved man by interrupting his nap, the child can thus be read as preparing for the day when he might exercise other forms of authority.

Bellew was simultaneously attracted and vexed by this tradition of representing children. On one hand, many of his comics show clear debts to the sentimentalized naughty children that appeared in popular prints and genre paintings. "Master Peter's Pranks with the Paint Pot," for instance, pays homage to D. C. Johnston's *Sound Asleep & Wide Awake* by reproducing its gag of the child with the paint can. Here, Peter cavorts about the barnyard with a paint can, turning gourds into monsters, the dog into a zebra, and a pig's backside into a giant smiling face.[41] Elsewhere, Bellew could be a sharp critic of the trope of the naughty child. Many of his comics and illustrations subvert the domesticating tendencies of this tradition by following the child's naughty "red-bloodedness" to its most absurd extremes. "Bad Boy's First Reader," a ruthless parody of a child's alphabet book, injects adult themes into children's nursery rhymes with its terrifying references to spinal meningitis and bizarre non sequiturs in which the platypus inexplicably appears under the caption "Z Zebra. Is this a Zebra? No, it is the ornithorhynchus paradoxus [scientific name for platypus]."[42]

These competing impulses are evident in Bellew's most sustained engagement with child subjects, the *Master Charley* series. Appearing in *Harper's Monthly* between 1857 and 1861, *Master Charley* follows the adventures of a fair-haired, upper-class child as he mingles with various lower-class street kids and other urban types.[43] Charley and his friends often imitate adult behavior, though they do so in a way that satirizes the affectations of the adult world. Because Charley and his urban companions are so indifferent to unspoken rules set by class and ethnicity, they often embody a tolerant cosmopolitanism. Charley himself is an unlikely match for the tough street kids he encounters. Dressed in lace and with the fine

---

41. Bellew, "Master Peter's Pranks," 4, 12, 13.
42. Bellew, *Bad Boy's First Reader*, 32.
43. Bellew, "Master Charlie's Sidewalk Acquaintances."

blond hair of a Victorian doll, he is hardly prepared for the rough-and-tumble lifestyle of the newsboys and street urchins, making him an easy mark for frauds and violence. At the same time, Bellew's Charley sees no contradiction in associating with these figures.

Later installments incorporated increasing complexity and irony into the clash of social and ethnic worlds that Bellew introduced in the first episode. As the series continues, Bellew increasingly makes Charley into a rabble-rouser who unconsciously violates invisible boundaries between class and ethnicity. The beating Charley sustains from the street children in the first episode is thus revealed as his initiation into their hardscrabble world rather than proof of his ineptitude. Bellew's artwork, in the meantime, added layers of irony by incorporating sentimental ornamentation and characterizations that further accentuated the tensions between Charley's angelic appearance and mischievous personality. In "Master Charley in the Snow" (fig. 2.8), the children take their snowball fight indoors, literally bringing the tough, public world of the street children into the parlor.[44] Another sequence, "Master Charley's First Pantaloons," features a variation on this theme as Charley receives a new pair of pants that he ruins first by stuffing the pockets full of trinkets from his play outside and then by roughhousing in the dressing room, a blunder that results in him being forced to wear a girl's dress at teatime.[45] In still another, Charley is spanked for ruining a wash bin while reenacting Washington crossing the Delaware. These antics all strike Charley and his friends as utterly logical, creating a satire that turns on the implicit contrast between adult affectations and the children's tolerance.[46]

Charley's status as a foil for the adult world brings readers full circle to Bellew's basic interest in the ideal he described as "merrymaking." The wisdom of Charley and his companions resides not with the entrenched beliefs of the adults who implicitly behave according to habit and convention but with the children who follow their intuitions. Bellew's subjects were not models of perfect behavior. They were simply themselves—complete with their flaws and eccentricities. For Bellew, this recognition of shared flaws and eccentricities offered a roundabout means of extending sympathy to his own subjects. Close observation of a character meant an understanding of the subject. And this was precisely what made them

44. Bellew, "Master Charley in the Snow," 429–30.

45. Bellew, "Master Charley's First Pantaloons," 717–18.

46. Bellew, "Master Charley's Fourth of July," 429–30.

His Sister has no more Idea who put Snow in the Doctor's Hat, than Master Charley has who hit the
Old Man in the Street.

Finishes the Day with a Snow-ball Party in the Parlor.

FIGURE 2.8. Frank Bellew, "Master Charley in the Snow," *Harper's New Monthly Magazine*, February 1860, 430. Courtesy of the American Antiquarian Society.

worthy of readers' sympathy. The disruption of polite social order either through eccentricity, naughtiness, or even violence is offered as the mechanism through which we, as readers, become aware of a common thread between all of his subjects.

John McLenan's Allegories of Social Mobility

Where Bellew's comics proposed play and idleness as potential solutions to the stultifying effects of middle-class convention, McLenan was far more pessimistic in his critique of American social life. In McLenan's comics, an undercurrent of psychological terror often lurked beneath the humorous façade. While his comics may initially seem like apolitical realisms or run-of-the-mill gag strips, they insinuate an ethical parody of myths about American social mobility. Many of his strips follow a well-meaning and optimistic social climber who finds that the promise of opportunity and social mobility was more mirage than reality. In McLenan's hands, the humorous sketch's repetitive qualities transform into evidence of unyielding obstacles and absurdities. Figures such as "Mr. Slim," "Mr. Bloemup," and "Mr. Elephant" all aspire to participate fully in American society through the achievement of social status or material wealth, only to be disappointed when class structures prove far more intransigent than advertised. But if the characters in McLenan's strips failed to comprehend their world, this had little to do with moral or ethical failings. Rather, their settings tended to be rife with obstacles and unresolvable paradoxes that make their demise seem inevitable.

McLenan's outsider characters are in this respect significant precursors to the "zany" aesthetic that Sianne Ngai identifies as a hallmark of twentieth-century cultural responses to capitalism. Like Lucille Ball's "Lucy" desperately attempting to fake her competence at occupations like window-washing or making chocolates, McLenan's characters are sent through a gauntlet of professions and social roles where their desperate attempts to maintain order reveal the precarity of their social positions. For Ngai, "the mix of desperation and playfulness" of the "zany" protagonist offers a vital allegory about labor within capitalism. "This playful, hypercharismatic aesthetic is really an aesthetic about work—and about precariousness created specifically by the capitalist organization of work . . . zaniness speaks to a politically ambiguous erosion of the distinction between playing and working."[47] This characterization of social precarity manifesting as an improvisational sort of clowning speaks strongly to the themes consistently seen in McLenan's comics.

The frustrations that emerged in McLenan's comics mirrored the artist's own lived experience. McLenan's life was typical of many working-class figures who flocked to New York's publishing scene in the 1850s and '60s. His route to urban periodicals paralleled that of the famous humorist Artemus Ward (Charles F. Brown). Both Ward and McLenan had traveled from humble beginnings in Ohio to New York, where they achieved international renown by first working their way up through the various humor magazines.[48] As the story goes, McLenan came to New York only after having been "discovered" at a pork packing plant in Cincinnati. D. C. Hitchcock noticed McLenan's drawings on barrel tops and sought to enlist him for publishing immediately.[49] His decision to write periodical comics seems to have been a conscious choice driven by personal and artistic preference rather than financial considerations. He was one of the most sought-after book and magazine illustrators of his generation. A favorite illustrator of both Charles Dickens and Wilkie Collins, McLenan doubtless had offers to do less taxing and more prestigious forms of magazine illustration. Despite these opportunities, McLenan chose to work as the primary illustrator for *Yankee Notions*. *Harper's* would eventually take note and McLenan's work for *Harper's* between 1855 and 1859 would establish a national following for his cartoons and comic strip.

Like many lives guided by artistic ambitions, McLenan ran into substantial financial difficulties. He was said to have died "in poverty and misery . . . overcome by [rheumatic gout] on his way to a valentine publisher's [office] in Chatham Street with some drawings he had to deliver to keep his wretched household in Brooklyn alive. McLenan's last sketches were auctioned off by friends in the newspaper industry to raise money for his family."[50] McLenan's sad fate underscores a central dilemma for the bohemian artists and writers living in New York. Social mobility was fragile even for the best-known artists. Status for the socially mobile seemed perpetually under threat, whether it be from the need to work tirelessly to

47. Ngai, *Our Aesthetic Categories,* 187–88.
48. "Bohemian Days at Pfaff's," 8.
49. Hamilton, *Early American Book Illustrators,* 120.
50. "Caricature in America," 109.

maintain one's position or the insidious suspicion that the dominant social classes would eventually restore the original order of things.

Undercurrents of disillusion in McLenan's background and art seem to be confirmed by his frequent collaborations with Doesticks, a humorist known for assaults on US culture's obsession with respectability. The two men appear to have enjoyed a close personal and professional relationship. McLenan is often cited as a companion of Doesticks, appearing at his side in both Gunn's diaries and in Doesticks's humorous writings. McLenan occasionally drew the illustrations that appeared alongside Doesticks's commentary in *The Picayune* and illustrated Doesticks's books, including the long mock epic *Pluribustah* (1856).[51] Their collaboration on *Doesticks' Letters and What He Says* resulted an exceptionally sharp critique of bourgeois values. In a chapter describing a drunken visit to Niagara Falls, Doesticks throws a series of barbs aimed at exposing the middle-class fascination with tourism as an "old swindling humbug"—a vapid affair in which the supposed "masterpiece" is at best "huge and nice" and at worst an outright "lie" whose chief merits are a "spray in one eye" and a "small lobster in one shoe."[52] At one point, Doesticks becomes so inebriated that a passerby fears he will dive headlong into the falls. The whole debaucherous scene is punctuated by a McLenan illustration titled "Doesticks on a Bender," depicting the humorist stumbling drunk and hallucinating as visions of Niagara swirl round his face with the word "beer" repeated in the background.[53]

The most extended of McLenan's explorations with "zany" protagonists was his series "Mr. Slim," which appeared in *Harper's Monthly* in 1855 and featured an effeminate protagonist who goes on various doomed excursions to the beach or the wilderness. McLenan's comic is primarily interested in the process of transformation through which Slim's optimism devolves into buffoonery and disappointment. For example, "Mr. Slim's Aquatic Experience" (fig. 2.9) follows the physical and psychological stages of a disastrous trip to the beach. McLenan's illustration makes light of Slim's discomfort with the elaborate dress of Victorian bathers, and he revels in

---

51. *Pluribustah*, an illustrated lampoon of Longfellow's *Hiawatha*, was among the most elaborate productions that either of the two men would create during their respective careers. Doesticks snuck a reference to McLenan into his book, *The Elephant Club*. Underhill and Doesticks, *History and Records of the Elephant Club*, 233–34.

52. Doesticks, *Doesticks' Letters*, 29–30.

53. Doesticks, *Doesticks' Letters*, 26.

430   HARPER'S NEW MONTHLY MAGAZINE.

Strikes out for the shore, and suddenly finds himself high and dry.

Recovers himself and is led in again by a friend who knows all about it.

Plunges in, and when he emerges finds himself surrounded by Mermaids.

In his flight he has lost the lower portion of his bathing-dress.

But fortunately recovers the article, and readjusts it.

He tries another dive. Further difficulty with his dress.

Resolves to "go out." View of the beach as seen by Mr. Slim on his way to the bathing-box. He makes a sensation.

Reappearance of Mr. Slim, after half an hour, spent in grumbling and efforts to dry himself with a wet towel covered with sharp sand.

FIGURE 2.9. John McLenan, "Mr. Slim's Aquatic Experience," *Harper's New Monthly Magazine*, August 1855, 429–30. Courtesy of the American Antiquarian Society.

the physical comedy as Slim is pulled away by the current and loses his pants to a group of suspicious "mermaids." In a particularly devastating frame, McLenan provides the caption "View of the beach as seen by Mr. Slim on his way to the bathing-box" with the image of a crowd including children and old women with spyglasses gawking at Slim's haggard appearance.[54] This captures a horror in public life that permeates many of McLenan's strips. The image of Mr. Slim, physically exposed and personally embarrassed on the beach, maps neatly onto a deeper set of fears in which demands for middle-class conformity could spoil even the simplest of pleasures like swimming or sunbathing.

In another installment titled "Mr. Slim's Experience at Sea," this central conflict of dashed hopes became a kind of tragicomic ballet. Here McLenan relies on a "two-step" rhythm in which the first beat sets up Slim's hopeful aspiration and is then followed by ironic understatement, which downplays the seriousness of each pratfall.[55] In an early frame, Slim nearly falls overboard while a droll caption reads, "He reaches the ship, but finds some difficulty getting on board"; another, in which Slim falls sideways, is accompanied by the internal monologue "Curious motion of the ship. He finds a difficulty in unlocking the door." In a raucous series of frames, McLenan pares this basic rhythm down to its barest essence as Slim tumbles head over heels: "Mr. Slim in his state-room.—Position Number One"; "Mr. Slim in his state-room.—Position Number Two"; "Mr. Slim in his state-room.—Position Number Three." The last frame of the strip punctuates the gag by returning to the two-step syntax: "Mr. Slim in his state-room again. Wonders if he is going to be sea-sick." McLenan's captions turn on the comedic tension between Slim's dogged attempts to maintain his polite, semi-aristocratic tone and the gruff, unyielding outside world.

McLenan's third installment of the Mr. Slim series, "Mr. Slim's Piscatorial Experience" (fig. 2.10), brings urban bohemianism into conversation with middle-class conformity through a sequence in which Mr. Slim's fishing trip serves as a wry send-up of the bohemian aspiration to establish an isolated space away from the materialism of bourgeois culture. In the comic, Slim sets about to go fishing (incidentally, a favorite pastime of McLenan himself).[56] Somewhat predictably, Slim is positioned as the effete, sensitive urban male who seems ill-equipped to embody the robust model of American masculinity that had been idealized in the frontier and seafaring romances of the time. Rather than simply go out and fish, Slim must first read books with titles like "Catfish Habits," "Last Run of Shad Tale," and "Porgies a Pome." Needless to say, he doesn't catch any

---

54. McLenan, "Mr. Slim's Aquatic Experience," 429–30.

55. McLenan, "Mr. Slim's Experience at Sea," 573–75.

56. McLenan, "Mr. Slim's Piscatorial Experience," 717–18.

FIGURE 2.10. John McLenan, "Mr. Slim's Piscatorial Experience," *Harper's New Monthly Magazine*, August 1855, 718. Courtesy of the American Antiquarian Society.

fish when he ventures out from his urban environs. But what he does find is intellectual and social fulfilment. In a scene reminiscent of Pfaff's beer hall, Slim "throws his line; has an awful bite; attempts to land his fish" and "discovers that instead of a fish, he has caught an artist—sketching. . . . Mr. Slim offers a suitable apology, which the artist readily accepts," conjuring a scene in which one can imagine the two kindred spirits drinking cognac, smoking tobacco, trading favorite lines of poetry, comparing sketches, and playing with the subversive theories of bohemian New York.

While the *Mr. Slim* strips generally projected a mild demeanor, they nevertheless evinced an undertone of tragedy that suggested a deeper frustration. Surface-level humiliations like those of Slim being laughed at on the beach or engaging in a failed fishing expedition implied a more general sense of intransigence in American social mobility. In this sense, they modulate away from the crass humor of many of the earliest imitations of the Töpfferian picture stories to a style of comic strip that emphasized subtler psychological tensions of living in a society where the thin line between success and failure seemed subjective at best.

McLenan's comics often treat the condition of the artist in ways that evince this very suspicion. In a single-panel self-portrait, McLenan depicts himself as slumped over and knocked out after feverishly pounding out dozens of illustrations. Another loosely autobiographical strip, "Our Artist, His Adventures in Pursuit of a Sketch of That Statue" (fig. 2.11), features an artist who runs afoul of the police for the simple offense of drawing strange and ugly pictures.[57] Like in many of McLenan's comics, the outsider figure appears to merely wish to participate in some version of respectable American society. In this case, the comic artist aspires to the ranks of a Gilbert Stuart type with his desire to depict a scion of American political culture in Daniel Webster, only to be turned away and shut out by the official establishment. The first frame depicts the frazzled artist with his sketchbook, drawing a full body sculpture of Daniel Webster. McLenan's caption punctures any appearance of would-be respectability, telling readers the artist is "lost in admiration, with the beautiful thought, 'How many pressed brick that pile o' dirt would make.'" As the comic continues, the artist's subtle transgressions catch the attention of a police officer, "C. P. Pellice No. 76," who informs him, "Mr. Puttyham" is the only artist allowed to sketch the statue. From here, a heated conversation and then a skirmish ensues. The final frame, captioned "What it was all about," provides a postscript, showing the artist's crude doodles. In bringing up these conflicts over who gets to approve works of art, McLenan positions the comic strip having a special role to play in public discourse.

---

57. McLenan, "Our Artist, His Adventures," 286–87.

Our Artist, HIS adventures in pursuit of a sketch of THAT Statue purporting to be a correct representation of the immortal D. Webster, Esq. We, (the Publisher,) having endowed the aforesaid artist with extraordinary powers to treat with the first "C. P. Pellice" that he came across, and to effect an entrance at all hazards, (even if it cost sixpence,) started him.

Scene 1st.—Artist seated before the Statue, lost in admiration, with the beautiful thought—"How many pressed brick that pile o' dirt *would* make,"—at length he sketches.

Didn't recollect her name.

An old farmer, residing within a short distance of Lancaster, visited that city a few days since on business, having disposed of a farm, and stepping into the office of a conveyancer, requested him to prepare the necessary title papers. When asked by that gentleman for the christen name of his wife, he gravely replied—

"Well, indeed, I don't recollect what it is. We have been married for upwards of forty years, and I always have called her mam."

The conveyancer left a blank in the deed, to be filled when "mam's" name was ascertained.

"I guess there an't much gammon about this," as the Yankee said when he tried a slice of wooden ham.

King Dick, having a note to pay on Monday, got into a muss on Saturday night, hoping some pugilist would knock him into the *middle of next week!*

April Fool.

The following anecdote, although out of season, is not out of place:

Among the many attempts to play off practical jokes upon the "green" ones on the first of April, that of a lady at one of the boarding houses of our city, is the best we have heard. It was this:

She procured from a marble yard several pieces of white marble, and breaking them into nice little lumps, put them into the sugar bowls. The counterfeit was complete. No unsuspecting person could have detected the fraud. Soon supper was ready—the tea was poured, and the sugar bowls were passed around the table. Everybody took one, two, or three lumps, according to their liking. Then followed a general tasting and stirring all around the table—nobody's tea was sweet enough, and the sugar positively refused to melt. They ground their spoons against it, and stirred again, but it was no go. The sugar proved to be marble, and they for once, proved to be *April Fools!*

Scene 2d.—Discovered by "C. P. Pellice," No. 76—agonizing expressions of despair, indignation, "Lager Bier," and just anger—to find a "feller drawin' rite under his nozz," flit across his intelligent face.

Scene 3d.—C. P. Pellice mutters forth the ominous word "quit, or I'll conform on yer. Mr. Puttyham has the ony rite here to draw."

A Good Excuse.

There is a society in existence in this city, which, like most other associations of the same kind, has a standing rule that all members who come late or absent themselves, shall be fined a certain sum, unless they are able to give sufficient excuse for their tardiness or absence. On one occasion a member came in after hours, and the chairman asked him his excuse for being late.

"Really, sir," said he, "I was not able to get here before—domestic troubles—perplexities of mind—I cannot say which will die first, my wife or my daughter."

"Ah," said the chairman, expressing much commiseration for the father and the husband, "I was not aware of that. Remit the fine, Mr. Secretary—the excuse is a good one."

The member consequently took his seat. The next morning another member met him; and with much feeling asked him how his wife and daughter were?

"In excellent health," replied he.

"How? I thought you said last night, that you did not know which one would die first."

"I did—and am still in a quandary. Time, however, will decide the question."

Scene 4th.—(*Note.*—Between Scene 3 and 4, an intermission of two minutes is supposed to have intervened, when Artist tells him—C. P. Pellice, No. 76—to go to thunder, and C. P. Pellice, No. 76, calls the Director.) Director thunders forth—

"Seize him, ossifers, seize him and bare him away!"

FIGURE 2.11. John McLenan, "Our Artist, His Adventures in Pursuit of a Sketch of That Statue," *Yankee Notions*, September 1853, 286. Courtesy of the American Antiquarian Society.

The fraught issue of social mobility could take on a downright night-marish quality in McLenan's work as the precarity of his protagonists occasionally tipped over into crushing humiliations and even violence. "Inconveniences of Living in a Uniform Row of Houses" features a resident of a row house who is mistaken for a vagrant, battered by police, and even shot at by a neighbor, simply for knocking on the wrong door at night. McLenan's "Mr. Elephant" was an especially acute example of a subject who seemed to embody the treacherous nature of an ever-shifting social landscape. In "Mr. Elephant at Mrs. Potiphors," McLenan uses the figure of a clumsy elephant at an elegant ball to embody this discomfort. Mr. Elephant flirts with ladies and challenges his romantic rivals but ulti-mately makes a fool of himself as his efforts to dance and fight see him falling down, shaking the walls, knocking pictures and chandeliers to the ground, and breaking through the front door. The final caption encapsu-lates the basic frustration of this social intransigence with Mr. Elephant's sad admission "that Fat Men Can't Be Graceful."[58]

The bleeding of observational humor into stark realisms in works like "Uniform Row Houses" and "Mr. Elephant" foreshadowed the persistent associations between comics and the important innovations in literary and artistic realism at the turn of the twentieth century. Critics such as Bill Blackbeard and Jean Lee Cole have observed that the street scenes of turn-of-the-twentieth-century comics like R. F. Outcault's *Hogan's Alley* and the immigrant characters of Rudolph Dirks' *Katzenjammer Kids* share the documentary impulses and preoccupation with urban social types that pervaded realist fiction and paintings of the period in works such as Jacob Riis's *How the Other Half Lives,* Stephen Crane's *Maggie: A Girl of the Streets,* and the paintings of the Ashcan School. In an oft-quoted passage, Outcault described how wandering about the slums of New York provided him with the inspiration for his phenomenally successful comic strip char-acter Mickey Dugan, or The Yellow Kid. "Seriously speaking," Outcault said, "The Yellow Kid was not an individual, but a type. When I used to go about the slums on newspaper assignments I would encounter him[,] encounter him often, wandering out of doorways or sitting down on dirty doorsteps. I always loved the Kid."[59] For Blackbeard and Cole, statements like this confer an air of respectability on turn-of-the-century Sunday Fun-nies because they at once suggest a kinship with the widely acknowledged

---

58. McLenan, "Mr. Elephant and Mrs. Potiphar's," 717–18.
59. Hancock, "American Caricature and Comic Art," 130.

accomplishments of American realism and a philosophical depth extending far beyond the comic strip's deceptively simple appearance.[60]

As this chapter has shown, mid-nineteenth century artists like Bellew and McLenan probably deserve similar plaudits for their finely textured portrait of urban life in the United States. Like their turn-of-the-century counterparts, Bellew and McLenan regarded comics as an artform that should simultaneously document and satirize the lived conditions of everyday people. In Bellew's case, observations of what he called "merrymaking" pointed to the conclusion that people retained underlying qualities of innocence and virtue amid the complexities of modern life. McLenan reached nearly the opposite conclusion, anticipating literary realism's preoccupation with characters ruined and humiliated by their unyielding circumstances. As we'll see in the next chapter, the observational impulse of mid-nineteenth-century American comic artists freely mingled with other types of formal and thematic inspiration, most notably the theater.

---

60. Blackbeard, "Yellow Kid," 21–24; and Cole, *How the Other Half Laughs*, 12–18.

CHAPTER 3

Drawn from the Stage

Theater Comics

"All the world is a stage, and all the men and women merely players."
Shakespeare's famous opening lines to *As You Like It* could have easily
applied to nineteenth-century America's comics pages. Much in the way
film was an inspiration to comic artists in the early twentieth century, the
visual language and themes of live theater offered a logical point of departure for depicting movement, inventing characters, and organizing narrative. For a significant subset of comics, to imagine the space between the
frames was to picture characters as actors upon a stage, whether those performances were bounded by the four corners of a theater's proscenium or
less formal performance spaces such as the street or the parlor.

Take the example of John McLenan's three-panel sequence "Three Tableaux in the Life of a Broadway Swell" (fig. 3.1), a comic that announces
itself as a theatrical performance. In the first frame, an effeminate dandy
named Mr. Blossom "sallies forth" across Broadway, prepared "to demolish
the fairer sex." Blossom's preening and posing resembles that of an actor or
an orator striking a pose, standing tall, head cocked to the side, shoulders
and hips opened wide, and cane placed delicately between his legs as a
prop. Blossom's posture seems drawn from one of the many nineteenth-
century acting manuals that prescribed precisely this type of gesture to
communicate charm and confidence. Predictably, Blossom's vanity does
not go unpunished. In the second frame, he slips on an orange peel and
his confident attitude turns into another acting convention: the slapstick
pratfall. His arms flail to the side, his hat pops off of his head, and his hind
quarters land with a thud beneath splayed legs. In frame three, a haggard

208   YANKEE NOTIONS.

THREE TABLEAUX IN THE LIFE OF A BROADWAY SWELL.

I.

MR. BLOSSOM HAVING MAGNIFICENTLY PREPARED HIMSELF, SALLIES FORTH TO DEMOLISH THE FAIR SEX.

A CLASS IN MUSIC.—"First class in sacred music, stand up. How many kinds of metre are there?"
"Three, sir– long metre, short metre, and meet'er by moonlight alone!"
"Who told you that, you booby?"
"Bill Jones, sir."

II.

HE MEETS WITH A SLIGHT INTERRUPTION IN HIS PROMENADE.

A PERSEVERING DRUMMER.—We are told of a remarkable case of perseverance on the part of a dry goods drummer. Seeing the name of a Western trader registered at one of the hotels, whom he knew would be a desirable customer, and anxious to secure him first, our drummer sat down in the office of the hotel to watch the key of the Western man's bedroom till he should come in to claim it. But something kept the stranger out very late, and the drummer fell asleep. When he woke, he found his customer had escaped him by coming in and going to bed. The drummer gave it up for that night, but early on the next morning he repaired to the door of the gentleman's bed-room, and seeing his boots, which had been nicely blacked, standing there, he, with a lead pencil, marked them across again and again, until they could not be mistaken, and once more took up his position in the office, but this time near the stairs, where he could examine the boots of all who came down. Finally, he discovered the ones with the well-known marks upon them, when he cordially addressed the wearer by his name, as if he had known him for years, and probably sold him a large bill of goods!

III.

AND RETIRES TO HIS SUITE OF ROOMS—FIFTH STORY BACK—TO REPAIR DAMAGES.

NOTE.—we are happy to state that Mr. B—— will be able to appear before the Broadway audience again to-morrow afternoon, in his favorite character, weather and orange-peel admitting.

At a ball recently given at the Hotel de Ville, Paris, a group, among which was the Secretary of Feruk Khan, were discussing the merits of the Euphrates Valley Railroad.
"Your country," said a lady to the Secretary, "will then be very near to us."
"Yes, if the project should be accomplished."
"Do you doubt it?"
"The difficulties of execution are very great and numerous."
"Certainly, but the English engineers will surmount them."
"Oh!" replied the young Persian, with an air of cunning, "there is one against which their science mustfail; all these deserts are peopled with ostriches."
"Well!"
"Well, these birds, you know, digest iron; they will eat the road up!"

FIGURE 3.1. John McLenan, "Three Tableaux in the Life of a Broadway Swell," *Yankee Notions*, July 1857, 208. Courtesy of the American Antiquarian Society.

Mr. Blossom, still relying on the visual language of stage acting, performs his dejection by dropping his head between his slouched shoulders and again using the cane as a prop, but this time as a means of showing the audience that his legs are buckling beneath his weight. In case readers have missed the theatricality of the sequence, McLenan advises them with this postscript: "Mr. B—will be able to appear before the Broadway audience again tomorrow in his favorite character, weather and orange peel permitting."[1]

McLenan's framing of "Broadway Swell" as stage performance before a "Broadway audience" highlights at least two mutually reinforcing patterns through which comics in mid-nineteenth-century America could take on a theatrical quality: First, conventions inspired by theater formed an important part of many comic artists' formal and thematic repertoires. As in "Broadway Swell," gestures were depicted in the visual vocabularies of elocution and pantomime. The tableau and mise-en-scène were used to establish scene and transitions between scenes. Instead of captions or word balloons, many illustrations were accompanied by lines formatted as playscript dialogues, with speakers identified by the common theatrical abbreviation "loq" (for "loquitur," a stage direction identifying the speaker). US comics featured themes, situations, and stock characters reminiscent of US theatrical productions, whether it be the crude antics and ethnic humor of the working-class Bowery theater and minstrel shows or the lively wordplay and splendor of genteel social comedies.

Second, there was also the matter of the implicit theatricality of American life overall. The comics serve as both records of a culture infatuated with the expectation that spontaneous performances could emerge almost anywhere *and* as direct participants in that culture. As theater historian Rosemarie Bank posits, nineteenth-century US "theater culture" was composed not only of productions taking place on actual stages but also interlocking displays—both public and private—of pageantry, orality, busking, and proliferating cultural forms.[2] Comics like "Mr. Blossom" both depict and promote this style of spectatorship. References to Blossom's return for the "Broadway audience" in "his favorite character" explicitly set up the expectation that performances could take place in settings that extended far beyond the interiors of theaters. Such expectations are recorded in the countless comics that (like "Mr. Blossom") depicted characters in public and private settings engaged in impromptu performances, ranging from the unintentional acrobatics of a man stepping on an ice rink for the first time to snappy dialogues between socialites in parlors.

A broader survey of McLenan's work reveals that "Broadway Swell" is only one of his many comics that reminds readers that they are viewing a kind of miniature performance on the page. Throughout McLenan's work,

---

1. McLenan, "Three Tableaux in the Life," 208.
2. Bank, *Theatre Culture in America*, 1–9.

we can notice consistent references to theatrical conventions and figures. He persistently presented his captions as theatrical dialogue, labeled his frames as "scenes" and "tableaux," and utilized stock characters such as Jim Crow and Brother Jonathan. In at least one instance, McLenan reproduced the text from an entire burlesque skit titled "The Lonely Pollywog of the Mill Pond" and then couched sequential illustrations between the lines of dialogue and stage directions (complete with malfunctioning special effects).[3] He also illustrated sequential strips of the actor William Burton in character as "Toodles," embarking on adventures in the Western Frontier and the East Indies.[4]

While McLenan himself was among the most explicit in his use of theatrical conventions, he was by no means unusual. Just as the novelistic approach of the Töpfferian picture story had become an important part of artists' storytelling repertoire through the 1850s and '60s, so too did the conventions and viewing practices associated with live theater. To speak of what this book calls "theatrical comics" in mid-nineteenth-century America is thus to engage these mutually reinforcing patterns of form and spectatorship. Comics adopted theatrical tropes to frame public and private space as inherently theatrical and, in doing so, they were both responding to and creating the suggestion that public and private life were indeed rife with performance.

Theatrical Engagements

The connection between theatrical performance and comics is rooted in a long tradition of visual satire that conceived of public performance and illustration as closely related. In English visual satire, entertainers and public performances were common subjects for conveying the experience of the vibrant urban landscape. In William Hogarth's prints and paintings, for instance, public entertainment offers both the carnival-like atmosphere of public performances and the social meanings that arose from observing the eighteenth-century crowd's reactions. This duality is evident in Hogarth's *Southwark Fair* (fig. 3.2), where a bustling English public interacts

3. McLenan, "Lonely Pollywog of the Mill Pond," 28–29.
4. McLenan, "Mr. Toodles' Adventures in the West," 4; and McLenan, "Mr. Toodles Goes to the East Indies," 4–5.

FIGURE 3.2. William Hogarth, *Southwark Fair*, 1734, print. Courtesy of the Metropolitan Museum of Art.

with a dizzying array of street performances.[5] Rustics gawk at the drummer woman, men dip their heads into the peepshow, and a throng gathers beneath the balcony to see the players and daredevils above. By directing the viewer's gaze to the paired spectacles of the performers *and* the crowd, Hogarth establishes a complex visual dialectic in which the gaze alternates between the personal sensations of awe that arise from live performance and the social meanings that become visible from watching others watch.

The interest in performance evident in Hogarth would in turn shape the graphic satire of subsequent generations. English artists Thomas Rowlandson and William Cruikshank made extensive use of performance tropes as did French and German artists such as Rodolphe Töpffer, Gustave Doré, and J. J. Grandville. Later publications such as *Punch* and its various

5. Hogarth, *Southwark Fair*.

imitators would follow suit. Indeed, the iconic first cover of *Punch* featured a cartoon of a crowd intently watching one of the famous "Punch and Judy" shows in a crowded London square. Other comics in *Punch* worked to emulate the farces and melodramas at the Drury Lane and Haymarket theaters through comics formatted in playscript dialogue or references to theatrical types and tropes.[6] By no means was the interest in theater solely the province of European comic artists either. In eighteenth- and nineteenth-century Japan, portraits of actors and depictions of theatrical scenes were indeed among the most common subjects of Ukiyo-e woodblock prints by artists such as Katsushika Hokusai, Utagawa Kunisada, and Utagawa Kuniyoshi.[7]

The long-standing connection between comics and live theater remained a prominent feature of comics at the turn of the twentieth century in America. Influential comics such as R. F. Outcault's Yellow Kid strips, Rudolph Dirks's *Katzenjammer Kids,* and George Herriman's *Krazy Kat* all relied on familiar conventions that were shared with vaudevillian entertainment. Repetitive gags, blackface minstrelsy, burlesque, verbal improvisations, and ethnic humor all continued as mainstays of both comics and live theater. Scholar Jean Lee Cole contends that the convergence of vaudeville and the early Sunday Funnies were vital to the development of a turn-of-the-century "comic sensibility," a new style of humor that served the needs of an important new immigrant readership and eschewed delicacy in favor of skits and situations that tapped into repetitive narrative structure and embodied the "guttural" humor of the vaudeville sketch as their core aesthetic values.[8] As Cole notes, George Luks's installments of *Hogan's Alley* were often presented to readers as theatrical tableaux, spotlighting the kind of entertainments associated with the vaudevillian variety theater. A single page might feature scenes of dancing, slapstick violence, ethnic caricature, verbal improvisations, and other forms of spectacle.[9]

If anything, mid-nineteenth-century US comics were even more closely attached to their local theater scenes than British or European counterparts. In no small part, this attachment played out through the physical geography of print and performance culture in the United States. The

---

6. *Punch,* August 1, 1841, 1.

7. Guth, *Art of Edo Japan,* 28–39.

8. Cole, *How the Other Half Laughs,* 6, 92. See also Meyer, *Producing Mass Entertainment,* 76–77, 118–19.

9. Cole, *How the Other Half Laughs,* 44–52.

dense concentration of publishing and theaters made city centers remarkably vibrant sites of exchange. Journalists, playwrights, actors, artists, and indeed cartoonists could trade ideas and inspiration in the nearby coffeehouses or discuss all manner of performances and spectacles. In New York City, an artist could walk from the offices of *Yankee Notions* or *Nick Nax* on Nassau Street, past the city's major newspapers and Barnum's American Museum, and into the center of the comic theater district around Lower Broadway and Fulton Street.[10]

The overlap between theater and producers of comics that resulted from this geographic and cultural proximity are extensive and persistent. In his diaries, illustrator Thomas Butler Gunn characterized theater-going as a primary pastime of the many comic artists who inhabited New York during the 1850s and '60s and described a persistent pattern of interactions between the two groups.[11] Frank Bellew wrote theater reviews and associated with many figures in New York's theater scene, including actress Ada Clare and owner of Wallack's Theatre, Lester Wallack.[12] In several cases, editors of humor magazines were themselves writers and producers in the theater scene. Cornelius Mathews, one of the most prominent humor editors of the period, wrote and staged several social comedies. Likewise, John Brougham, primarily known as the playwright and producers of plays such as *Metamora, or The Last of the Pollywogs*, dabbled in illustrated humor with his short-lived magazine, *The Lantern*. Jesse Haney, the publisher of *The Picayune, Nick Nax*, and *Comic Monthly* was also a minstrel performer who appeared under the name Julius Hannibal Caesar.[13] One could doubtlessly list interactions between comics and theater ad nauseum. But most importantly, the geographical proximity of entertainment districts and publishing houses correlated with cultural and intellectual affinities.

For their part, US humor magazine editors and artists were eager to remind audiences that the activity of viewing comics was linked to performance culture. Comics were to be seen as their own peculiar variety of performance, capable of transporting readers to the imagined space of

---

10. Reilly, "Comic Drawing," 15.

11. References to attending theater with various figures from the illustrated press recur throughout Gunn's diaries. Some representative examples include Gunn, *Thomas Butler Gunn Diaries Volume 9*, January 12, 1858, and March 22, 1858; Gunn, *Thomas Butler Gunn Diaries Volume 11*, December 13, 1859; and Gunn, *Thomas Butler Gunn Diaries Volume 14*, November 27, 1860.

12. Bellew, "Brigham Blake," 92; Gunn, *Thomas Butler Gunn Diaries Volume 18*, January 13, 1862; and Gunn, "Restaurants of New York," 100–101.

13. Gunn, *Thomas Butler Gunn Diaries Volume 5*, November 17, 1852.

New York or Philadelphia's theaters. The characters, dialogue, situations, audiences, and even the architecture of American theaters were a persistent presence in the comics.

We need look no further than the covers of humor magazines from the 1840s through the 1870s to appreciate the extent to which comics were presented to readers in this way. Covers persistently featured images of characters depicted as performers on stage. Curtains, tents, and audiences were often the borders for cover design. Henry Louis Stephens's illustration for *Punchinello* featured the magazine's eponymous mascot in a doublet standing on the apron of a stage, pulling back a curtain to reveal ballerinas, jesters, and swordsmen in the wings (fig. 3.3).[14] To the left is an audience filing in alongside a ticket booth with an advertisement stating, "Will Exhibit Every Saturday, Admission 10 cents." Thomas Nast's cover illustration for *Mrs. Grundy* likewise featured that magazine's mascot, facing an auditorium with "one hundred easily recognizable faces" that readers were guided to pick out from the crowd as part of a contest.[15] Meanwhile, the covers for *The Comic Monthly* typically featured images of stage actors in character like Edmund Forrest as a gladiator or Burton as Toodles. The implicit promise to audiences was clear: The content within the magazines themselves would approximate the excitement of live performance.

The suggestion that comics were miniature performances was also evident in artists' visual composition. Characters were often arranged at a three-quarter angle toward the viewer, creating a line of vision similar to that of viewing actors on a stage or in the promotional lithographs. The panel itself emulated the proscenium view with side wings bounding the image to the left and right and the proscenium or upper arch bounding the top of the frame. Such conventions remained widespread not only in comics but also in other sectors of the illustrated press such as broadside prints and newspapers like *Frank Leslie's Illustrated Newspaper*.[16]

Among the most important tools in comic artists' visual repertoire were the conventions of the expressive tableau. In a tableau, an actor would hold a pose or gesture, giving the audience time to absorb what scholar Peter Brooks describes as a "visual summary of the emotional situation."[17] In this manner, viewers were presented with a pregnant moment in which they

14. *Punchinello*, April 2, 1870, 1.
15. Paine, *Thomas Nast*, 100.
16. Brown, *Beyond the Lines*, 72–73.
17. Brooks, *Melodramatic Imagination*, 48.

FIGURE 3.3. Cover illustration for *Punchinello,* April 2, 1870, 1. Courtesy of the American Antiquarian Society.

were invited to project forward or backward in time, anticipating the next action, emotion, or scene. Underpinning theatrical tableau was a sophisticated visual language of gesture and emotion. Nineteenth-century British and American acting and oratory manuals drew nuanced distinctions between different gestures and the corresponding emotions and passions

FIGURE 3.4. Gilbert Austin, *Chironomia or, A Treatise on Rhetorical Delivery*, plate 10. Reproduced in Gilbert Austin, Lester Thonssen, and Mary Margaret Robb, *Chironomia; or, A Treatise on Rhetorical Delivery* (Carbondale: Southern Illinois University Press, 1966).

that they might evoke onstage. Leman Rede's influential *Road to the Stage*, for example, featured a list of seventy-four distinct gestures with detailed directions for how an actor should adjust their body to convey a particular emotion.[18] The charts and diagrams that populated acting manuals featured a similar level of detail. Gilbert Austin's *Chironomia* (1806), the most well-known, offered readers a single-page chart through which different stances could be compared and contrasted (fig. 3.4).[19]

18. Rede, *Road to the Stage.*
19. Austin, Thonseen, and Robb, *Chironomia*, 617.

The influence of tableaux in the comics readily appeared in the close resemblance to gestures in acting manuals. Comics that utilized tableaux organized their frames as chains of emotional resolutions that readers would momentarily ponder before moving on to the next frame. If done correctly, such tableaux would create what theater critic Percy Fitzgerald described as an "anticipatory gesture" in which the viewer experienced suspense before the next gesture resolved to either fulfill or overturn expectations.[20] Some artists would even label their frames as "tableau" in order to signal to readers that they were looking at a chain of emotional resolutions, implicitly advising them to slow down and absorb the frame's emotional information before moving on to the next frame.

This anticipatory quality of the tableau forms the basis for "The First Cigar," a popular gag that recurred in different forms across multiple US periodicals.[21] In this 1864 version from *Merryman's Monthly* (fig. 3.5), a young boy discovers his father's cigars, smokes one, and then proceeds through a series of expressive poses, telegraphing his progress from curiosity to ecstasy to confusion to terror to abjection. At each panel break, the viewers are implicitly asked to anticipate whether each succeeding tableau will follow as a continuation of the current emotional state or result in an ironic reversal. In each case, the captions and gestures combine to signal the progress of the emotions of the boy, who is cheekily named "Master Hopeful." The boy's gestures build from the inquisitive tilt of his head in panel 1 at "find[ing] one of his father's Havanas" to his triumph at finding himself "the envy of smaller boys," expressed by his striking the pose of a victorious army general with puffed-out chest and raised arm. Of course, the victory is short-lived, and so we see the progression reverse itself. Thus, his increasingly anxious states of mind reach their climax in panel 9, where the simple caption "Remorse" is conveyed by the classic Victorian convention of a character swooning and falling backward onto a couch.

Importantly, sequences in the vein of "The First Cigar" operate as a series of emotional situations in the vein of the melodrama's approach to using tableaux. The movement of the eye from frame to frame thus proceeds as a sequence of momentary contemplations of isolated emotions. The comic does not depict any single sustained emotion for more than a frame or two as much as it guides the plot forward by progressing through a series of distinct tableaux, each featuring an easily legible emotion. The

20. Qtd. in Mayer, "Encountering Melodrama," 152.
21. Hopkins, "First Cigar," 5; McLenan, "First Segar," 92–93; and "First Cigar," 244–45.

The First Cigar.

1. Master Hopeful finds one of his Father's Havanas on the Shelf.

2. Is induced to imitate his Father in sundry respects.

3. Is the envy of smaller boys—and the admiration of larger ones.

4. Somehow he thinks there isn't so much fun in a Cigar after all

5.

6. Thinks it grows quite warm.

7.

8. Curious phenomena—surrounding objects go round and round—playing "Wind! tobacco, Joshuay" about Master Hopeful.

9. Remorse.

10. The Doctor.

11. Reads about the evils of using tobacco and resolves never more to touch the vile weed.

12. Ten years after.

FIGURE 3.5. Scenes from "The First Cigar," *Merryman's Monthly,* September 1864, 244–45. Courtesy of Hathitrust.

use of tableaux in this manner tends to create a droll, understated style of humor reliant on halting rhythms and pregnant pauses. One might imagine the effect as analogous to a narrator in the side wings calling out the emotion suggested by the actor's body language and pausing for laughter before moving on to the next tableau.

The dialogue-driven comedic skit emerged as another theatrical convention that became significant in mid-nineteenth-century US comics. Artists made a common practice of depicting stock characters with a caption featuring playscript dialogue. Dialogues could feature stage directions, the abbreviation "loq" to label a speaker as "loquitor," or a caption identifying

THE CALIFORNIA VOLUNTEER.

A DRAMA OF INTENSE INTEREST

*Written expressly for the rejection of our principal theatrical managers,
and dedicated, without permission, to every body,
and the public in general.*

DRAMATIS PERSONÆ.

SAM BUTCHERBIRD,   TWO NEWSBOYS,
MAJOR SWILL.   SARAH BUTCHERBIRD.
TWO POLICEMEN.

NATIONAL PROPERTIES, *Sundry Volunteers.*—THEATRICAL PROPERTIES,
*A Lamp-post, two Rum Bottles, a People Boat, a Plate, a Chatham-
street Deal Table, and two Policeman's Staffs.*

ACT I.

*SCENE I.—A chamber, at the nominal rent of six shillings per week,
with suitable furniture. SARAH discovered in a disconsolate mood, seated at
a table, on which is a bottle of Rum, and fragments of a hasty meal. Curtain rises to music descriptive of half-past four o'clock, P. M.*

SARAH—Ah, gracious me ! this is a wretched day !
What can detain my darling Sam away !
He never was behind his time before—
Confound them Mexicans what caused this war !
Sam's mind is addled, and he " goes for glory"
I guess that when he fights, he'll tell another story.
How changed ! e is, oh my ! how sunk his eye !
How red his nose ! his mouth is all awry.
His beard is stubby—holler is his cheek—
I guess he hasn't had a clean shirt for a week.
Oh, wretched day, that ever I was born !
Done up, forsook, unfortunate, forlorn !

*[She sings a melancholy song, which draws tears from the eyes of
the spectators, and during the symphony thereof, she helps herself
abstractedly to rum. A husky cough is heard—chord of music.]*

'Tis he, my Sammy !—On the gentle breeze
I hear his cough, and recognize his sneeze !

[Music descriptive of double-soled brogans. Enter SAM.]

Oh, welcome home, dear Sam ! You're late to-day.
Say, what has kept my dear bo-hoy away ?
SAM—(grasping her wrist) Come forad, dearest Sal, and
                pay attention,
To wot your Sammy is about to mention.
I am inlisted, and got my commission
As Seargeant in the California expedition.

[Hysterical chords of music. SARAH falls in a fit.]

SAM—(running to her) She's in a fit—'tis fit she should be so.
'Twould be much fitterer if I'd fit the foe.
Come, rise my gal, throw off these false alarms !
And throw yourself into a husband's arms
SARAH—(recovering) Bear me no longer—sooner let me fall.
I'd rather you would not bear arms at all !

SAM—'Tis now too late— I cannot tarry here.
I'm booked, and am a reg'lar Volunteer.
To-morrow morning I must go on drill,
At Gov'ner's Island, under Major Swill !

SARAH—(her hair in wild confusion)   Oh, do not go !
SAM—I must—Swill won't be braved
Consent my gal—
SARAH—(after a pause and evincing unequalled emotion,) I do !
SAM—(waving his hat triumphantly) Hurray ! the country's
                saved.

*[They dance the " Redowa Polka," to the unequaled delight of an
overflowing house, and the Act drop falls.]*

☞ *A lapse of sixteen hours and a quarter is supposed to have taken place
between the first and second Acts.*

ACT II.

*SCENE I—The Parade Ground on Governor's Island, SAM discovered
on drill under MAJOR SWILL. Slow music as the Act drop rises, descriptive
of a balmy morning, and patient individuals fishing in the bay. When Act
drop up, grand flourish of fife and drum.*

MAJOR—Toes out—head up—eyes right—and stand at ease !
Shoulder musket—good !—Attention ! turn out knees !
Advance—right foot !—that's the left—the other one !
Fall back—draw ramrod—fix bayonet—not your gun !
Hold up your head—and keep your eyes on me ! &c &c.

*Music from a cracked fife and drum. A boat approaches, from which
several hampers of live recruits are landed, dressed in California regimen-
tals. Major Swill entertains them with a military hornpipe, and the scene
closes.*

*SCENE II—A Street with lamp post. Enter SAM in a copious state
of brandy, a bottle of which he carries in his hand.*

I got old Swill's permit to come on shore,
Whilst he [hic] danced hornpipes to recruits afore.
This brandy's stiffer than I calculated,
And yet I'm sure, [hic] I'm not intoxicated.
A raw recruit at least mought take a sup
Of raw material [hic] to keep his spirits up.

He clutches lamp post affectionately. Enter two untamed News Boys.

a speech as a "soliloquy." In the most elaborate instances, the script for an entire theatrical skit was placed on a full-page spread alongside illustrations of characters acting out the scenes. Works like "The California Volunteer" (fig. 3.6) and McLenan's "The Lonely Pollywog of the Mill Pond" embedded entire skits that could be acted out over the course of a few minutes.[22] Far more common were simple, single-panel cartoons featuring a dialogue between a couple of immediately recognizable stock characters. These dialogue-driven skits adopted a stable structure of characters and styles of clowning, thereby setting up a highly predictable framework in which jokes could be executed efficiently, as audiences watched for repetitions of interactions that they already knew quite well. This semi-allegorical structure found its roots in the harlequin figures of commedia dell'arte and nineteenth-century melodrama where character types stood in for particular styles of clowning that were immediately recognizable to the audience and displayed little to no psychological depth.[23] Yet, the voices that appeared in the comics were diverse. Artists presented dialogues from an array of character types and voices ranging from the sludgy brogue of urban toughs and rustic clowning of Jim Crow minstrels to the banter of upper-class mistresses and effeminate affectations of dandies and swells in comfortable parlors.

Dialogue-driven skits departed from the Töpfferian picture story in both narrative style and theme. Works like *Obadiah Oldbuck* and others in the Töpfferian style typically relied on captions that were "extradiegetic" in the sense that the text was narrated in a third-person voice outside of the action or what narratologists call the "storyworld." On the other hand, comics that utilized playscript dialogue were "intradiegetic" in the sense that the text depicted utterances that took place inside of the storyworld.[24] Similar to the modern convention of the speech bubble, playscript offered a sound image, meant to evoke the rhythms and timbre of the spoken word. The importance of this distinction to both narration and theme cannot be overstated. Where the Töpfferian style was organized around picaresque misadventures and character studies, comics utilizing playscript were typically structured around whip-smart exchanges between two characters and turned on a quick punchline. Captions frequently featured the

---

22. See McLenan, "Lonely Pollywog," 28–29; and "California Volunteer," 16–17.

23. Jones, *Captive Stage*, 50–74.

24. See Exner, "Creation of the Comic Strip"; Thon, "Who's Telling the Tale?," 68; and Smolderen, *Origins of Comics*, 137–47.

classic comedic routine in which a "straight man" serves up a deadpan line to be foiled by a quick-witted comedian or buffoonish clown. Other captions played with the sounds of dialect, using exotic spellings to evoke the embodied voices of the social types being depicted.

These single-panel dialogues were attractive to magazine editors because they provided a self-contained gag that could be inserted into virtually any section of the magazine without breaking up the flow of adjacent articles or comics. In some cases, they were slotted as filler when blank space on a page became available. In others, they were laid out in sequence, creating a succession of short comedic skits. A *Harper's Weekly* page from 1858 exemplifies editorial practices regarding comic dialogue skits.[25] The page features skits by three different artists with each identifying a distinct locale as a potential site for viewing an impromptu performance. The top sequence by McLenan entitled "Broadway Sketches" captures the snarky remarks of working-class children during clashes with fashionable women on the street. Bellew's "Country Sketches" turns on the irony of farmers admiring comments on the "elegance" and "purty smart" looks of barnyard animals. The bottom row, signed by an artist with the initials "CS" and titled "The Pugilistic Revival," identifies yet a third locale with dialogues appearing both inside and outside the home with humorous one-liners lampooning the craze for prizefighting. The effect of laying the cartoons out as independent vignettes rather than sections of a unified story creates the implication that spontaneous humorous dialogues were available to the observant spectator in virtually any locale in American life.

By no means were formal devices such as the tableau and dialogue-driven skits entirely unique to US comics. These methods for composing comics did indeed find parallels in British, French, and even Japanese traditions in the nineteenth century. But what was distinctive about US comics was their active engagement with the still-developing, US-born theatrical traditions. As we will see in the rest of this chapter, theatrical styles of organizing narrative were inseparable from a larger suite of performance conventions arising out of settings, including the working-class milieu of the urban variety theater and more genteel settings such as productions of domestic comedies. In each case, artists attached local, identifiable performance settings, audience responses, and thematic conventions to their work.

---

25. McLenan, Bellew, and C.S, "Comicalities Page," 672.

Burlesques and B'hoys:
Comics and the Urban Variety Theater

The humor and conventions of the urban variety theater endured as a site of exchange between theater and comics. A raucous precursor to vaudeville, the urban variety theater incorporated broad comedy, burlesques, and ethnic humor while catering to notoriously rowdy audiences of white working-class men. Theaters such as the Bowery and William Mitchell's Olympic hosted diverse audiences of what the British writer Francis Trollope described as "the shirtsleeve crowd" in her travels to the US. Working-class mechanics and firemen as well as immigrants, especially from the German and Irish communities, packed into halls for burlesques, ethnic humor, minstrel routines, and even spectacles like horse shows. Star actors turned to robust theatrics that utilized exaggerated gestures and emphasized hypermasculine, occasionally crude personas, as exemplified by Frank Chanfrau. Audiences also watched travesties that targeted familiar works such as Shakespearean drama or frontier melodrama. Macbeth interacted with Irish immigrants or was reimagined as a minstrel figure, and humorists such as John Brougham took on America's cultural myths with lampoons of frontier melodramas that bore titles like *Last of the Pollywogs* and *Poc-a-hontas*.

Audiences themselves were often as much a part of the performance as anything taking place onstage. Theatergoers stopped performances to heckle actors, appeal for changes to scripts, demand that scenes or speeches be repeated or simply call for the singing of "Yankee Doodle" and other patriotic songs.[26] Figures like the writer George Foster were horrified, describing the Bowery Pit as heaving "in wild and sudden tumult, like a red flannel sea agitated by lurid storm[s] . . . the roaring crush and clamor of [the] tobacco chewing, great coat wearing [. . .] second tier, the yells and screams, the shuddering oaths and obscene songs, tumbling down from the third tier."[27] But, as sociologist Richard Butsch notes, the rowdiness of the famed Bowery b'hoy youth culture is not so easily reduced to rowdiness for its own sake. Rather, in this setting, the outbursts and social drinking were just as easily interpreted as expressions of self-determination and loyalty

26. Constance Rourke goes so far as to say that "the legitimate theater came to a standstill" in this period, as "a vigorous burlesque usurped the stage, turning serious drama upside down." Rourke, *American Humor*, 119.

27. Qtd. in Butsch, *Making of American Audiences*, 46–47.

in opposition to the conformist tendencies of middle- and merchant-class values.[28]

The expansive quality of urban theatrical spectatorship extended out into the areas around theaters as well. As historian Peter Buckley observes, the areas around urban theaters became centers for "networks of male sociability" in which "plebian flaneurs" loafed about in search of the spectacles to be offered by the city. Merchants and newsboys engaged in colorful banter with potential customers while minstrel performers did "breakdowns" and "eel-dancing," often with the sponsorship of a butcher who wished to attract customers to his shop.[29] The permeable barriers between stage, audience, and street thus created a complicated dialectic in which the stock characters of prevaudevillian plays and skits were imagined as available for observation in both the audience and in the streets—and eventually, the comics page.

The perception that public space offered entertainment to the urban loafer was evident in "Humorous Police Reports," a story which appeared alongside multiple comics depicting urban space in Benjamin Day's *Brother Jonathan*. In the story, spectators gather at the police office to observe a succession of defendants who resemble the racial and ethnic caricatures appearing on the prevaudeville stage. The spectators guffaw at a woman minstrel who becomes so drunk that she performs "an extemporaneous Nubian war dance," a country rustic who is brought up on charges of making a "lamp-post oration to an attentive audience of butcher boys," and a vagrant who pleads innocent in a heavy German accent, "Me awagrant! I wenture to say as there mus' be some mistake."[30] As in many depictions of urban life, "Humorous Police Reports" implies that the activity of viewing the stock characters of the urban theater did not end merely because one had left the auditorium but was instead a persistent, thoroughgoing process. This perceived fluidity between stage and street proved a potent means of naturalizing the racist and xenophobic tropes of the urban theater. After all, it was one thing to observe grotesque stereotypes on a stage; it was quite another to apply those same viewing practices to real passersby on the street.[31]

---

28. Butsch, *Making of American Audiences,* 47.

29. Buckley, "To the Opera House," 345. See also DiGirolamo, *Crying the News*.

30. "Humorous Police Reports," 6.

31. On the use of stage-inspired racial and ethnic stereotypes to divide the city into legible social types, see Clytus, "Visualizing in Black Print," 29–66.

For comic artists, this complex and unruly form of spectatorship offered the foundation for a textured vocabulary of movement, dialogue, and most importantly, a working-class ethos. Those artists who worked in this vein drew upon the variety theater's racial and ethnic codes, cues for comedic timing, and norms for communal spectatorship. They turned to slapstick violence, crude language, and ethnic clashes as expressions of white working-class identity. The stock characters that rose to fame amid the early burlesque theater became many of the primary actors in the earliest comic strips. This varied approach to theatrical viewing was driven by these publications' attempts to offer themselves to readers as a means of maintaining ongoing engagement with the public life of the city. Broadly construed, the viewing of theatrical performances was central to one's sense of participating in the collective experience of public life. The early humor publications were especially quick to recognize this participation through comics that reproduced urban spectatorship in its varied dimensions.

The many comics featuring racist images of blackface minstrels are perhaps the most well-known works from this period to engage with this shared visual and theatrical vocabulary. Arguably the most widespread style of entertainment in nineteenth-century America, blackface performance was so pervasive in graphic humor in no small part because its tropes and figures were so recognizable to a vast swath of the American public. To that end, Douglas A. Jones describes minstrelsy as a "blackface salve" insofar as it created a common grammar that served to unify the disparate sociopolitical groups who identified as white.[32] As Jones observes, blackface minstrelsy's garish dialogue, pantomime clowning, racist humor, and stock characters like Jim Crow (a plantation rustic) and Zip Coon (a buffoonish urban dandy) solidified ideas about whiteness through the suggestion of Black inferiority.[33] Amid the ongoing exchanges between theater and graphic humor, this well-developed collection of visual and verbal figures was immediately recognizable to a disparate array of social demographics and thus a powerful means for publishers and artists to appeal to white audiences.

But blackface was just one part of a larger roster of stock characters and subjects shared by comics and urban theater culture. In addition to blackface minstrels, comics featured a diverse range of theatrical stock characters

32. Jones, "American," 403–9.

33. See also Cockrell, *Demons of Disorder*, 66–162; and DuComb, *Haunted City*, 58–76. Lott, *Love and Theft*, 19–38.

that included lewd b'hoys, Yankee rustics, drunken Irishmen, mischievous newsboys, as well as real actors and actresses such as Frank Chanfrau and Lola Montez. Comics depicted these figures performing onstage, emerging spontaneously on the streets, and being viewed by audiences. Parallel to the function of blackface, the presence of this broader repertoire of tropes and figures served to imbue both comics and live performance with the aura of a communal experience.[34]

Philadelphia native Felix Darley's work in *The John Donkey* marked an early sustained set of experiments with elements of working-class theater.[35] Darley figuratively announced this project on the cover of each issue of the magazine in which his own harlequin character, "Dr. John Donkey," stood in the center with various tableaux surrounding the periphery as if to announce the magazine's cover as the entre to an evening's entertainment (fig. 3.7).[36] Darley's promise of a theatrical experience was born out in an impressive array of experiments with different burlesque rhythms and routines. His *John Donkey* illustrations work featured stagings of musical numbers as in "A Rare Musical Treat," tableaux vivant, and scenes from inside the theater itself. He depicted Bowery b'hoys in and around theaters, interacting with the performances as in "Modern Drama," where two Bowery b'hoys debate in heavily accented dialect whether a military hero onstage is wearing a helmet or an ice cream freezer.[37] Throughout his run in *John Donkey*, Darley relied upon the thematic hallmarks of burlesque conventions: his work donned the guise of artistic tradition and authority, only to devolve into irreverent lampoons and travesties.

Darley was the period's most prolific book illustrator and would have found many entry points into the antebellum urban theater scene. Darley's parents were both actors: his father John Darley was a comedian, and his mother Eleanor Westray was a popular actress.[38] Darley's work on the memoir *Sol Smith's Theatrical Apprenticeship* seemed an especially

---

34. Bank, *Theatre Culture in America*, 75–119; Hodge, *Yankee Theatre*, 11–81; and Seymour, *Lola Montez: A Life*, 283–308.

35. Darley's illustrations in *John Donkey* are unsigned. He is cited as the principal illustrator of *John Donkey* and as a staffer for *Yankee Doodle* in *American Bibliopolist*, 263. See also Sloane, *American Humor Magazines*, 105. This book concurs with these attributions based on stylistic similarities to signed Darley illustrations including Smith, *Theatrical Apprenticeship*; and Avery et al., *Harp of a Thousand Strings*.

36. Darley, "Cover Page."

37. Darley, "Modern Drama," 4.

38. King, *Darley*, 1–2.

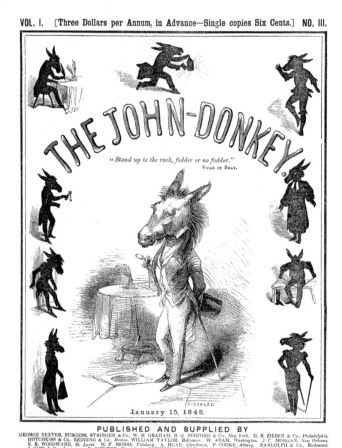

VOL. I. [Three Dollars per Annum, in Advance—Single copies Six Cents.] NO. III.

FIGURE 3.7. Darley's cover illustration featuring John Donkey performing various tableaux, *The John Donkey*, January 15, 1848, 1. Courtesy of the American Antiquarian Society.

important precursor to his theatrically inspired comics. *Theatrical Apprenticeship* recounts Smith's life as a stage comedian and leader of an acting troop as well as his short-lived career as a preacher. Smith's rich account of stage productions and theater culture provided Darley with an occasion to depict costume, character actors in action, and shenanigans in the wings.[39] Several of the book's illustrations feature Darley's approach to theatrical performance as a complexly layered style of spectatorship that would characterize his comic strips in *John Donkey*.

Darley's most elaborate theatrical project arrived in the form of *Shakespeare Illustrated*. The series features short snippets of *Othello* accompanied

39. Smith, *Theatrical Apprenticeship*.

by illustrations in which the characters are illustrated as popular stock characters of urban theater such as the b'hoy, drunken Irish immigrant, burlesque drag queen, or black minstrel. In this manner, Darley closely reproduced well-established burlesques and travesties on Shakespeare that enjoyed popularity in Jacksonian theater. As historian Lawrence Levine notes, blackface productions of Shakespeare were raucous affairs that mingled literary language, ethnic spectacle, and crude humor. "Audiences roared at the sight of Hamlet dressed in fur cap and collar . . . listened with amused surprise to his profanity" when "commanding Ophelia 'Get thee to a brewery' or . . . heard him recite his lines in black dialect or Irish brogue."[40] Yet, even as these productions engaged in crude parodies of Shakespeare, they could also feature straightforward drama. Antebellum Americans relished Shakespearean language and possessed a deep knowledge of the plays. This combination of raucous entertainment and sincere appreciation meant that performances could shift rapidly between modes of lampoon and drama in ways that can be quite alienating to an outsider.

Darley's *Shakespeare Illustrated* was calibrated to evoke these rapid shifts between racist spectacle, slapstick humor, and melodrama. Most obviously, Darley adapts and exaggerates the minstrel show's sight gag of blackface makeup by depicting Othello as a completely black silhouette rather than fully illustrating him. In depicting Othello this way, Darley uses the tools available to him as an illustrator to fully realize one of the minstrel show's central racist fantasies. Minstrel shows commonly made jokes about blackface characters being invisible or indistinguishable from shadows because of their dark skin, relegating the Black subject to the status of a nonthreatening sight gag. In Darley's hands, this spectacle is pushed to its most absurd and extreme limits with its implication that the visual effect of race was so compelling that it could create the illusion of a character literally disappearing into shadows. When played in earnest, Shakespeare's Othello is a character who potentially serves as an intellectual and romantic rival to white masculinity. Reimagined through the tropes and visual vocabulary of minstrelsy, he is stripped of these qualities, literally and figuratively rendered invisible.

Verbal and visual ironies also give occasion for the burlesques of social identity that formed the foundation of working-class theater. Garish-looking figures deliver lines and act out scenes that undercut the seriousness

---

40. Levine, *Highbrow/Lowbrow*, 13–14.

JOHN-DONKEY'S SHAKSPEARE ILLUSTRATED.
OTHELLO.

Oth. Oh, my fair warrior!
Des. My dear Othello!
Oth. It gives me wonder great as my content,
To see you here before me.—Oh, my soul's joy!—
If after every tempest come such calms,
May the winds blow till they have wakened death!
And let the laboring bark climb hills of seas
Olympus-high; and duck again as low
As hell's from heaven. If it were now to die,
'Twere now to be most happy; for, I fear,
My soul hath her content so absolute,
That not another comfort like to this
Succeeds in unknown fate.
Des. The heavens forbid,
But that our loves and comforts should increase,
Even as our days do grow.

             ACT II. SCENE I.

Iago. If this poor brach of Venice, whom I track
For his quick hunting, stand the putting on,
I'll have our Michael Cassio on the hip;
Abuse him to the Moor in the rank garb—
For I fear Cassio with my night-cap, too—
Make the Moor thank me. love me, and reward me,
For making him egregiously an ass,
And practising upon his peace and quiet,
Even to madness. 'Tis here, but yet confused;
Knavery's plain face is never seen till used.

             ACT II. SCENE I.

Iago. Oh, sweet England!

        [*Sings and gives more wine to Cassio.*

     King Stephen was a worthy peer,
       His breeches cost him but a crown;
     He held them sixpence all too dear,
       With that he called the tailor—lown.

     Cas. 'Fore Heaven, this is a more exquisite song than the other!
     Iago. Will you hear it again?
     Cas. No, for I hold him unworthy of his place that does those things.—Well—Heaven's above all; and there be souls that must be saved, and there be souls that must not be saved.

             ACT II. SCENE II.

Oth. Hold, for your lives.—
Why, how now, ho! from whence ariseth this?
Are we turned Turks: and to ourselves do that
Which heaven hath forbid the Ottomites?

FIGURE 3.8. Felix Octavius Carr Darley, "Shakespeare Illustrated," *The John Donkey,* April 15, 1848, 244. Courtesy of the American Antiquarian Society.

Promotion in the Navy.

Commander Mayo is now a Post-captain, having posted Colonel Davies. As the latter has taken the post so quietly, he has been ordered into action—but we believe it is an action at law.

JOHN-DONKEY'S SHAKSPEARE ILLUSTRATED.

OTHELLO.

Oth. What needs this iteration, woman?
I say, thy husband:—dost understand the word?
My friend, thy husband—honest, honest Iago.
Emil. If he say so, may his pernicious soul
Rot half a grain a-day! He lies to the heart:
She was too fond of her most filthy bargain.

ACT V. SCENE I.

*Des. And have you mercy, too! I never did
Offend you in my life; never loved Cassio,
But with such general warranty of Heaven
As I might love. I never gave him token.*
Oth. By Heaven, I saw my handkerchief in his hand.
Oh, perjured woman! thou dost stone thy heart,
And mak'st me call what I intend to do,
A murder,—which I thought a sacrifice!
I saw the handkerchief.

ACT V. SCENE I.

Oth. It is too late. [*Smothers her.*] [*Emilia knocks,* L.
ACT V. SCENE I.

And say, besides,—that in Aleppo once,
Where a malignant and a turbaned Turk
Smote a Venetian, and traduced the state,
I took by the throat the circumcisèd dog,
And smote him—thus!— [*Stabs himself.*]
ACT V. SCENE I.

END OF OTHELLO.

FIGURE 3.9. Felix Octavius Carr Darley, "Shakespeare Illustrated," *The John Donkey,* May 13, 1848, 311. Courtesy of the American Antiquarian Society.

of the original Shakespearean text (fig. 3.8).[41] For example, in the scene where Iago plants Desdemona's handkerchief in Cassio's room, the fine silken cloth is replaced with a soiled rag that Iago, who is dressed as an urban tough, ironically describes as a "trifl[e] light as air" and "holy writ." Meanwhile, Othello himself is depicted as Zip Coon, a minstrel figure who affects the manner and dress of white upper classes or nobles. Similar to Zip Coon onstage, Darley's Othello is offered to readers as a clown-like figure whose ambitions and pretensions result in farce. This racist spectacle becomes particularly intense as Othello's attempts to woo Desdemona are construed as vicious parodies of Black desire and sexuality. Thus, when Othello declares his longing for Desdemona by declaring "as hell's from heaven," his clownish appearance as Zip Coon and Desdemona's appearance as a man in drag trivialize the import of the dialogue.

Perhaps most surprising, *Shakespeare Illustrated*'s ironic burlesques can rapidly give way to a secondary reading mode based on a more straightforward style of melodrama. In this manner, Darley's comic shares the volatile tonal shifts that characterized actual Jacksonian productions of Shakespeare between irony and sincerity. This quality becomes particularly apparent in the last installment of the comic, as the play hits its tragic climax (fig. 3.9).[42] There is nothing terribly funny about the final frames nor was there intended to be. Instead, Darley's cartoon takes an ominous turn as the crude humor of the burlesque gives way to a frightening set of panels that depict Desdemona's murder. Where Othello is depicted as being shorter than the other players in early parodic scenes, he is now taller than any of the other characters. His body language turns from comedic pantomime to threatening, aggressive gestures. He tenses his arms and legs as Emil tells him of a "filthy bargain" and shakes his fist, standing over Desdemona who begs, with folded hands, "Have you mercy too!" Othello's sheathed sword even resembles a devil's tail in the shockingly explicit depiction of him smothering Desdemona. After Othello's self-inflicted impalement, the final frame of the sequence leaves readers with the stark image of a sword crossing a theater mask of Melpomene, the muse of tragedy. With this, Darley leaves readers on a surprisingly sinister note. In doing so, Darley strives to capture a body of cues and conventions that not only seem bewildering and alienating to the modern viewer but would have looked that way to non-American viewers of the time as well.

41. Darley, "Shakespeare Illustrated," April 15, 1848, 244.
42. Darley, "Shakespeare Illustrated," May 13, 1848, 311.

Attempts to adapt the stage productions of burlesques and travesties like Darley's were a consistently recurring feature of US humor magazines between the late 1840s and early 1870s; however, they were, on balance, less significant than the ongoing world-building process in which comic artists engaged.[43] To that end, artists persistently referred to theatrical conventions and each other's comics in ways that constructed an internally coherent narrative world parallel to the performance onstage. Over time, the repetition of stock characters, situations, gags, dialects, styles of clowning, and predictable resolutions served to construct rules and conventions that would have been immediately legible to a reader of the time. This world-building process could play out on a single page or over the course of multiple issues. In each case, these dialogue cartoons were presented to readers as miniature performances that one might happen upon while loafing through the busy city. Individual characters and scenarios were largely devoid of psychological complexity and yet would have been entirely coherent to readers with the accumulated knowledge of the stock characters and the rules of the social world that they implicitly inhabited.

Benjamin A. Baker's play *A Glance at New York* became an important touchstone in establishing the rules for the culture of urban loafing and ethnic humor that composed this narrative world. Baker's play is most famous for introducing the character of Mose the B'hoy, a hard-drinking fireman modeled on the working-class mechanics who mulled around Manhattan and attended performances at the Bowery and Olympic Theaters. In Baker's play, Mose loafs about the streets visiting the "Hall of Novelty" and the Irish bar "Loafer's Paradise," spoiling for a fight (what he describes as a "muss") with any upper-class snob or urban tough who crosses his path.[44] In both appearance and manner, Chanfrau's version of Mose, with his tattered plug hat, red shirt, and blue trousers, established the look and feel of the character for live performances and on the printed page.

For all of his hedonism, Mose embodied an egalitarian brand of social justice that thrilled New York audiences. The nineteenth-century theater

---

43. For example, in 1872 Livingston Hopkins published a series of burlesques on Shakespearean dialogue that featured Jim Crow– and Zip Coon–style minstrels and other urban types delivering lines from *The Merchant of Venice* and *Hamlet* while performing slapstick comedy. Hopkins, "Shakespeare Illustrated," October 24, 1872, 5; Hopkins, "Shakespeare Illustrated," November 7, 1872, 11; Hopkins, "Shakespeare Illustrated," December 5, 1872, 13; and "Shakespeare Illustrated," December 19, 1872, 4.

44. Detsi-Diamanti, "Staging Working-Class Culture," 11–26.

critic Thomas Allston Brown recalled the audience's response to Chanfrau as a reaction tinged with an underlying class consciousness:

> For a moment the audience eyed him in silence; not a hand or foot gave him welcome. Taking the cigar stump from his mouth and turning half-way round to spit, he said: "I ain't a goin' to run wid dat mercheen no more!" Instantly there arose such a yell of recognition as had never been heard in the little house before. Pit and galleries joined in the outcry. It was renewed several times, and Mose was compelled to stand, shifting his coat from one arm to the other, and bowing and waiting. Every man, woman, and child recognized in the character all the distinctive characteristics of the class.[45]

Mose's reputation as working-class antihero was further buffeted by his penchant for violence, which the character primarily inflicted upon predatory swindlers and unscrupulous capitalists. In a scene from *A Glance at New York*, Mose roughs up a group of "foo foos" who attempt to swindle George, the country rustic. This scene, like others in the play, disavows the possibility that the slapstick violence carried any deeper class or social implications. Thus, when asked about his motivation for kicking the foo foos out of the bar, Mose simply exclaims "Cos I want ter pick up er muss," denying any motivation beyond the mere fun of getting into a fight. However, the message to the audience was clear: Mose's penchant for violence and his coarse mannerisms signaled clear assertions of populist, working-class power.[46]

The class allegories exemplified by Baker's play were echoed especially in the comics of John Goater, Gunn, McLenan, and Stephens among others. Works in this style depicted stock characters from the urban variety theater loafing around the city like Mose, viewing public spectacles, exchanging snappy insults, and entering into the occasional fight. Similar to *A Glance at New York*, this potent combination of slapstick violence and ethnic humor celebrated white working-class masculinity, usually at the expense of upper classes and racial minorities. Moreover, it did so in ways that were heavily embodied. Parallel to Mose's laugh line of "Cos I want ter pick up er muss" in *A Glance at New York*, the protagonists of these single-panel dialogues most typically disavowed explicit social consciousness. Instead, they exacted revenge on perceived class enemies through

45. Brown, *History of the New York Stage*, 284.
46. Bank, *Theatre Culture in America*, 82–86; and Tomc, *Fashion Nation*, 90.

bodily acts with ambiguous social meaning such as laughter and slapstick violence.

Depictions of Chanfrau's Mose emerged as a staple of mid-nineteenth-century US graphic humor. Mose remained a common subject for broadsides and made frequent appearances in earlier humor magazines such as *The Old Soldier* (1852), where he was depicted wreaking havoc upon the sensibilities of the upper classes.[47] One of the most elaborate graphic narratives about Mose was itself among the first full-length picture albums to be produced in the United States, Gunn's *Mose among the Britishers* (1850).[48] In Gunn's album, Mose travels to Britain and encounters a succession of effete Londoners. Gunn himself was a British immigrant to the United States and, by all accounts, held little sympathy for the working-class mechanics and bohemians who populated the New York theater district. However, apparently in hopes of commercial success, Gunn depicted Mose's adventures in London as a triumph of working-class authenticity over the superficiality of British snobbery.[49] In the album's climax, Mose causes an uproar at an aristocratic masked ball and is hauled off to prison. The humorous closing scenes show him falling into a "muss" with a nobleman named Don Cesar, dancing with other inmates in prison, and then appearing in a courtroom full of unsympathetic aristocrats who are nursing bruises and black eyes from their previous scrapes with Mose. The captions in Gunn's closing scene put a decidedly nationalist gloss on the sequence. Upon his conviction, Mose "denounces the British Lion" and returns to New York where he regales his friends with tales of his adventures, all the while concluding "there is no place like home."[50]

The class allegory represented by Mose was echoed in magazine comics in the form of myriad characters who adapted Mose's egalitarian brand of social justice to a wide range of comedic situations. Stephens's single-panel dialogues in *Vanity Fair* in the early 1860s are among the best examples of these class allegories. Stephens's cartoons feature a variety of straight man / comedian combinations of social and ethnic types who rove about the city engaging in heavily accented verbal jousts and slapstick violence. Like the set pieces of *A Glance at New York*, Stephens's *Vanity Fair* cartoons typically

47. "Mrs. C. Sinclair," 5.

48. Gunn. *Mose among the Britishers.*

49. See West, "Britisher among the B'Hoys," 16–29.

50. Gunn, *Mose among the Britishers*, 19–20.

end with a white working-class figure emerging victorious through a rough-and-tumble brand of social justice.[51]

In one Stephens cartoon, an omnibus driver does verbal battle with a gentleman on the street who becomes the butt of his joke. The gentleman's complaint that there is no room in the coach invites the driver's heavily accented retort.

> Driver: Plenty of room for one more, sir.
> Gent: There's no room.
> Driver: No room—there's cords—afraid of bein' squeezed, hey? You oughter have a whole coach to yerself. You ought A.H! H! H! (*Sarcastically*)[52]

Here, Stephens takes great pains to render audible elements of the exchange, including the driver's heavy accent, embodied laughter (signified by "A.H! H! H!"), and even a stage direction "(*Sarcastically*)" to indicate the tone of voice. Like Chanfrau's portrayal of Mose, Stephens's cartoons express their protagonist's class identification through embodiment rather than textual description. In this case, sarcastic laughter becomes a bodily response that exacts revenge upon the "Gent" and, by extension, upper-class snobbery.

Another Stephens dialogue inverts this class dynamic with a scene of a white newsboy who acts as a straight man for the follies of a black minstrel boy (fig. 3.10). In this manner, close attention to dialect and ethnic caricature serves to set boundaries even among figures within the culture of loafing. The cartoon depicts the two boys viewing a poster for Barnum's freak show "What is It?," an exhibit in which Barnum invited audiences to consider Darwinian evolution by speculating whether an African American actor might be a descendent of modern-day homo sapiens. While the newsboy models the typical Barnum audience response by guessing that the actor is a "G'rilla," the minstrel misunderstands the exhibit's racist intent, exclaiming that the actor is of noble birth, "Don't you see it's de new Prince 'er Wales? Sha—a—aw."[53] Reminiscent of Stephens's omnibus driver dialogue, the white working-class figure prevails, and the gag is executed through an embodied response (in this case, the minstrel's guttural

---

51. Stephens, "How the Boys Take It," 84; Stephens, "Incident for a Book," 143; Stephens, "Plenty of Room for One More," 130; and Stephens, "What Else Could They Be," 27.

52. Stephens, "Plenty of Room for One More," 130.

53. Stephens, "How the Boys Take It," 84.

FIGURE 3.10. Dialogue cartoon, Henry Louis Stephens, "How the Boys Take It," *Vanity Fair*, August 11, 1860, 84. Courtesy of the American Antiquarian Society.

laughter). However, rather than serving up retribution to upper-class snobbery, the exchange consolidates the newsboy's claim to racial superiority, thereby setting a lower boundary from which to demarcate white working-class identity. Taken together, Stephens's cartoons follow the blueprint for world-building laid out in Baker's original play. They offer readers a repertory of immediately recognizable social and ethnic types who loafed about the city providing what were imagined as spontaneous performances that highlight the borders of ethnicity and class.

The universe of caricatures and settings that focused on prevaudevillian working-class figures like Mose and Jim Crow are relatively well known to historians and critics of US graphic humor. The same cannot be said of another strand of theater- and performance-inspired comics, drawn from the more genteel side of US theater culture. As we'll see in the next section, a variety of lesser-known comics, emphasizing domesticity with humor and dialogue reminiscent of the period's social comedies, were also an important site of exchange between comics and theater.

At Home Onstage: Social Comedy Comics

Starting in the 1860s and continuing into the 1870s, US humor magazines and the comics sections of variety magazines increasingly began to feature comics that emulated the conventions of social comedies such as Anna Mowat's *Fashion* (1849) and Bronson Howard's *Saratoga* (1870). These "social comedy comics" addressed a more middle-brow, family-oriented audience and appeared in a variety of places, including *Nick Nax, Frank Leslie's Budget of Fun,* and C. J. Howard's work in *Wild Oats.* Both the plays and the comics emphasized a subtle comedy of manners, lively banter, and a light and sentimental tone that focused on themes about domesticity and family. Social comedy comics featured elements such as playscript and staging conventions that implied to readers that viewing their comics was tantamount to watching a performance. But where the Bowery-inspired comics of Darley and McLenan idealized the culture of urban loafing as an occasion to observe spontaneous acts of theatricality, social comedy comics imagined the home as a figurative stage.

The late 1850s, a pivotal time for live theater in the United States, saw a notable increase in the prominence of genteel social comedies. Under pressure from the city's wealthy elites, theater managers turned away from the raucous, male-dominated Bowery audiences in favor of productions and practices welcoming to genteel clientele, especially women and families. These class tensions were punctuated by the Astor Place Riot, an ugly incident in which violence erupted between working-class supporters of Edwin Forrest and the state militia, leading to at least twenty deaths and around one hundred injuries.[54] Historian Robert Allen describes the mid-1850s as a time of "social transformation." Women moved "from their traditional place in the boxes into the heretofore masculine domain of . . . what had formerly been called the pit and was now called the parquette."[55] The

---

54. For a brief synopsis, see Burrows and Wallace, *Gotham,* 761–66. For a book-length treatment, see Cliff, *Shakespeare Riots,* 125–37.

55. Allen, *Horrible Prettiness,* 70.

conservative audiences who were driven out of the theater by the rambunc-
tious mechanic class found a hospitable environment in establishments
such as William Burton's Chambers Street Theater. These more respectable
performance spaces eschewed broad humor and crass ethnic caricature in
favor of lush pageantry, sentimental melodrama, comedy of manners, and a
subtler style of burlesque. Rather than three or four short sketches, a single, full-length production with a shorter accompanying piece comprised
the evening's entertainment.[56] This style of entertainment was more closely
related to the urbane theater scenes of London and Paris.

The American social comedy was foremost among these stage genres
to gain traction in the comics. This genre remained a close relative to the
British and French versions of the domestic comedy and comedy of manners. It used lively dialogue and improbable plots to offer a gentle satire
on the manners and fashions of America's urban elites. As the genre of the
social comedy came into prominence through the 1850s and 1860s, playwrights provided audiences with diverse scenes of leisure and high society.
Courtship, vacations, balls, and even attendance at other theatrical events
were among the subjects of plays like Anna Mowatt's *Fashion* (1849), Cornelius Mathews's *False Pretenses* (1856), Edward Wilkins's *Young New York*
(1856), Sidney Bateman's *Self* (1857), Irving Browne's *Our Best Society* (1868),
and Bronson Howards's *Saratoga* (1870).

From the standpoint of plotting, social comedies homed in on the
dynamics within and between affluent families while presenting a sentimental view of white upper- and middle-class life. Plays focused on the
problems of marriage and challenges of maintaining respectable appearances amid snobbery and materialism. They were populated with common
character types: henpecking wives, eccentric husbands, frivolous society
women, and ambitious (and sometimes unscrupulous) social climbers.
These plays rarely presented hardship or gave prominent roles to characters from outside the narrow confines of affluent white society apart from
butlers, maids, and foreign visitors who served as comic relief. Instead, the
plays celebrated a harmonious balance between genders within the domestic sphere with each character fulfilling a prescribed role in the family. The
ideal consisted of a loving wife who oversees the household but ultimately
submits her authority to a kind, if bumbling, husband.[57] Conflicts hinged

---

56. Rinear, *Stage, Page, Scandals, and Vandals*, 149.

57. The social comedy in America was in this respect similar to the domestic comedy in
Britain. See Booth, "Comedy and Farce," 129–44.

on some disruption that upset this ostensible balance: wives who assumed too much authority, husbands who became complacent or neglectful, disagreements between families, or the unscrupulous social climber who endears himself to a daughter or wife. By the final curtain, each of these conflicts would be resolved as misunderstandings were revealed and benevolent paternal authority was restored.

More often than not, playwrights' jibes were directed at the foibles of the upwardly mobile nouveau riche who tried—and typically failed—to affect the tastes and mannerisms of the aristocracy. Mrs. Tiffany, the protagonist of Anna Mowatt's influential play *Fashion*, portrays this type of humor, declaring, "I heard the other day that poets were the aristocrats of literature. That's one reason I like them, for I do dote on all aristocracy!"[58] Through these types of productions, audiences were invited to indulge in the fantasy of encountering scenes of leisure and luxury. Stage directions commonly included detailed instructions for directors about the elaborate decorations and furniture that were to adorn the stage. The onstage pageantry often entailed a succession of dialogues with interesting and elegant people whom the upper-class subjects might encounter, whether it be foreign dignitaries, artists, or other cultural elites.

Among humor magazines, *Nick Nax* most fully embraced the genteel aesthetics of the social comedy in its comics. This emphasis on social comedy in *Nick Nax* arose largely out of changes that took place when Mary A. Levison took over as publisher and executed an ambitious plan to create a humor magazine that catered to an audience of women. During its early years, *Nick Nax* had been published by Jesse Haney and Mary Levison's husband, William H. Levison. The contents of the early *Nick Nax* issues closely resembled the humor and visual experimentation of other humor magazines of the 1850s such as *Yankee Notions*, *The Picayune*, and *The Lantern*. Upon William's death in 1860, Haney sold his share of *Nick Nax*, and Mary Levison became sole owner and publisher. At the time of the purchase, an incredulous Thomas Butler Gunn was dismissive of Mary Levison's belief that she could lead *Nick Nax*. In a statement reflecting the sexist attitudes of New York's male-dominated publishing scene, Gunn lamented, "The woman has an eager, clutching idea that there's money to be made in the enterprise," and he sneered that her "desig[n] to purchase and edit" *Nick Nax* was "a fancy at once foolish and mean."[59]

---

58. Mowatt, *Fashion*, 7.
59. Gunn, *Thomas Butler Gunn Diaries Volume 12*, May 3.

Nevertheless, resistance from Gunn and others hardly seemed to stifle Mary Levison's efforts to transform *Nick Nax* into a humor magazine that featured content for women. With Mary Levison in control, *Nick Nax* underwent dramatic changes and apparently achieved some success with its new strategy. The humor and illustrations often took place in domestic settings and focused on sympathetic woman protagonists. Illustrators avoided the sketchy, expressive doodles that characterized the earlier comics in *Nick Nax* in favor of more realistic illustrations that gave meticulous attention to dress and furniture. Many plates were now printed as full or half pages to highlight the elaborate illustrations. The quality looked extraordinary for a humor magazine of the time, as the illustrations rivaled the detail in fashion magazines such as *Godey's Lady's Book* and *Harper's Bazaar* for their accurate renderings of clothing and manners. They also published advertisements for products such as sewing machines, hoop dresses, and patterned bonnets, with women regularly listed as winners for their monthly contests.[60] This woman-friendly version of *Nick Nax* lasted about ten years, which was an impressive achievement given the short lifespan of most humor magazines during the nineteenth century.

The aesthetics of genteel theater culture constituted an important part of Mary Levison's strategy to appeal to women audiences. The 1860s version of *Nick Nax* published an array of theater-related comics alongside its other woman-centered content. These theatrical comics included illustrations of extravaganza and dance routines with ballerinas, "soliloquys" of fashionable subjects, scenes from sensation melodramas, and of course, many comics that emulated the dialogue and look of the social comedy. Within *Nick Nax*'s social comedy–themed comics, follies of the wealthy and well-heeled remained common tropes. These simple conceits were largely captured through series of lushly illustrated single-panel cartoons. In "Mr. Bear (Soliloquizing)," Mr. and Mrs. Bear closely resemble the fascination with art of a Mrs. Tiffany type. After purchasing an opera box so that Mrs. Bear can show off her wealth, Mr. Bear is unable to see anything because of his wife's elaborate hairstyle. His "soliloquy" emulates the social comedy's stock character of the well-meaning patriarch who is perpetually beset upon by his wife's social ambitions:

---

60. For representative advertisements and promotions, see the February 1867 issue of *Nick Nax for All Creation*, especially "Fashions for 1867," 258; "Madame Rallings" 287; and "Notice to Rebus Solvers," 288.

Mr. Bear (*Soliloquizing*)—*Last year I enjoyed a Seat in the front of the House or in the Parquette! But now Wife must have a Private Box to show what she calls her grand Toilette; and I can't see anybody, nor anything! Well I suppose one must make some sacrifices in order to be considered a millionaire.*[61]

Parallel to the social comedy, the indulgences of the ambitious "Mrs. Bear" produce humorous tensions that arise in the social comedy's idealized, affluent household. Mr. Bear, the patriarch, is a master of the public sphere. The "sacrifices" that he must make are played as charming and ultimately harmless absurdities of family life (rather than legitimate sources of tension). Like the dynamics of social comedies onstage, Mrs. Bear's ambitions thus signify momentary overreaches that will inevitably resolve in the restoration of order with Mr. Bear's kindly paternal authority.

Among the most significant contributions of *Nick Nax*'s new approach to comics were its ambitious experiments with longer-format projects. Under Mary Levison's ownership, artists were allowed to devote an entire issue's worth of illustrations to comics organized around a single theme. These longer sequences rarely, if ever, featured a definite plot; instead, they were structured as a series of comedic vignettes that took place within a single fashionable social scene, such as an elegant vacation spot or a horse race. As a narrative device, this structure emulated the convention in the social comedy to offer a succession of dialogues or monologues, highlighting each character's peculiarities and social foibles, with the sum of the vignettes adding up to a larger social spectacle.

One such series, entitled *At the Springs*, appeared in *Nick Nax* between 1863 and 1870 and featured a premise virtually identical to that of Bronson Howard's *Saratoga*. Both the play and the comics record the joy and folly of upper classes as they descend upon Saratoga to bathe in the freshwater springs. Each installment introduces readers to a cross-section of upper-class characters and the complex social world of high-class leisure: young lovers canoodling by the sea, elegantly dressed women putting on airs, newly rich stockbrokers trying to fit in, and whip-smart children, all with clever witticisms and snappy retorts at the ready. Some characters are played for laughs while others are to be admired for their dress and manners. In each case, *At the Springs* introduces a distinctive mix of satire and escapist daydream based on the complexities of the upper-class social world.

---

61. "Mr. Bear (Soliloquizing)," 234.

The fashionable women who recur throughout the series are especially important to establishing the series' sophisticated sense of play with manners and fashion. Like those characters who appeared onstage in American domestic comedies, the fashionable women of *At the Springs* are canny negotiators of the status-obsessed world of the leisure classes. They mask their shrewdness behind a façade of naivete and charm even as they jockey for status. In particular, meanness holds special importance in this social world because it becomes a way of asserting authority. A cutting remark about a dress or a subtle put-down can thus signify a complex power play. Figure 3.11 demonstrates this intricacy in showing a husband frothing with rage at his wife over her flirtations with other men. She deftly takes command of the situation with a breezy admonition that diffuses his masculine bluster:

> JEALOUS SPOUSE.—I swear to you Madame, *that if I see any more of these flirtations, I'll blow his brains out.*
>
> AGGRAVATING DEAR CREATURE.—You make yourself appear more ridiculous than you already are. This is the third man you have sworn to KILL! *and they are all alive and remarkably well and strong.*[62]

Another scene features a variation on this theme in which a fashionable woman's cutting remark against a fellow vacationer at first seems frivolous or unthinking but is in reality a sharp assertion of her status in the pecking order:

> ELEGANT CREATURE—*Well I declare! if it isn't* Mrs. Simpson *with a dress on that she wore last summer. If I was the landlord of a hotel, I wouldn't take such tiresome people.*
>
> HUSBAND OF EXQUISITE CREATURE (WHO HAS MADE A LUCKY HIT IN STOCKS)—*You see my dear, these kind of people always say they only come for the* Water.
>
> ELEGANT CREATURE.—*Stuff and nonsense, they can get the Water at home, of* [sic] *any Druggist.*[63]

Both of these dialogues exemplify the woman-driven power plays seen not only in *At the Springs.* Each of these two woman protagonists performs

---

62. "At the Springs," 137.
63. "Saratoga," 135.

the role of the naive socialite even as she is engaged in a proverbial game of chess. She presents herself to the public and her partner as an inconsequential figure whose concerns do not seem to extend beyond the trivial manners of dress and social propriety. However, in both cases, the roleplay ultimately helps each character accomplish her goals: Aggravating Dear Creature is allowed to continue flirtations with other men while Elegant Creature asserts her status within the social hierarchy. Ultimately, the cleverness of these power plays thus prompts the humor. Rather than laughing at the women's frivolity, readers are guided to laugh with them. Each of these two exchanges invites readers to admire the sly manner in which each of the two women has played her partner and social competitors for fools.

Another important element of this subgenre of comics emphasized the visual appeal of luxury. As much as a series like *At the Springs* might offer a satire on wealth and materialism, it also invited its reader to linger over the elegant fashions and furnishings enjoyed by the characters. Lush illustrations like those featured in figure 3.11 are displayed to readers as objects of intense interest as the fashionable women are posed in ways that place the emphasis squarely on the details of their clothing. For example, the face of the character "Dear Creature" is turned away so that the viewer might admire the immaculate folds of her dress and the delicate curls of her hairstyle. Likewise, "Elegant Creature's" billowing dress, feathered sun hat, and tasseled parasol dominate the space of the frame. Here, the images are notable for their relative *lack* of dynamic motion. Instead of emphasizing motion, the sequence operates as a series of visual tableaux that build toward a general atmosphere of luxury and splendor that unfolds over the course of a single issue of *Nick Nax*. Rather than dynamic or action-based transitions between frames, the sequence builds momentum through repetition of visual details, as the fashionable clothing and furnishings recur again and again to produce a multilayered effect of leisure and ease.

The framing of domestic space as performance space in Levison's *Nick Nax* could occasionally cross over into a style of voyeurism in which readers were invited to witness intensely private behavior. In this manner, the implicit theatricality of the cartoons served a very different purpose than in *At the Springs*. Rather than translating the aesthetics of the social comedy, it appropriated them as a means of exploring taboo fantasies of sexuality and debauchery.

This erotic variation on the domestic comedy is a particular emphasis of *Masquerading*, a long-running series that appears to have been inspired

At the Springs.

JEALOUS SPOUSE.—*I swear to you, Madame, that if I see any more of these flirtations, I'll blow his brains out!*
AGGRAVATING DEAR CREATURE.—*You make yourself appear more ridiculous than you really are. This is the third man you have sworn to* KILL! *and they are all alive, and remarkably well and strong!*

Spiritual.

The Knickerbocker is responsible for the following :
"Tom, a three-year old, like many others, has received his due quantum of theological information, some of which exuded the other day in the following form. Tom was standing at the window, and just before him buzzed one of the first flies of spring, which he addressed in the sweetest tones imaginable. 'How do you do, little fy ? do you love your God, little fy ? do you want to *see* you God, little fy ? [Suddenly, with a vicious "jab" of the finger,] Well, you *shall ! There !*' The unfortunate insect was smashed, and its spirit sent off to the land where the good flies go."

STATISTICS OF INFANTRY.—A young officer who was always "hard up," upon being asked by a lady whether he liked babies, replied that he did not think them very interesting until they were able to stand *a loan*.

Oh, My !

One Sabbath afternoon, a Sunday School teacher observed two boys playing at marbles by the road side. He stopped, told them how wicked it was, and succeeded in persuading the worst one to accompany him to school. The lad was decidedly a fast youth of about eight years of age. In the class, among other things, the teacher told him that " God make this beautiful world, and all that is in it ; we must thank Him for all good things we enjoy ; He gives us our food and clothes." "Does he give me my clothes, too ?" broke in the lad. "Yes, He gives us every thing." "Now, there's where you got your eye shut up, for ma'am made these trowsers out of dad's old ones !"

THE man who took everybody's eye, must have a lot of them.

WANTED—The hammer that broke up the meeting.

FIGURE 3.11. "At the Springs—Jealous Spouse," *Nick Nax for All Creation,* September 1863, 137. Courtesy of the Billy Ireland Cartoon Library & Museum, The Ohio State University.

by French cartooning and applies the storytelling style of the domestic comedy to various dalliances at a masked ball.[64] Like *At the Springs, Masquerading* contained many of the hallmarks of domestic comedies. The glamorous upper-class social world, snappy dialogue, and lush fashions were all present. However, unlike the wholesome depictions of upper-class life in *At the Springs, Masquerading* embraced a brand of naughtiness and titillation that would surely have scandalized audiences at places like the Chambers Theater. The series itself featured an array of immaculately illustrated characters dressed as coquettish Pink Dominoes, impish Harlequins, lewd cross-dressers, and spooky goblins who engage in a free love bacchanalia. Characters flirt, drink, and smoke as they compete for partners or commiserate about being rejected. Thus, where *At the Springs* produced a vicarious experience of the ways in which privilege allows cultural elites to spend their leisure time, *Masquerading* turns to the question of how that same privilege allows for diverse forms of bacchanalia and sexuality.

The themes and humor in *Masquerading* revolve around the bawdy verbal exchanges in which characters use puns and innuendo to seduce or reject one another. In this way, *Masquerading* redirects the flirtations and satire on manners of the social comedy toward lascivious titillation. One characteristic scene features a scantily clad woman dressed as a butterfly delivering an innuendo-laced warning to an unwanted suitor, "You will find I have the sting of a Bee, if you do! You'd better try some of the Animals!"[65] Others are even more forthright in their sexual tone. For instance, a pair of flirty come-ons between the characters "Miss Eva" and "Old Beelzebub" leaves little to the imagination: "Have a bit of my Apple, Old Beelzebub!" meets with the churlish response, "Yes, my little dear, I will devour you, Apple and all, if I get a chance."[66]

---

64. The visual style and premise of *Nick Nax*'s series *Masquerading* resemble a series of lithographs titled *Au Bal Masque*, which were reprinted in *Le Charivari* in the early 1860s. It is unclear whether the editors of *Nick Nax* plagiarized artwork or created their own version for their American audience. See, for example, "Au Bal Masque," March 8, 1862, 19; "Au Bal Masque," March 15, 1862, 20; "Au Bal Masque," March 18, 1862, 21; and other issues of *Le Charivari* throughout 1862–63. There are important distinctions between the images in *Charivari* and *Nick Nax*. Unlike those in *Au Bal Masque*, the images in *Nick Nax*'s *Masquerading* are arranged in series and appear to be drawn by a different artist. What seems significant here is less the provenance of the artwork than the surprising fact that the editors of *Nick Nax* chose to include this potentially scandalous material in their magazine at all.

65. "Witticisms of the Masquerade," 4.

66. "Masquerading," April 1865, 185.

Apart from titillation, the witty repartee of *Masquerading* also extends to characters finding liberation and acceptance in the naughtiness of the masquerade. In some cases, young lovers find legitimate romance and confess their love through veiled references to their disguises; in others, conventionally unattractive characters find kinship through their common rejection or find that norms of attractiveness do not apply in the masquerade. A notable frame near the end of the series explores these nonnormative models of attraction with a sequence that affirms the appeal of both older men and of older women. Jones, an older man, dances vigorously with two heavily disguised women. He ignores a friend's warning that his dance partners are "neither young nor pretty" and instead focuses on the pleasure that dancing brings by exclaiming, "I don't believe it, for they've taken a great liking to me, and are mighty dancers! This makes me feel ten years younger!"[67] As in other installments from *Masquerading*, the use of disguise in the masquerade flattens out conventional norms of attraction. Sexual attractiveness is no longer the sole province of the young and beautiful but instead opens up to a wider array of figures.

The diverse styles of eroticism of the masked ball also provide occasion for *Masquerading* to explore queer identity and desire in ways that are reminiscent of twentieth- and twenty-first-century drag shows. In *Masquerading*, women pose as men, men as women, whites as blacks, criminals as nobles, humans as animals, creating scenes that call to mind theorist Judith Butler's famed celebrations of drag. For Butler, the over-the-top aesthetics and parodic elements of the drag show are precisely what make them such powerful heuristics for imagining queer gender and sexuality because they call attention to how gender and sexuality are reiterated social performances rather than essential realities. Thus, the "giddiness of the [drag] performance is in the recognition of a radical contingency in the relation between sex and gender," and "in the place of the law of heterosexual coherence, we see sex and gender denaturalized by means of a performance which avows their distinctness and dramatizes the cultural mechanism of their fabricated unity."[68] If heteronormative gender and sexuality are themselves performances rather than inevitable identities, so this logic goes, then diverse styles of performing gender become available as possibilities. Under these terms, the costumes and pageantry of drag become less about disguise or concealment than the use of performance to

---

67. "Jones (to Himself)," 341.
68. Butler, *Gender Trouble*, 187–88.

FIGURE 3.12. "Masquerading," *Nick Nax for All Creation*, March 1869, 336–37. Courtesy of the Billy Ireland Cartoon Library & Museum, The Ohio State University.

reveal something about one's underlying authentic self. *Masquerading*, with its framing of disguise as a means of sidestepping norms of attractiveness and gender, features these qualities in spades.

Masquerading's exploration of queerness through a drag-like use of costuming and disguise is the centerpiece of one of the series' most extraordinary sequences, a diptych in which transvestitism becomes a powerful weapon against male sexual advances (fig. 3.12).[69] The left side of the two-page layout depicts a woman in a top hat and tuxedo, plunging her hand into her pocket with a masturbatory gesture as she declares her intention to pursue a lesbian sexual encounter. These encounters offer a means of imagining styles of sexuality sensitive to the desires and needs of women. She remarks, "I am going to make love to Sallie Myers tonight, in earnest. She shan't know it is not a man" to which her friend responds, "Then, don't say the things the stupid animals say to me, or you will have but poor success." Meanwhile, the right side portrays a large mustachioed man in

---

69. "Masquerading," March 1869, 336–37.

a wig and ball gown, who has just cheerfully seduced and punched out an unfortunate male seducer. The figure declares that he will "teach a fellow like that to know he's not to take too many liberties because he treats to a glass of punch." With the winking quality of the dialogue and illustrations, the sequence leaves the reader to decide whether the sequence's gender-bending and queer seductions are a lighthearted satire on the social conventions of courtship or a not-so-thinly-veiled exploration of how queer identity and desire might offer means of redressing the humiliations and injustices of patriarchal authority.

As demonstrated in this chapter, the convergence of comics and theater culture proved a potent combination for imagining and defining the public and private spaces of American life. The inadvertent Broadway performances of McLenan's Mr. Blossom, the loafing of working class b'hoys and newsboys, and the witty repartee of *Nick Nax*'s sea bathers were all offered to audiences as figures and types who could readily be observed and enjoyed on the page, stage, street, or home. This circuit of exchange can seem positively utopian in a work like *Masquerading*. After all, *Masquerading*'s alliance of print and performance not only deploys drag performance as a liberating exploration of queerness; it also wills queerness out from the margins, placing it at the center of domestic space and domestic experience.

It was not, of course, *Masquerading*'s liberating visions of domestic drag that lodged themselves in the imaginations of artists and audiences as either subject matter for the theater or stereotypes of public and private space. This distinction, of course, would go to the racist minstrel imagery of works like Darley's *Shakespeare Illustrated* and countless caricatures of Jim Crow and Zip Coon. As any student of nineteenth- and twentieth-century American visual culture can recount, minstrelsy's blending of theatricality with racial caricature is probably the strongest evidence for the mutual influence between comics, theater, and perceptions of lived experience. And here one cannot help but feel a pang of regret at the route that the alliance of theater and comics took through the late nineteenth and early twentieth centuries.

CHAPTER 4

Impressions of Places
Augustus Hoppin and Travel Comics

Americans like to travel—or at least read about it. Travel was among the most popular and enduring of literary genres in the nineteenth century. Writing in *Trubner's Bibliographic Guide to American Literature* (1859), Benjamin Moran went so far as to declare that publishing was seeing "the age of *travel literature*," commenting that "no nation has given more good books of this class to the world since 1820 than the United States, with regard to styles or information."[1] Indeed, virtually all of the period's major and minor writers published travel books, viewing it as reliable income in light of a public whose curiosity about travel seemed insatiable. Conservative accounts recorded at least two thousand travel books published in the US over the course of the nineteenth century, with the most popular volumes recording sales in the tens of thousands. For some readers, curiosity about travel was stoked by technologies such as the steamship and railroad, which created unprecedented access to travel for the average person. For others, it provided vicarious access to experiences and forms of self-education that remained elusive.[2]

Comic artists did not miss the proverbial boat on the craze for travel writing. Themes and experiences relating to travel remained a major feature of US graphic narratives almost from the moment that multipanel comics began appearing in the late 1840s. Usually, these travel strips followed a single character, creating loosely related tableaux that transported readers between various locales. The subgenre encompassed a wide spectrum of

1. Qtd. in Melton, *Mark Twain, Travel Books, and Tourism*, 17.
2. Melton, *Mark Twain, Travel Books, and Tourism*, 16–19.

different tones and styles. Many travel comics featured slapstick gags and light humor that simultaneously satirized and simulated the physical and psychological experience of travel. Others animated imperialist fantasies of taking domain over exotic regions. Still others were directed more squarely toward the process of self-discovery that nineteenth-century readers associated with travel and tourism.

At first glance, it may seem curious that travel would emerge as a dominant theme in nineteenth-century US comic albums and humor magazine comics. After all, the sketchy quality of comic illustration hardly lent itself to the sublime and picturesque scenery or precise ethnographic renderings of clothing and cultural practices, often associated with eighteenth- and nineteenth-century landscape paintings and illustrated travelogues.[3] In many cases, nineteenth-century US travel comics seem to willfully avoid common conventions for detail and verisimilitude. Most travel comics feature surprisingly little in the way of scenery or ethnographic detail and are instead organized around the evolution of the individual character as they move between new contexts. The paradox of travel comics' pervasiveness seems even more acute when considering their emergence alongside technological advancements in lithography and photography, which allowed illustrated travel books and periodicals such as *Harper's Monthly* and the *New York Illustrated News* to incorporate imagery that featured unprecedented levels of detail and verisimilitude.[4]

But an emphasis on intricate scenery or documentary realism overlooks a key reason that travel writing appealed to many nineteenth-century European and Anglo-American readers. Namely, travel implied a sense of personal transformation. As critic Carl Thompson notes, romantic and Victorian audiences increasingly shifted from seeing travel literature as a "knowledge genre" tasked with communicating objective facts about the places they visited to a "a narrative emphasis on personal development and growing self-knowledge."[5] Where eighteenth-century travel writers had been scolded for self-reflection or expressions of emotion, later travel writers like Lord Byron, Charles Dickens, and Mark Twain were celebrated for weaving their real-time thoughts, feelings, and sensory impressions

---

3. See Leitch, "Visual Images in Travel Writing," 456–73.

4. Stafford, *Voyage into Substance*, 1–7; Micklewright, *Victorian Traveler in the Middle East*, 9–11.

5. Thompson, "Nineteenth-Century Travel Writing," 123. See also Melton, *Mark Twain, Travel Books, and Tourism*, 64–78.

into their travel narratives. This shift toward a novelistic approach was buttressed by the immersive travel experiences offered by visual attractions like the moving panorama, which used a mechanically driven succession of images to pull the viewer's gaze through a progression of sights along an itinerary. In both cases—the novelistic travel narrative and the panorama—the reader/observer was invited to imagine the experience of travel as a succession of sensations and psychological displacements that transformed and informed the traveler's internal self. To read or view travel was to experience real-time contrasts with other regions and thus come to a better sense of one's own regional and national identity.

In this light, the sketchy quality of comic illustration hardly deterred artists from conveying the feelings of displacement and transformation that fascinated audiences. In fact, the casual spontaneity of comics made them uniquely suited to connecting a reader to an artist's or character's experiences of the activity of travel itself. As cartoonist Scott McCloud contends, simpler cartooning tends to produce an effect of "iconic abstraction" in which complex concepts such as emotions are rendered down to their most essential elements, allowing for quicker and more efficient expression. "By stripping down an image to its essential meaning," McCloud writes, "an artist can amplify that meaning in a way that realistic art can't."[6] In the context of nineteenth-century travel comics, cartooning allowed artists to emphasize immediacy in their rendering of travel experiences. Like a hastily written journal entry, comic illustration was thought to strip away artifice and connect the viewer to the real-time feelings and sensory impressions of the artist-traveler. This spare, efficient art style proved to be a powerful combination with the multipanel comic's capacity to animate movement. With only the most essential information presented, comic artists that initiated a play of perspectives that evoked the artist-traveler's immediate sensory impressions and feelings of psychological displacement.

This approach to travel comics finds striking expression in the work of Augustus Hoppin, an artist who maintained the long project of refining his own version of this subgenre over the course of about thirty years. One reviewer of Hoppin's work could thus confidently state, "As all know, an apparently careless etching is usually far more spirited and natural than an elaborate steel engraving. . . . Mr. Hoppin's etchings tell those who have not been in Egypt far more about the country, its wonders, and its ways

---

6. McCloud, *Understanding Comics,* 30.

than even a series of photographs would do."[7] Another credited Hoppin's ability to capture a "more correct and satisfying impression of places and people abroad . . . than volumes of mere words" to the fact that his sketches "were the thought of the moment—inspirations; that they were taken on the wing, done 'on the spot.'"[8] Hoppin's reviewers articulated a premise that underlay many travel comics of the period: The hastily sketched comic provided a quick, efficient means of connecting the reader to the feeling of seeing or experiencing something for the first time. Its object was to instigate a lasting connection between the reader and momentary subjective experience of an artist or character.

This chapter pursues two major threads of inquiry in its exploration of the travel comic as it emerged in long-form picture albums and humorous magazine comics. First, discussion focuses on how US comic artists reimagined the Töpfferian picture story to emphasize travel themes and maximize the new visual technology of the humorous picture story. In presenting the picture story as recognizably "American," artists both satirized and engaged with audience preoccupations with travel in ways that established a lasting set of conventions. The second half of this chapter delves into Hoppin's efforts to craft the genre of the travel comic into a more earnest medium, paralleling both the sophisticated narrative voice of literary travel writers and the immersive qualities of visual attractions.

Hoppin's attempts to elevate the medium of travel comics are interesting partly due to what happened later. Despite the apparent popularity of Hoppin's periodical comics and travel sketchbooks, few artists would follow in his footsteps. In this sense, Hoppin's works were true "lost literacies" insofar as they were uniquely a project of the 1850s through 1870s. Rather than false starts, they represent the sense of possibility for comics at a crucial moment in the medium's development.

The Travel Narrative and the Töpfferian Picaresque

The interest in using sequential comics to animate travel sprung up from the very emergence of the picture story in the United States. In fact, virtually every long-form picture album produced in the first decade of the

---

7. "Unromantic View of Egypt," 6.
8. "New Sketch-Book by Augustus Hoppin," 1.

genre's existence in the United States included some element of a character undertaking an arduous journey or touristic excursion. This use of travel humor must have seemed like an irresistible way for artists to adapt the picaresque ramblings of Töpffer's picture stories for the US market. Works such as *Journey to the Gold Diggins* (1849), "The Adventures of Mr. Tom Plump" (1850), *The Wonderful! And Soul Thrilling Adventures of Oscar Shanghai* (1855), and *Sad Tale of the Courtship of Chevalier Slyfox-Wikof* (1855) all adopted travel as their thematic point of entry. Magazine comics followed suit in ways that developed the basic setup into a repeatable formula. Countless shorter works signaled their satirical association with travel narratives such as "Trip to California" (1852), "Mr. Toodles' Adventures in the West" (1857), and "Professor Tigwissil's Trip to the Nile" (1876).[9]

In the early years of the travel comic subgenre, regionalist humor provided an important reference point for how travel was depicted by comic artists. Travel was central to regionalist humor that appeared in sources like the *Crockett Almanacs*, the fiction of James Kirke Paulding, and the monologues of Artemus Ward. The travel narratives embedded in US regionalist humor featured a parade of hypermasculine frontiersmen who charged into foreign terrain with a comedic disregard for the cultures they encountered. For instance, in Paulding's story "Jonathan's Visit to the Celestial Empire" (1831), a Yankee rustic named Jonathan travels to China where he runs roughshod over local values by misunderstanding Chinese norms for corporal punishment and then courting the daughter of the village elder. True to the conventions of the subgenre, Jonathan's trespasses do not lead to misfortune and instead set off a chain of events that leads him to return home with half a million dollars and a hero's welcome. In framing Americans' travel in this way, authors like Paulding promoted myths of US exceptionalism. Whether characters were wrestling alligators or scandalizing the sensibilities of "natives," readers were consistently reminded that Americans were rugged individualists, destined to conquer vast swaths of territory (often in spite of their own buffoonish tendencies).

The medium of the picture story offered a vital new dimension in the way that regionalist travel humor could be presented to audiences. Artists were not bound by the long verbal yarn upon which figures like Paulding and Ward depended. The picture story could bring these plotlines into the realm of visual spectacle. Slapstick action and the wild swings in plot and

9. "Trip to California," 79; McLenan, "Mr. Toodles' Adventures in the West," 4; and Hopkins, "Professor Tigwissil's Trip up the Nile," 8.

character could thus be depicted instantaneously in a kinetic frenzy. Even more importantly, the implicit distinctions between the American protagonists and their "foreign" counterparts and landscapes could be viewed and inspected for comparison.

If US artists were eager to make use of the picture story's capacity to animate fantasies of exploration and imperial expansion, they found an especially apt vessel in comedic narratives about the California gold rush. Works including *Journey to the Gold Diggins* (1849) by J. A. and D. F. Read, *Expedition to California* (1849) by the pseudonymous XOX, *Tom Plump* (1850), and *The Miner's Progress* (1853) by Alonzo Delano all tracked fortune hunters on their way to California. Works that were not squarely about the gold rush often snuck in a subplot about an excursion westward (or simply put a gold miner on the cover, as in the case of *Ferdinand Flipper* and *My Friend Wriggles*). Gold rush picture stories condensed westward expansion into an accessible visual spectacle. Viewers could survey the various regions, trade relations, and social identities of the country with the turn of the page. Characters traversed North and South America in their various journeys to California along the overland routes, through the Panama Canal, and around Cape Horn. The stories' plots almost always featured a protagonist from New York who, after all the farcical adventures, returned home.

Early US picture stories' impulse to narrate imperial conquest paralleled the way that visual spectacles had been deployed in the river panorama, a form that had been received tepidly in Europe but enjoyed intense popularity with American audiences. Spectacles such as Banville's *Panorama of the Mississippi River* and Fredric Church's *Heart of the Andes* provided a thrilling display where armchair travelers could imagine themselves being transported to exotic and treacherous destinations. As scholar Angela Miller notes, these types of spectacles tended to confirm tropes of US conquest over North and South America as "the image of a mechanically controlled narrative with a definable beginning, middle, and end[, which] encouraged a view of history as a series of unfolding scenes fluidly connected with one another, giving to audiences the illusion of mastery over random, distant, or otherwise incomprehensible events."[10]

In the moving panorama, the entire process of US conquest was thus presented as a deceptively simple, orderly, and inevitable process that audiences could view passively by dint of the spectacle's thrilling illusionism.

---

10. Miller, "Panorama, the Cinema," 41.

Miller continues, "The beginning of the journey is shown in relation to its conclusion; the local passages of scenery in the context of a larger extent of territory; and the particular moment in the cycle of trade in relation to an unfolding vista of national progress and western settlement."[11] With images of westward conquest confronting audiences as an automated visual spectacle, the river panorama thus fostered the implication of inevitability. This sense of movement was as much about psychological movement toward a certain conception of the meaning of Anglo-American identity as it was about anything to do with the visual perception of landscapes. The mechanically driven story would always proceed to the telos of "Manifest Destiny" in the form of Anglo dominance over the North American continent. This plot would in turn proceed without any obvious protagonist turning the crank but instead the invisible force of the panorama's machinery.

The scene-to-scene transitions of *Journey to the Gold Diggins* provide precisely this neatly circumscribed visualization of Anglo-American domain over the West. Undergirding each adventure of the gold-hunting protagonist lies the implication that he will conquer and domesticate the wild terrain, even if he does so unwittingly. In turn, this device of the hapless rube-turned-conqueror becomes the occasion to explore a fascination with traversing the continent. Each frame introduces a new locale that displaces Jeremiah, giving him a fresh set of location-specific challenges to which he reacts in slapstick fashion (fig. 4.1).[12] One moment, he comes ashore from the Pacific Ocean and encounters South American natives; the next, he is on the Mississippi River battling alligators; at another he banters with Natives on the plains. In turn, these challenges lead to a physical and psychological transformation of Jeremiah himself. He dons an array of disguises that allow him to embody and subsume the various Indigenous people and frontier types whom he meets. He is transformed from his original state of wig-donning swell to a variety of new roles, depending on his new haircut or acquisition of goods. He becomes a shipmate swabbing the deck and then, aloft on a crow's nest, a pirate, haggard prospector, Mohawk Indian, and even a member of a pack of coyotes. In each case, the movement from frame to frame animates not just a change in landscape but a larger change in subjectivity as readers fantasize, at some level, about Jeremiah's simultaneous hybridization into the cultures and environs of the frontier.

---

11. Miller, "Panorama, the Cinema," 41.
12. Read and Read, *Journey to the Gold Diggins.*

Mr. Saddlebags hires a mule to carry him over the mountains.

30

He finds the road anything but level.

On condition that he will become a native his life is spared, and he is taught the war-dance.

57

He rushes to his lady-love, who does not recognise him.

61

FIGURE 4.1. Scenes from James Alexander Read and Donald F. Read, *Journey to the Gold Diggins* (New York: Stringer & Townsend, 1849). Courtesy of Beinecke Rare Book and Manuscript Library, Yale University.

The dialectic between the landscape and Jeremiah's physical and psychological transformations are particularly striking in *Gold Diggins*'s closing sequence in which he is captured by Natives and then escapes home to New York. The sequence opens with Jeremiah wandering the plains, physically and mentally battered by the hardships of life in the wilderness when he meets "a native, who arrests his progress."[13] From here, Jeremiah assimilates into the group, begrudgingly cutting his hair into a mohawk, donning "Native" clothing, wielding an ax, and doing a war dance in exchange for his life. Jeremiah's supposed physical transformation plays out as a parody of the many early nineteenth-century novels and plays that featured white men who donned redface in order to imbue themselves with mystical qualities associated with the "authentic" Native identity.[14] As Jeremiah makes his escape to New York still attired in the dress of his captors, he is rendered unrecognizable to friends and family who are apparently easily fooled by the simple changes to his appearance. "Supposing him to be a savage," they react by alternatingly recoiling in horror at his strange appearance and pursuing him with pitchforks and rifles.[15] But the revulsion does not last long. Once Jeremiah's wife recognizes him, these terrifying new features of his appearance become reinterpreted as evidence of his newfound worldliness and masculine gravitas as an adventurer. With this revelation, the book closes with the transformed Jeremiah regaling his wife and family with his tales of fortune-hunting.

Throughout *Gold Diggins*, the medium of the comic album itself plays an important role in framing the meaning of Jeremiah's conquest of the wilderness and his personal transformation. While Jeremiah's blunders may seem like mere slapstick, they speak volumes to the underlying logic at play: Jeremiah, the perpetually accidental conqueror, lacks any agency in the Anglo-American conquest of North America. Instead, the white imperialist is pushed in mechanistic fashion between shifting places and shifting social identities by the simple animation produced by the reader's act of turning the page. The conclusion of Anglo-American Manifest Destiny

13. Read and Read, *Journey to the Gold Diggins*, 56.

14. Redface actors such as Edwin Forrest loudly announced their claims to Native American authenticity, touting research and use of so-called Native mannerisms and clothing. Although these efforts were received with praise by many of Forrest's critics, his claims to authenticity were mocked and satirized by later humorists and playwrights. A similar sequence of episodes would also play out with James Fenimore Cooper's Leatherstocking Tales book series. See Hughes, "Indispensable Indian," 32–35.

15. Read and Read, *Journey to the Gold Diggins*, 60.

is advanced not by the rhetoric of God or fate but instead by the passive visual spectacle inherent in the format of the picture story.

Far-flung locales and imperialist expansion were not always necessary to initiate the sense of dislocation that drove the fascination with humorous travel comics. Many works depicted shorter excursions. Artists wrote recurring gags about weekend trips to the country, fishing excursions, scientific expeditions, or technologies such as the train, hot air balloon, and omnibus. The basic formula for these comics about shorter excursions was often similar to the comics about more exotic destinations: track the experience and reactions of an individual traveler through a series of scene-to-scene transitions as he or she undergoes various forms of physical and psychological displacement. In comics that took place closer to home, regional quirks and scrapes with local wildlife provided ample basis for meaningful contrasts between the protagonist and their new surroundings.

One of the most persistent storylines was domestic tourism narrative, where an urban dweller does battle with overgrown wildlife. Fish, mosquitos, and other creatures drove outsiders away in ways that foreshadowed the animal antagonists of many twentieth-century comics and animated cartoons such as Woody Woodpecker. An especially lively version of the animal comic strip came in the form of comics about the "Jersey Mosquito," a dog-sized insect who preyed upon tourists while they slept.[16] The mosquito storyline proved an appealing topic for the way it flipped the narrative of the cavalier intruder. The tourist rarely, if ever, came out on the winning side and this result generated a dual-sided lampoon in which the consumerist tendencies of the leisure tourist were satirized even as the countryside became a source of fun as a cartoonish exaggeration of the wilderness. By turns, artists could exaggerate the features of the mosquito, fashioning it as an object of macabre horror or a gleeful antihero.

An early mosquito strip from *Yankee Notions* in 1860 handles the action in an almost parenthetical fashion, making light of "Mr. Tourist's" sense of disorientation at finding himself in a strange, new place (fig. 4.2). The normally plump Mr. Tourist awakens confused to find that he has lost a great deal of weight. The cause is only revealed when a giant, grotesque mosquito perches upon his chest and "commences operations."[17] Later artists

---

16. Multiple variations of the Jersey Mosquito sequence appeared in the 1860s and 1870s. See "Adventure with a Jersey Mosquito," 5; "Englishmen's First Night in America," 348–49; "Mr. Tourist's Experience," 304; Hopkins, "Out of the Frying Pan," 8; and "Mosquito Guard," 9.

17. "Mr. Tourist's Experience," 304.

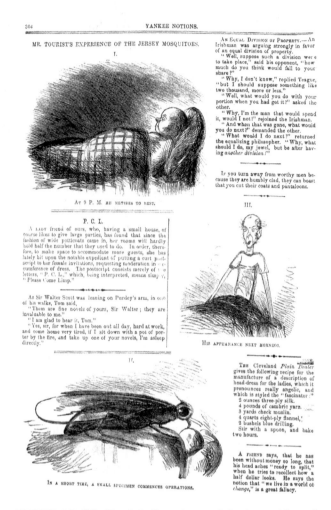

FIGURE 4.2. "Mr. Tourist's Experience of the Jersey Mosquitoes," *Yankee Notions,* October 1860, 304. Courtesy of the American Antiquarian Society.

would develop the gag into more overt and elaborate forms of slapstick, reminiscent of the German artist Wilhelm Busch.[18] "An Adventure with a New Jersey Mosquito" from 1873 features a dynamic back and forth that begins with "Mr. Snags" waking up to find a mosquito playing guitar and serenading him at his bedside. At this point the action escalates into a dynamic back and forth as Snags and the mosquito tussle. The upper hand shifts with each frame, with Snags gaining the advantage at one moment, the mosquito the next. All the while, the captions use comedic

18. For a discussion of the exchange between the American Jersey Mosquito comics and Busch's animal comics, see Kunzle, "Precursors in American Weeklies," 159–85.

overstatement, presenting the battle in melodramatic terms. Snags burlesques Shakespeare, shouting "Blood! Blood, Iago, blood!" while the
mosquito's momentary retreat inspires a reference to Psalm 137:2 with the
mawkish declaration, "The harp is hung on the willow."[19]

The physical sensations associated with traveling by ship, rail, or car
also emerged as common points of fascination and terror. As scholar
Wolfgang Schivelbusch notes in the case of the railway, the nineteenth
century marked a period of intense adjustment to the new visual and physical experiences presented by mechanized travel. While early nineteenth-
century train passengers expressed terror at the disorienting sensation of
looking out a compartment window at an "evanescent" landscape, later
travelers understood these experiences as "sources of enrichment," enliven-
ing and animating an otherwise "monotonous landscape."[20] Comic artists
commonly poked fun at the terror inspired by these adjustments even as
they used transitions between frames to illustrate the thrilling sensation of
speed and motion.

A mainstay of this vehicle-based humor was the recurring gag of passengers tossed about the deck of a steamship or railcar, often suffering motion
sickness. This stock sequence offered an opportunity to explore the line
between modern and premodern sensibilities. The motion-sick victims of
these stock gags were typically depicted as rustics or rubes who were unable
to cope with the speed of modern life and thus experienced literal vertigo.
This formula can be seen in action in "Mr. Spinks Adventures on the Trial
Trip of the Steamer Earthquake" where an out-of-touch gentleman has
his snobbish affectations quite literally pounded out of him. Spinks begins
the strip as a snob who "goes on board with the confidence an elegant
exterior always inspires."[21] These pretensions are figuratively blasted apart
in the ensuing frames as Spinks is shot into the air by steam, exposing him
as just the sort of sheltered rustic he claims to disdain. The sequence that
follows seems equally interested in punishing Spinks for his arrogance and
in showcasing the power of modern steam technology. Failing to secure
himself, Spinks is tossed from the upper deck into the steerage with the
lower-class passengers, jetted to the engine room where shipmates curi-
ously inspect him, and finally shot into the ship's funnel. Spinks's demise
provides a bit of schadenfreude in its insistence that upper-class snobs lack

19. "Adventures with a Jersey Mosquito," 5.
20. Schivelbusch, *Railway Journey*, 59–61.
21. "Mr. Spinks' Adventures," 236–37.

the savviness of their comparatively modern working-class counterparts even as the succession of blasts make a visual spectacle of steamship travel. Variations of this gag remained alive and well in the 1870s with works like Woolf's "Railway Journey" and Worth's "Mr. and Mrs. Thumper's Experiences in a Sleeping Car," which employed sophisticated visuals to record and replicate the impressions and sensations of riding on a train.

While the Jersey mosquito and vehicle gags may seem far afield from the roving adventures of *Gold Diggins,* they exemplified a common approach to situational comedy that made madcap fun from various forms of physical and psychological displacement. Dislocated and disoriented, these early comic travelers bumbled through slapstick encounters with an array of social others, exotic landscapes, and vertigo-inducing transportation with an occasional hint of social allegory and inward reflection. With the work of Hoppin and a few others, these basic conventions turned toward an increasingly ambitious and reflective array of themes and sensations.

Augustus Hoppin and a Genteel Turn

Augustus Hoppin would stand out as the most prolific and accomplished US producer of travel comics and sketchbooks in the mid- to late nineteenth century. More than any figure of the period, Hoppin adopted the conventions of the travel comic as a space for formal and thematic innovations, refining his own version of the subgenre over the course of twenty years. The first of Hoppin's travel-related works appeared around 1854 with his earliest series in *Yankee Notions,* continuing through his work in *Harper's Weekly* in the late 1850s and early 1860s, and concluding with a series of lush book-length travel albums in the early to mid-1870s. Through all of this output, readers can observe a steady progression toward self-consciously literary ambitions as Hoppin undertook sophisticated experiments with perspective and self-reflection.

Born in Providence, Rhode Island, to an affluent family of artists, Hoppin marked a contrast from the bohemianism and financial hardship that characterized the lives of so many cartoonists in the 1850s, '60s, and '70s. In the same period that artists like Bellew and Gunn were renting rooms in boarding houses, Hoppin was investing in real estate and leasing office space to businesses.[22] Hoppin's brother William was a founding member of the Century Club in New York. Another brother, Thomas Frederick,

---

22. Hoppin advertised office and rooms for lease in "To Be Let."

designed the chancel window at Trinity Church in New York.[23] As a boy, Hoppin was acquainted with George Curtis, the eventual editor of *Harper's Weekly*, who would later give him his first opportunity to publish as the illustrator for *The Potiphar Papers* in 1853. Hoppin's education remained equally distinguished. In 1848 he graduated from Brown University and then spent time as a student in England at Cambridge Law School. After a year of attempting to practice law, Hoppin gave up on his first career and set off for Europe where he studied art and toured the Continent.[24]

Apart from his travel sketches, Hoppin was one of the premiere illustrators of middle-class life in the mid- to late nineteenth-century United States. Even as Hoppin was starting his legal practice, he worked as a principal artist for *Yankee Notions*. Later, he published comics in *Young America* as well as *Harper's Weekly* and *Harper's Monthly*. As a book illustrator, Hoppin illustrated works by many of the most well-known American authors of the period, including Mark Twain, William Dean Howells, Oliver Wendell Holmes, Louisa Mae Alcott, as well as a significant number of children's works.[25] Hoppin was also an author himself, publishing a children's book titled *Carrot Pomade* (1864) and a pair of semiautobiographical works, *Recollections of the Auton House* (1881) and *A Fashionable Sufferer* (1883).

Late in Hoppin's life, an observer would note that his skill as a storyteller seemed to go hand-in-hand with his travels: "Wherever he goes, he carries a pencil with him and, be it ten days on a steamer, a tour through Europe, or any trip he may happen to take, he can spread it on a few broad pages in a truly graphic manner."[26] This account of Hoppin as a peripatetic artist, constantly taking stock of his surroundings is supported both by his published and unpublished artwork and illustrations.[27] In particular, Hoppin's private sketches reveal him using his travel experiences as the basis for experiments with graphic narrative. In the year after he abandoned his career as a lawyer, Hoppin created (but never published) a series of 6" × 9.5" pen-and-ink sketches in which he depicted his own travels through

23. "Famous as an Artist," 2.

24. Hoppin's travels are described in newspaper articles including, "Famous as an Artist"; and "Mr. Augustus Hoppin."

25. Representative and notable examples of Hoppin's book illustration work include Alcott, *Kitty's Class Day*; Holmes, *Autocrat of the Breakfast Table*; Howells, *Their Wedding Journey*; and Twain and Warner, *Gilded Age*.

26. *Hartford Daily Courant*, 1.

27. Hoppin consistently drew images of the people in his life, often using them as models for his published work. Hoppin also incorporated the activity of drawing directly into his personal relationships, presenting short comics and drawings as keepsakes for private entertainment. For an account of Hoppin's drawing practices, see *Hartford Daily Courant*, December 22, 1874.

France, Belgium, Holland, Germany, Switzerland, and Egypt. In many of the sketches, Hoppin turns to the formal hallmarks of comics—captions, word balloons, and sequential illustrations—to record his momentary impressions and emotions. Some sketches are witty and droll, depicting mishaps or funny bits of dialogue; others capture more somber impressions in which Hoppin is charmed by someone that he meets or struck by the beauty of his surroundings.

Hoppin's choices of subjects and the dialogues in these private sketches suggest an artist-writer preoccupied with conveying how his experiences as a traveler contribute to shifting moods and an evolving sense of self rather than merely recording sites and scenery (fig. 4.3).[28] For instance, a two-frame sketch captioned "Dutch Dance House/Bad Smell in Street" depicts a humorous contrast between Hoppin's experience of Amsterdam over the course of two days. In the first frame, Hoppin jubilantly dances the polka with a Dutch woman at the Shul house; in the next, Hoppin's infatuation with Dutch culture gives way to disgust as the foul smells emitting from Amsterdam's city center send him racing for his boarding house. Other scenes convey Hoppin's evolving sense of self by emphasizing his friendship with his traveling partner, Cunny. Here, Hoppin's internal growth takes precedence over the specifics of the landmarks and scenery. Hoppin's emphasis on the friendship appears in his depiction of their visit to a cathedral in Cologne. Rather than rendering the visit itself, Hoppin's sketch depicts a quiet scene in which the two men share a bottle of wine reflecting on the day's sights and events. Hoppin's composition prioritizes the shared process of reflection over the scenery. With Hoppin and Cunny portrayed in the foreground and the faintly sketched cathedral relegated to the background, Hoppin directs the viewer's gaze to the two companions reminiscing about their day while the cathedral is framed as a hazy dream image conjured up by the men's recollections. Hoppin's consistent focus on internal psychological states and relationships position the sketches as something akin to diary entries. Each sketch preserves a momentary insight that arises from visiting a place rather than the specifics of the place itself.

Hoppin's earliest published travel comic, *Jonathan Abroad*, which ran 1854–55 in *Yankee Notions*, appears to have been based loosely on his private travels and sketches as a young man. In adapting his own travels into a

---

28. Hoppin, "Travel Sketches."

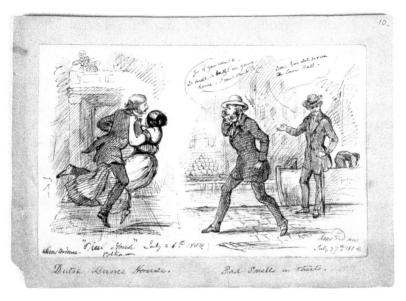

FIGURE 4.3. Augustus Hoppin, "Travel Sketches," ca. 1854. Courtesy of the American Antiquarian Society.

series for *Yankee Notions,* Hoppin vacillated between conventional Yankee humor and a more cosmopolitan vision of the travel comic and the American's role in the world. On the surface, *Jonathan Abroad* looked like another in the line of regionalist slapstick; however, when viewed carefully, readers can notice that the series uses the travel comic as a vehicle for subtle, introspective modes of expression. In this manner, Hoppin would foreshadow the complex blend of Western slapstick and cosmopolitan reflection that Twain would undertake fifteen years later with *Innocents Abroad* (1869).

Early episodes of *Jonathan Abroad* hewed closely to the stock conventions of works like *Journey to the Gold Diggins* or *Oscar Shanghai*. Jonathan's encounters often have less to do with exploring these cultures than situating the American Yankee as a gadfly among other cultures of the world. Hoppin gleefully thumbs his nose at European institutions by positioning Jonathan as a wise fool. Speaking in his thick Yankee dialect, Jonathan expresses his confusion at Europeans' apparent tendency to worship their own landmarks and history and, in doing so, unwittingly exposes their pretensions (fig. 4.4). He is bemused by the English fascination with London's St. Paul's Cathedral, where an ascent to the dome yields only a view of "the thickest fog that was ever got up, regardless of expense."[29] Meanwhile, a trip to the Royal Academy results in a sly contrast between Jonathan's folksy empiricism and the pretensions of English socialites. In his naivete, Jonathan glides straight past the artwork and fixes his gaze on the strangeness of the visitors who crowd the gallery, fawning over the unremarkable paintings: "I hain't got time nor room in this screed to tell you all about my visit to the royal Akaddamme, where the picturs are, but you kin jist see by looking at the cut's I'v whittled out, that the folks air abeout as great curiosities as the pictures."[30] In each case, encounters with the locals provide the occasion to draw contrasts between stereotypes of the brash American cavalier and uptight European snob.

Later installments of *Jonathan Abroad* offer a much different vision of the American's presence in the Old World. Shifting away from Jonathan's breaches of social etiquette, Hoppin depicts the American encounter with ethnic others with delicacy and admiration. *Jonathan Abroad*'s episodes in Paris and the Middle East are especially attentive to Jonathan's sincere attraction to other cultures. In one series of frames, Jonathan finds himself so taken with French culture and urban sophistication that he cannot stop himself from giving money to the various charming French merchants whom he encounters (fig. 4.5). Grisette, a charming glove saleswoman makes him feel "as skittish as a four year old."[31] Jonathan is "so pleased with the operation" that he "is in danger of exhausting all of his floating capital in gloves, to the detriment of his pocket, and his vows to Jermima."[32] This

29. Hoppin, "Jonathan Abroad," September 1854, 280–81.

30. Hoppin, "Jonathan Abroad," September 1854, 281.

31. Hoppin, "Jonathan Abroad," December 1854, 369.

32. Hoppin, "Jonathan Abroad," December 1854, 369.

JONATHAN IN THE BALL OF ST. PAULS.

arter I'd nearly kirflumuxed two or three times for want of breath I got up inter a grate round hole, from which she, the old woman, sed I should git a splendid vew. I went to the side a holdin' on like a pair o'nippers, and looked eout but I se'd nothin' but a leetle the thickest fog that was ever got up regardless of expense. It was so thick, you could jist pick it up in chunks, and I couldn't see one darned inch beyont my nose. I'd hearn tell of London fogs, but I didn't think they was so all fired solid. Well, as I couldn't see nothin' I went deown agin. and baring a slip up, by which I tore my trowserloons behind, I got deown all right side up. I telled the old woman I hadn't seen nothin' for the fog, and she told me I must come some other day when it was clear, but though I waited three weeks it warnt no better, it was fog all the time.

I hain't got time nor room in this screed to tell you all abeout my visit to the Royal Akadamme, where the picturs are, but you kin jist see by looking at the cut's I'v whittled eout, that the folks air abeout as great curiosities as the picturs.*

* I feound out since it was a dead suck in, cause there ain't no window into it.

deown with a curry comb if he warnt a policeman and nothin' shorter. They're cute critters, they are ; they make love to all the pretty helps on their beet, and if there's any thing to eat or drink areound, they know jist where to find it, and by their looks it aint no two to one that they don't know what to do with it.

Well, I shotted along and bimeby I kim to a meetin' house, with a steeple on it higher than forty seven telegraff poles set up on end, one on top o' 'tother; and I ax'd a feller, what meetin' house it was, 'that hair' said he is 'Sent Pauls'. Well, the door was open and in I went. and I be chewed up if a feller did'nt come up and make me give him tuppence afore he'd let me see any o' the sights. So I gin him the tuppence and I see the clock, well the old mill wheel deown in the creek warnt nothing to the big wheel here. It looked like the daddy of all the clocks in creation. I aint got time to tell you all I se'd, but I'll tell you what I didn't see. An old woman told me I should go up in the ball; well I did'nt no where the ball was, or I'd never a done it, but she pointed the way and I clim and clim, and clim ; I thought I should never be done climing and

JONATHAN IN THE ROYAL ACADEMY.

FIGURE 4.4. Augustus Hoppin, "Jonathan Abroad," *Yankee Notions*, September 1854, 280–81. Courtesy of the American Antiquarian Society.

attraction to French beauty then recurs with a flower girl, a peripatetic postal worker, and a lemonade vendor on the Champs-Elysées. Each time, Hoppin dispenses with slapstick in favor of a sentimental tone that idealizes the cross-cultural interaction as a moment of growth and personal insight. In doing so, he depicts his American subject as growing from the foul-mouthed outsider into a potentially cosmopolitan figure. Like Twain's

FIGURE 4.5. Augustus Hoppin, "Jonathan Abroad," *Yankee Notions*, December 1854, 369. Courtesy of the American Antiquarian Society.

narrator in *Innocents Abroad*, Hoppin's persona of Jonathan offers a dual satire. It simultaneously confronts the uncouth tendencies of American travelers even as it chips away at the pretensions of Old World culture.

In fact, there is ample reason to believe that Twain drew inspiration from Hoppin's travel comics. Many of Twain's early writings appeared in *Yankee Notions* alongside Hoppin's work while Hoppin himself was the illustrator for the first edition of *The Gilded Age* (1873). In fact, Twain even includes a scene in *Innocents Abroad* that closely resembles Hoppin's purchasing of the gloves from the French saleswoman. Upon his arrival in

said, and invisible to the naked eye, could be clearly distinguished through those same telescopes. Below, on one side,
we looked down upon an endless mass of batteries, and on the
other straight down to the sea.

While I was resting ever so comfortably on a rampart, and
cooling my baking head in the delicious breeze, an officious
guide belonging to another party came up and said :

"Senor, that high hill yonder is called the Queen's Chair "—

"QUEEN'S CHAIR."

"Sir, I am a helpless orphan
in a foreign land. Have pity
on me. Don't—now *don't* inflict
that most in-FERNAL old legend on me any more to-day !"

There—I had used strong language, after promising I would
never do so again ; but the provocation was more than human
nature could bear. If you had been bored so, when you had
the noble panorama of Spain and Africa and the blue Medi-

FIGURE 4.6. Mark Twain, *The Innocents
Abroad, or The New Pilgrim's Progress*
(Hartford, CT: American Publishing Com-
pany, 1869), 67. Courtesy of the American
Antiquarian Society.

Gibraltar, Twain contemplates the "English and Spanish female loveliness" as a "handsome young lady in the store" convinces him to purchase
ill-fitting gloves, convincing him that it would be "a stylish thing to go
to the theatre in kid gloves."[33] Twain expands on the scene, spinning out
into an elaborate debate over the relative virtues of the well-fitting gloves
versus the momentary pleasures of the saleswoman's charms. Deciding
that "we had entertained an angel unawares," Twain, like Hoppin twenty
years earlier, arrives at the conclusion that being conned is a small price
to pay for the memorable experience.[34] The resemblances extend to the
visuals of *Innocents Abroad* as well. To that end, Twain's publisher utilized
a visual layout similar to *Jonathan Abroad* in which the illustrations are cut
into the space of the paragraph, creating a comics-like synergy between
image and text (fig. 4.6). The evidence that Hoppin directly inspired Twain

33. Twain, *Innocents Abroad,* 73.
34. Twain, *Innocents Abroad,* 75.

seems largely circumstantial, but the resemblance is anything but a coincidence. Hoppin, similar to Twain, used the wildly popular genre of travel narratives as a means of transforming his own medium. In Twain's case, this transformation meant using travel as a means of reinventing popular humor through reflection upon the self and the outside world. In Hoppin's, the engagement with travel narratives meant reimagining travel-themed comics as the starting point for a distinctive authorial point of view.

Where *Jonathan Abroad* presented a façade of Töpfferian slapstick, Hoppin and a few others soon embraced a more earnest approach, framing the travel comic as a means of offering vicarious access to the experiences of middle-class tourists. These genteel works often navigated a middle ground between humorous comics and the pictorial reporting appearing in publications like *Frank Leslie's Illustrated Newspaper* and *Harper's*. Many incorporated elements of photorealism, featured layers of psychological complexity, and eschewed the crass slapstick of works like *Journey to the Gold Diggins* and *Oscar Shanghai*. Artists identified their cartooning with personal experiences through titles like "Travels of Our Artist in England," "How Our Artists Travel," and "Our Artist in Search of the Bald Mountain Volcano."[35] In the process, they established the humorous picture story as a space for relating personal travel experiences and recollections. A few US artists, including G. W. Carleton, Horace Cope, Abner Perk, and Hoppin, produced elaborate full-length books that followed entire trips from beginning to end.[36] These "travel sketchbooks," as publishers called them, delved into autobiographical and semiautobiographical experiences, often including names and descriptions of fellow passengers or visually accurate depictions of local clothing and architecture.

This strand of genteel travel comics had important precedents in a tradition of autobiographical travel albums that appeared in Britain and France throughout the 1850s and '60s by artists such as Richard Doyle, Gustave Doré, and Cham.[37] These travel albums typically adapted the Töpfferian format and narration style to lightly fictionalized, serio-comic accounts of the artist-author's own travels. The most widely circulated example in

---

35. "How Our Artists Travel," 3; "Our Artist in Search," 193; and "Travels of Our Artist in England," 12.

36. Representative examples include Carleton, *Our Artist in Cuba*; Cope, *Reverend Mr. Sourball's European Tour*; and Perk, *Merry Maple Leaves*.

37. Cham's travel albums are collected in Kunzle, *Cham*, 307–480. Doré's travel albums appear in Kunzle, *Gustave Doré*, 142–92.

the US was *The Laughable Adventures of Messrs' Brown, Jones, and Robinson* (1851) by the British artist Richard Doyle.[38] Doyle utilized a refined visual style and realist approach that would provide a model for the more earnest graphic travel comics from the United States. The album depicted the titular "three illustrious individuals" on their excursion through France, Austria, and Italy, capturing their reactions to exotic sites and social types. Doyle's piece often resembles a series of postcards in which each frame offers a glimpse of the travelers' stop at a landmark of interest. In contrast to the absurdist picaresque of *Oscar Shanghai* and *Gold Diggins,* Doyle's *Laughable Adventures* referred to the lived experiences of middle-class travelers in ways that his audiences understood as reflecting their own experiences.

Graham Everitt, a contemporary of Doyle's, described the book as "graphically relating the experiences of the most ordinary class of continental tourists" in a manner "sufficiently possible to remind one of personal vicissitudes encountered off the track or on the frontiers."[39] In turn, claims of a vicarious insider experience were buttressed by light satire on British middle-class peculiarities. Doyle intersperses depictions of landmarks on the European Grand Tour with observational humor about the mannerisms and mundane logistics of middle-class travelers. For instance, the album lampoons British travelers' tendency to insulate themselves from the cultures and places that they visited. The tourists in *Laughable Adventures* refuse to learn foreign languages and pack excessive amounts of luggage, confirming the suspicions of Washington Irving who interpreted British caravans as "a little morsel of the old island rolling about the world—everything so compact, so snug, so finished and fitting."[40] Doyle's emphasis on the mundane situates *Laughable Adventures* as a blend of satire and self-reflection, offering humorous reminiscences for those who had been lucky enough to travel and vicarious access to such memories for those

---

38. Doyle first published the work as a serial titled "The Pleasure Trips of Messrs Brown, Jones, and Robinson" in *Punch* 1851 during a period of heightened excitement about travel amid the first London international exhibition with an English book edition released in 1854 under the title *The Foreign Tour of Messrs Brown, Jones and Robinson,* followed shortly by a newly retitled American edition, *Laughable Adventures* in 1855. The American edition of *Laughable Adventures of Messrs Brown, Jones and Robinson* from Dick & Fitzgerald does not include a date. Advertisements place it as a new publication in 1855. See back wrapper of A.L.C. (pseud.), *The Wonderful! And Soul Thrilling Adventures by Land and Sea of Oscar Shanghai.* For a discussion of the book's publication history, see Walkiewicz, "Humor of Circumstance," 29–47.

39. Graeme, *English Caricaturists and Graphic Humourists,* 391–92.

40. Graeme, *English Caricaturists and Graphic Humourists,* 308.

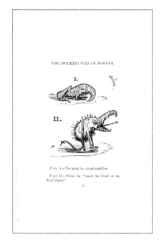 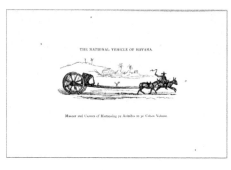 

FIGURE 4.7. Scenes from George Washington Carleton, *Our Artist in Cuba: Leaves from the Sketch-Book of a Traveller during the Winter of 1864–5* (New York: Carleton, 1865). Courtesy of the American Antiquarian Society.

who had not. Like a series of photographs, the comics offered snapshots of spontaneous, never-to-be-repeated moments observed by an individual.

Carleton would make the analogy to photography explicit in describing the "photographic value" as the primary appeal of his own Doyle-inspired travel sketchbook. Carleton thus reflected that the value of the travel comic lay less with producing beautiful or accurate drawings than delivering the "crispy freshness of a first impression."[41] Instead, travel sketches intended to offer "the chance results of idle moments" that arise "as every one, with both eyes open, sees."[42] The spontaneity of the sketch was crucial because the emphasis lay with creating "sketchy little impressions" and "exaggerations of actual events, on the spur of the moment jotted down, for the same sort of mere pastime as may lead the reader to linger along its ephemeral pages."[43] This minimalist approach widely appears in Carleton's own comic travel albums. Most pages consist of simple line sketches. As figure 4.7 shows, a typical page will either zero in on a minute detail of local mannerisms or reimagine an episode of Carleton's travels in terms of a joke or caricature. Carleton renders a Havana flea as a strange bird-like caricature; his sketch of a farmer is drawn in silhouettes, favoring exquisite attention to the curve and motion of his whip and the detail of the donkey's gait; his spare illustration of Chanticleer the rooster favors understatement

41. Carleton, *Our Artist in Cuba*, vii.
42. Carleton, *Our Artist in Cuba*, vii.
43. Carleton, *Our Artist in Peru*, vii.

depicting only its simple and spontaneous peck at the ground. Here and elsewhere in Carleton's rendering, a full, detailed landscape was not necessary to create an artifact of the "idle moment." Far more important is the way that the irregular curve of a line or simple observation allowed readers to trace experiences backward from illustration to place.

US writers and artists embraced the suggestion that comics could offer vicarious touristic experiences. Comics with semiautobiographical undertones featured tourist destinations along the famed Grand Tour of Europe or America's version of the Grand Tour, a route that curled through New York City up the Hudson River into the Catskill Mountains and Saratoga Springs and over into Niagara Falls.[44] Through comics, these artists implicitly tied their work to a distinctively literary sensibility. Travel on the famous European "Grand Tour" had long been identified with popular writers such as Irving, Bayard Taylor, and Twain. Meanwhile, tourism along the American Grand Tour held special significance for its identification with the search for the American natural sublime. Writers such as Ralph Waldo Emerson, Margaret Fuller, Henry David Thoreau, Benjamin Silliman, and the artist Thomas Cole were all known to frequent the White Mountains, with others making trips to Niagara and the Great Lakes regions.[45]

This newer semiautobiographical approach to travel comics appeared in the tourism stories that Hoppin created for *Harper's Weekly* in the late 1850s. Like *Laughable Adventures* and *Our Artist in Cuba*, these pieces poked light fun at the inconveniences of tourism even as they implicitly offered vicarious access to a luxury excursion. Here, Hoppin adopted the fictional personas of a variety of fashionable tourists. Where his "Jonathan" character from *Yankee Notions* provided a humorous contrast to the affectations of the upper-class tourist, newer characters like "Miss Juniata Rowe" and "Mr. Peter Plum" embody the affectations of the upper-class tourists. In doing so, Hoppin offered a significantly different style of satire. Sending his characters on the Grand Tour of Europe and its American counterpart, Hoppin's *Harper's Weekly* comics were as much about exploring the fantasy of the fashionable American tourist's experience as they were about poking fun at it.

---

44. See "Adventures of McTiffin at Long Branch," 16; Crayon, "Artists' Excursion over the Baltimore," 1–19; "Travels of Our Artist in England," 12.

45. For a discussion and bibliography on the substantial amount of scholarship on the European Grand Tour, see Colletta, "Introduction," ix–xx. On the American Grand Tour, see Sears, *Sacred Places,* 49; and Brown, *Inventing New England.*

7.—THE SCENE FROM A NEW POINT OF VIEW.

9.—BEFORE WE WENT INTO THE CAVE OF THE WINDS.

At intervals, all night it seemed to me, gymnastic feats—in the way of getting in and out of berths—were executed by "ladies of the Company," and, tired and sleepy as I was, I couldn't help laughing at the droll figure some of them cut.

At last we were at Albany—our first view of which consisted of a foreground of Hibernian carriage drivers, each with a whip in his hand, who seemed prepared to lay on our backs if we didn't engage him; and a background of fog and dingy houses covered with monstrous signs about "feed" and "cheap transportation." The day was spent by mamma and me in sleep; in the evening we took the Central Railway for Niagara. Alfred would have me take a walk through the cars after we had started—in order, as he said, to study physiognomy, and human nature undisguised. I don't know what benefit he may have reaped from our excursion: he talked a good deal about the different expressions of the human countenance, and so forth, afterward. For my part, I saw nothing but rows of boots on the top of seats; and I confess I am not enough of an observer to detect physiognomies in shoe-leather. I was glad enough to get back to my seat, and to snooze quietly in my uncomfortable position.

I was in the middle of a half-waking dream, in which I was reasoning with myself whether I would wear my flounced plaid silk or my blue barège at dinner on our arrival at the Falls, when the conductor shouted something in our neighborhood, and papa roused us all very violently, and bade us get out. It was pitch dark, and of course neither mamma nor I could find our traveling-bags, or our parcels, or our parasols for ten minutes at least, and the conductor and papa seemed (to judge from their language, which was any thing but Scriptural) very angry indeed; but we got every thing at last and were pushed out, and there was a shout, and a whistle, and a rumble, and away the train went; and there we stood, in Egyptian darkness, on a platform, with nobody near us but a few sleepy-looking railway people.

My first thought was to listen for the Falls. I heard nothing but the distant sound of the train. Papa went to look after the luggage. In a few moments he came back.

"By Jove!" said he, "it's scandalous. They've carried off our luggage, and left us without even a hat-box."

"Where are we?" said mamma, bridling up in wrath.

"I guess you're to Geneva . . . or Rome" (I forget what the fellow said; he was a sleepy-looking porter, or something of the kind).

"Isn't this the Falls!" I screamed.

"Reckon not, by no means," drawled the sleepy personage.

So we had missed our landing-place, but could go on, as a stern official with a lantern informed us, by an early train in the morning; and no doubt we'd find our luggage there, if it hadn't been sent back to York. There was one consolation, papa said. A party bound to the place where we were had also missed their destination, and had gone on to the Falls.

We recovered our good temper when the morning train landed us safely at the Falls. There, sure enough, was the mighty roar, and there, in the distance, was the spray falling in great clouds. Alfred and I determined to walk to the Falls—just to have one look—before we went to the hotel. A number of our fellow-passengers, imbued with the like feeling, accompanied us, and a few moments' walk brought us face to face with Niagara.

8.—ON BOARD THE "MAID OF THE MIST."

Oh Aunt! what can I say that shall give you the least inkling of that wonderful sight! We were silenced, awed by the scene. Alfred, poor fellow! squeezed my hand—I shouldn't wonder if, in my emotion, I returned the pressure—such scenes are so overpowering and absorbing. As for Alfred's friend Plendergrath, he would do nothing but suck the end of his cane, and ejaculate "By God!" at intervals.

We staid five days at the Falls. Oh! dearest Aunt, your poor niece will never know such happy days again—there are so many delightful points of view in which the Falls can be studied, and each time with additional luxury. (Papa, who, after dinner, is very sarcastic after a fashion, one evening stepped out and came upon Alfred and me as we were admiring the scenery: it was blowing so fresh, that Alfred, like a kind, good fellow, held me tight, lest I might be blown over; and papa sneeringly observed to all the company that evening that he had discovered a new point of view from which to enjoy the Falls.

"Where? where?" every body cried.

10.—AFTER WE CAME OUT OF THE CAVE OF THE WINDS.

that it was the sickness that made her so cross. Mamma climbed up to an upper berth, and couldn't sleep a wink; for the lady under her was a leader of the Woman's Rights party, who kept repeating over to herself all night a speech she intended to make—the doctrines of which were so horrid and dreadful, mamma says, that they kept her in a fever till daybreak.

11.—TABLE-ROCK.　　　　　12.—OUR CANADIAN FRIENDS.

FIGURE 4.8. Augustus Hoppin, "A Trip to Niagara Falls," *Harper's Weekly Magazine*, October 2, 1858, 633. Courtesy of Internet Archive.

The *Harper's Weekly* sequences play upon the discrepancy between expectations and realities of the Grand Tour. He crowds his frames with hordes of tourists, rushing to board steamships or catch site of a picturesque view in pleasure excursions that never turn out to be so pleasurable. At Niagara Falls, well-dressed sightseers enter the cave of the winds only to find their fine clothes and coifed hair doused with water as they creep around the tight passages underneath the falls (fig. 4.8).[46] Similarly, "Trip to the White Mountains," plays on the ironic juxtaposition in which innocuous captions (like "Old Man of the Mountain" or "Notch of the White Mountains") are paired with scenes of tourists tumbling down cliffs and hanging tight to a runaway stage coach.[47] Through scenes like this, Hoppin envisioned the American Grand Tour as both object of satire and aspirational goal.

Certainly, the vanity and materialism of Hoppin's tourists are called up for consideration. However, the humor stops short of outright ridicule and instead frames the pratfalls as snapshots, capturing spontaneous and amusing memories. The *Harper's Weekly* comics would serve as a prelude to his most productive period. In these later, more mature works, Hoppin would mobilize the complex ironies and sophisticated treatment of the perspective of "Going to Europe" in the service of book-length works that ranged through a diverse array of themes and stylistic tones.

Hoppin's Sketchbooks

The early 1870s marked a prolific period for Hoppin as he produced four full-length travel sketchbooks in the space of four years: *Ups and Down on Land and Water* (1871) was an account of a grand tour through Europe; *Crossing the Atlantic* (1872), a fictionalized account of a voyage aboard a Cunard steamer; *Hay Fever* (1873), a humorous send-up of medical tourism; and *On the Nile* (1874), a densely textured visual diary of Hoppin's trip through Marseilles, Malta, and Egypt. In these books, Hoppin expanded the blend of situational comedy and light satire that he had been developing in *Harper's Weekly* into longer, more complex works. The sketchbooks of the 1870s embarked on the fashionable tours as their subject matter, covering the Grand Tours of both Europe and America as they would have been experienced by upper-class tourists. However, in contrast to the *Harper's*

46. Hoppin, "Trip to Niagara Falls," 632–33.
47. Hoppin, "Trip to the White Mountains," 536–37.

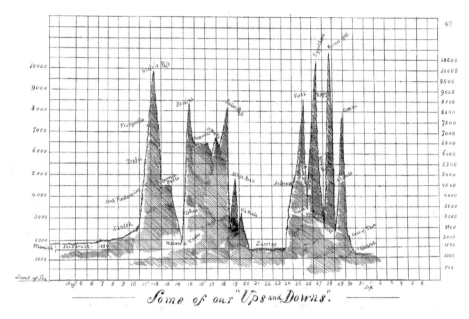

FIGURE 4.9. Augustus Hoppin, *Ups and Downs on Land and Water* (Boston: James R. Osgood & Company, 1871), 74. Courtesy of the American Antiquarian Society.

Weekly series, these sketchbooks evinced an ambition to reframe the travel comic as a distinctively literary genre through which Hoppin aspired to match the thematic and narrative scope of American prose travel writing. Hoppin purported to educate his readers through travel writing, incorporating rich detail about the places and cultures that he visited. He expanded his use of autobiographical reflection into complex, sustained meditations on his growing consciousness as a traveler.

In pursuing these heightened ambitions, Hoppin incorporated a variety of new formal techniques that imbued his travel comics with multiple, shifting perspectives. Occasionally, he turned to a first-person perspective to take readers directly into the sights and experiences of a traveler. He used collages of souvenirs and diagrams of passengers to offer glimpses into the entire collection of goods and memories accumulated over time. He even placed maps and charts into his books to create a macroscopic perspective, depicting abstract and quantitative information like travel routes and elevation (fig. 4.9).[48] In this manner, these books achieve a level of artistic and thematic sophistication in travel comics that would arguably go unmatched until the late twentieth century.

---

48. Hoppin, *Ups and Downs*, 47.

The ambition that Hoppin brought to his run of travel sketchbooks reflected broader developments in US travel writing at large. Over the course of the nineteenth century, US travel writing had matured into a multilayered genre that blended elements of education, entertainment, and autobiography. The best-regarded travel writers were at once journalists who informed audiences of interesting facts and lively commentators who burnished those facts with penetrating insights that explored the dialectic between the region and the traveling writer's thoughts and inner-self.[49] Authors like Irving, Taylor, Melville, Fuller, and Twain dabbled in a diverse array of stylistic tones ranging from the adventurous and sensational to the humorous and witty to the reflective and philosophical. In each case, the powers of the traveler to establish their personal perspective and skill as a storyteller were understood as vital to the overall appeal of the work.

This emphasis on self-reflection in travel writing (and in Hoppin's comics) was driven partly by the powerful need of US audiences to define their place and themselves in relation to the rest of the world. As scholar Jeffrey Melton notes, "American travel writers could fill a need in American readers' psyches that could never be addressed by British masters; they could offer views of the world from an avowed *American* perspective. Scott and Dickens might entertain a massive audience with their novels, but they could never give American readers the picture of an English countryside or the 'real' London that an American travel writer like Irving could."[50] By identifying the travel narrative with the gaze of an identifiably American personality, writers set up an implicit comparison between the perspective of the commentator and that of the rest of the world. These comparisons traced varied trajectories, depending on the location of the travel. Travel writers who looked eastward to Europe typically reflected on how the relatively new "American" subject descended from the wisdom of the Old World, even as it looked toward the future. Meanwhile, westward travel was more likely to chart the potential for rejuvenation and perpetual youthfulness offered by the pursuit of resources and acquisition of land.

Hoppin's first full-length travel sketchbook *Ups and Downs on Land and Water* strongly reflected the genre-blending, multilayered qualities of

---

49. For instance, E. F. Atkins's celebrated account of hay fever travel recounted a transcontinental rail journey from Boston to Sacramento in which the author tracked his vacillating symptoms, which, by turns, disappeared while passing through Omaha but reemerged upon crossing into Denver. See Savoy, "Subverted Gaze," 287.

50. Melton, *Mark Twain, Travel Books, and Tourism*, 22.

the period's more sophisticated works of travel writing. An autobiographical account of Hoppin on the Grand Tour of Europe, the book consists of a meticulous account of the sights and raw data as well as a record of Hoppin's growing consciousness. Hoppin took pains to establish an intimate, autobiographical tone both in the visuals and themes. The physical layout of the illustration replicates the look of a personal notebook. Unlike the standardized layout of most illustrated magazines or books, Hoppin's illustrations display as free-floating sketches accompanied by Hoppin's delicate cursive scrawl instead of typeface. His comic vignettes emphasize attention to minute details that might escape the notice of a less astute traveler. He eschews attention to grand landmarks and sublime scenery in favor of unadorned illustrations of peculiarities and quaint customs such as Belgians using dogs to pull carts in the market or a meal that he enjoys in a London pub. Transitions between frames form a loose chronology that navigates among the general impressions that Hoppin gathers along the way. Consequently, Hoppin rarely arranges his plates as tightly circumscribed actions or movements between landmarks. Instead, they are composed of collections of souvenirs and impressions that form an intimate portrait of his experiences as a traveler.

Hoppin's attempts to establish his travel comics as a space for personal reflection akin to American travel writers are evident in a sequence about the idiosyncrasies of an Austrian lodging house run by a peasant named Joseph Mair. Mair's sequence mingles commentary on the quirks of the lodging house with affectionate portraits that serve to humanize Hoppin's hosts. All this detail provides far more than an anthropological account of Austrian living practices. Rather, it becomes a record of Hoppin's own evolving consciousness as his whole way of seeing is reformulated. The focus of his gaze shifts from Austrians' funny eccentricities to a more intimate awareness of Austrian life. On their arrival at the lodging house, Hoppin and his companions are greeted by Mair, a peasant whom readers are told "acted the part of the Saviour in the Passion Play."[51] Hoppin orchestrates the subtlest of ironies with Mair's dual roles as "Saviour" and lodging house manager. In the first frame, Mair's physical appearance at once suggests an ethereal Christ figure *and* the more grounded role of peasant-valet. His flowing hair, delicate features and faraway gaze strike a contrast with his gruff work clothes, tattered hat, and rustic surroundings.

---

51. Hoppin, *Ups and Downs*, 21.

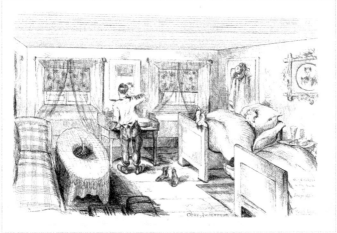

FIGURE 4.10. Augustus Hoppin, *Ups and Downs on Land and Water* (Boston: James R. Osgood & Company, 1871), 21–23. Courtesy of the American Antiquarian Society.

Hoppin does not play this duality for broad laughs as much as he uses it to add texture to his portrait of everyday Austrian life in which the distinction of performing in the Passion Play carries such great import (fig. 4.10).

As the sequence continues, Hoppin drops in subtle clues that mingle light comedic eccentricities with observations to fill out the story of Hoppin's expanding consciousness of his surroundings. Upon ascending the staircase, the travelers arrive at their cramped room. Hoppin himself is depicted lying uncomfortably in a short bed, knees crunched into his chest, feet dangling over the footboard. At the same time, Hoppin balances the joke about his discomfort with other details that highlight Mair's efforts to make their quarters feel cozy and inviting. A portrait of a family member hangs above the beds, shades carefully drape over the windows, and the matching drinking glasses lie at the bedside. These intimate details provide an important tonal break as Hoppin shifts attention away from a joke about the inconveniences of travel to reflection on the emotions and hopes of Mair's family.

Hoppin's next book, *Crossing the Atlantic*, closely resembled the style and tone of *Ups and Downs*, but the volume marked one significant change in its approach: *Crossing the Atlantic* was a work of fiction. Rather than describe landmarks and cities on the European Grand Tour, Hoppin fictionalized an account of a voyage aboard a steamer that he named *Ethiopia*. He populated the imaginary *Ethiopia* with a diverse cross-section of fictional American passengers and followed their struggles and pleasures as they made the trip between New York and Ireland. Despite its fictional origins, *Crossing the Atlantic* retained the implicit claims that the sketches could offer readers vicarious access to the experience of a fashionable tourist excursion to Europe. Hoppin filled the sketchbook with the sort of details that readers had come to expect in actual accounts of Cunard steamer trips. The opening pages feature an extensive ship manifest with the names of passengers along with their places of origin and illustrations depicting their various idiosyncrasies. Hoppin also took care to include beat-for-beat accounts of the various stages of the voyage. The book includes scenes of everyday occurrences, such as passengers eating meals and relieving their monotony by socializing on the main deck as well as logistics like spotting a pilot boat ahead of the port and the process of disembarking with luggage. These observations, while seemingly mundane, were conventional for travel writers because they appealed to readers' appetite for knowledge about the overall experience of a voyage and the spontaneous impressions that a guest aboard a steamer accumulates as they travel from one place to another.

Hoppin's background as a comic artist remained vital to the narrative techniques of *Crossing the Atlantic*. In particular, he continued to rely upon many of the old stock sequences about travel that had appeared in earlier humorous travel comics; however, Hoppin reimagined them as occasions for reflection and growth. For example, depictions of seasickness and turbulence were reliable ways for comic artists to elicit laughs and create visual spectacles through lively animation. Hoppin himself had been no stranger to this technique. In fact, the entire first two installments of *Jonathan Abroad* revolved around slapstick gags playing on steamship turbulence as a

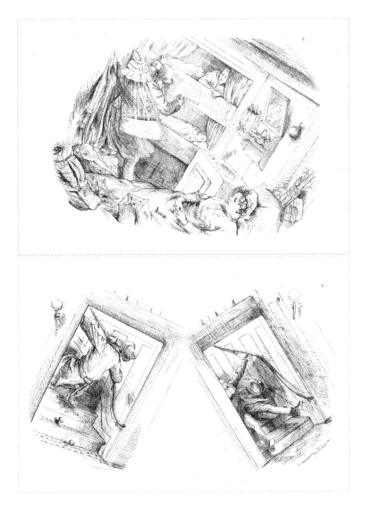

FIGURE 4.11. Augustus Hoppin, *Crossing the Atlantic* (Boston: J. R. Osgood & Company, 1872), 6–7. Courtesy of the American Antiquarian Society.

succession of passengers fall ill and are blown back by the wind. Such stock sequences do indeed appear in *Crossing the Atlantic*. But the situations and type scenes that had resolved as slapstick pratfalls in works like *Jonathan Abroad* were now reframed in ways that extended a sympathetic eye to passengers and reflected upon how the vagaries of travel led to personal growth.

As shown in figure 4.11, Hoppin intersperses sentimental and comedic modes as he depicts the effects of turbulence from a storm. In the first scene, Hoppin presents his reader with a tenderly illustrated Sir Mungo Murgatroyd gently soothing his bedridden wife while the caption sympathetically recounts, "The two Misses Murgatroyd prostrate.

Lady Murgatroyd considerably discouraged, and Sir Mungo Murgatroyd endeavoring to relieve the distress of his family with a little hot toddy."[52] Hoppin's tone takes a sharp turn toward slapstick in the next plate as a now-grizzled Sir Murgatroyd and Mr. Brownstone are tossed to and fro in the stairways. Hoppin accentuates the comedic effect by tilting his frame to simulate the shifting angle of the ship (and presumably, Murgatroyd and Brownstone's shared sense of vertigo). Following these two frames, the sequence resolves with a return to its original sentimental mode as a panoramic layout shows the peaceful repose of "the sick ones getting better and the ship dandling along at fourteen knots."[53] Quite apart from objects of a quick laugh, the experiences of figures like Sir Mungo represented the mixture of pleasure, hardship, and absurdity that Hoppin wanted his readers to imagine as part of a transatlantic steamship journey. The emergence of these complex characters, whose suffering is by turns cause for humor and sympathy, marked a significant departure from the pratfalls of earlier travel comics.

Hoppin's strategy of reimagining familiar humor conventions remained crucial to *Crossing the Atlantic*'s claims to realism. In the view of his contemporary reviewers, these humorous elements added a folksy component that must surely have come from Hoppin's own experiences. One writer commented that "scenes of 'life on the ocean wave' are reproduced with curious fidelity, presenting in their comic aspects a whimsical contrast to the somber experiences of reality."[54] "The gallery of characteristic portraits" and details such as "popping of champagne and wit of happy voyagers" would allow readers to relate to the passengers "as old acquaintances, if he has ever enjoyed the supreme felicity of crossing the Atlantic in a Cunard steamer."[55] This logic of encountering the passengers as "old acquaintances" reaches the heart of Hoppin's project in *Crossing the Atlantic*: traveling was not just about taking in sights or learning about culture on an intellectual basis but instead exploring spectrum of the spontaneously occurring impressions of the voyage.

Hoppin's interest in conveying the experiences of fashionable tourists took an idiosyncratic turn in *Hay Fever*, a very funny send-up of the mid-nineteenth-century craze for fashionable medical tourism. The piece

---

52. Hoppin, *Crossing the Atlantic*, 6.
53. Hoppin, *Crossing the Atlantic*, 9.
54. "Crossing the Atlantic Illustrated," 6.
55. "Crossing the Atlantic Illustrated," 6.

follows "Mr. Weepy," who suffers from allergies and travels throughout the United States in search of "non-catarrhal" regions free from nasal irritants. The central gag of *Hay Fever* hinges on the way that the various travel scenes, which *should* provide relief from his allergies, consistently fail to do so. Hence, Mr. Weepy visits various sites of rejuvenation throughout America only to find that the problems that plague him in the city continue to torment his sensitive mucus membranes. At first glance, *Hay Fever* seems to share little in common with the interest in fashionable tourism that characterized many of Hoppin's works through the 1870s. After all, it adopts a cartoonish visual style and relies on absurd situations that feel more at home with Western humor or children's literature than genteel travel sketchbooks like *Ups and Downs* and *Crossing the Atlantic.* However, *Hay Fever* did, in fact, form its basis in real touristic practices. Like his other sketchbooks, it was invested in offering comics as a means of celebrating the charms of travel and even offering vicarious access to the experiences of the fashionable traveler.

As early as the 1820s, well-to-do Northeasterners had begun indulging in what was known as "hay fever patronage," setting off in droves for popular resort areas along the American Grand Tour such as the White Mountains, the Adirondacks, the Great Lakes, and the Western Plateau in search of relief from seasonal allergies. By the 1870s, hay fever patronage had become something of a national pastime. Glistening hotels like the Maplewood Hotel and the Sinclair House catered to hay fever sufferers amid the White Mountains' social festivities and renowned outdoor walks. Accounts of the lively hay fever resort scene became common features of the society pages of urban newspapers, and hundreds of hay fever-related travel narratives were produced.[56] The craze reached its peak with the release of Morrill Wyman's 1872 treatise *Autumnal Catarrh.* Wyman lent scientific credence to the long-held belief that hay fever included a regional component. Wyman's book itself bears close resemblance to travel writing, featuring maps and personal accounts of Wyman's journeys through the White Mountains, where he walked on foot between hotels and resorts to interview people about their allergies as they moved from city to country.[57]

Hoppin presented *Hay Fever* as a satire of the craze, even adopting an extensive quote from Wyman as the preface. Hoppin's satire of hay fever patronage can hardly be said to function as a robust critique

---

56. Mitman, "Hay Fever Holiday," 601.

57. Mitman, "Hay Fever Holiday," 623.

of the phenomenon. Instead, it fits more comfortably into the category of an inside joke directed to others who were familiar with the pleasures and foibles of hay fever tourism. In this manner, *Hay Fever* corresponded with the broader discourse surrounding hay fever patronage, which was often distinguished by humorous banter making light of the annoyances of allergies as well as the convenient solution of using tourism as a cure. Prominent theologian Henry Ward Beecher, who regularly scheduled a late-summer vacation to the White Mountains, once remarked that "he could never be grateful enough for having been thought worthy of enrollment in the ranks of Hay Feverites" while noting "I can't get well and won't get well. . . . I esteem my six weeks' vacation in the mountains too well."[58] Beecher's comments exemplified the self-effacing stance taken by hay fever patrons. With hay fever patronage defined as light-hearted leisure rather than urgent medical treatment, there was plenty of room for inside jokes and gentle ribbing of travelers.

Hoppin filled *Hay Fever* with sights and experiences that would have been familiar to insiders or those Americans who had read the many written accounts of hay fever tourism. In this manner, the satire struck an important parallel to Hoppin's other travel sketchbooks. Like *Ups and Downs* and *Crossing the Atlantic*, Weepy's journeys tracked the experience that a fashionable tourist might expect on a hay fever excursion (fig. 4.12). Leaving his dreary existence as a clerk in the city, Mr. Weepy travels first to the tourist areas of the Northeast, visiting scenes reminiscent of the baths at Saratoga and the White Mountains; he heads to "Indian country" where he becomes "a companion of the Prairie Dog: but that affords him no relief"; he even boards a hot air balloon.[59] The climax comes with the fictive "great catarrhal belt" in which the ineffable geographic feature plays as a kind of lampoon on the mythic language of the Great Plains or the Sierras.[60] Hoppin even peppered in jokes and episodes that would seem obscure to those readers unfamiliar with hay fever tourism. For example, Weepy's miserable train ride to the seashore closely resembles a common complaint among hay fever tourists that, in attempting to escape the pollutants of the city, they were required to suffer through a train ride in which they inhaled the smoke and soot that belched from the engine.

58. Qtd. in Mitman, "Hay Fever Holiday," 620.
59. Hoppin, *Hay Fever*, 18.
60. Hoppin, *Hay Fever*, 21.

XVIII. *The coal-dust " sets him frantic:" so he flies to the Indian country, and becomes a companion of the Prairie-Dog : but that affords him no relief.*

FIGURE 4.12. Scene from Augustus Hoppin, *Hay Fever* (Boston: J. R. Osgood & Company, 1873). Courtesy of the American Antiquarian Society.

Hoppin also made light of the symbolism that hay fever tourists attached to their resort areas. In many travel accounts, hay fever tourism allied the act of locating a "non-catarrhal" region with a search for the natural sublime, verging on the spiritual. As historian Greg Mitman notes, sites like the White Mountains offered hay fever sufferers "a place whose history affirmed their social identity and shaped their relationship to the natural environment . . . a landscape devoid of their dreaded enemy, and infused with the romantic sublime."[61] The purported restorative powers prompted descriptions that aligned the White Mountains' hypoallergenic qualities with something resembling Emersonian transcendence. One writer observed, "the climate, the soils, the hotels, and the railway [were] arranged by a special kind of providence to ameliorate [their] sufferings."[62]

Hoppin's *Hay Fever* turns these lofty aspirations on their head as Mr. Weepy's dual search for physical relief and natural sublime devolves into a series of clownish antics. In each of the episodes, the recurring conceit

61. Mitman, "Hay Fever Holiday," 623.
62. Qtd. in Mitman, *Hay Fever Holiday*, 615.

plays on the way that Mr. Weepy's symptoms overshadow and undercut the claims to divine providence in picturesque landscapes. Sublime scenes of the seaside, mountaintops, and sky are literally obscured from view by the effusion of Mr. Weepy's handkerchiefs. His incessant sneezing prevents him from achieving the much-idealized unity with nature. His face contorted from a sneeze, Weepy remains unable to look upon the prairie dogs who stand at attention or the majestic panoramas of the Rocky Mountains. The juxtaposition of Hoppin's cartoonish illustration style and these sublime natural sights deflates some of the most hallowed ideals of literature and painting about traveling through the United States. Where the audience of Emerson, Taylor, and Hudson River School paintings were encouraged to understand sublime and picturesque scenery as restorative, the presence of the heavily caricatured figure of Mr. Weepy creates an intense visual irony that makes these pretensions impossible to sustain.

On the Nile, Hoppin's last travel sketchbook, stands among the most significant of his visual travelogues due to its concerted effort to push graphic narrative in increasingly ambitious directions. Unlike the earlier works, *On the Nile* demands a much slower and more attentive reading. The book features long blocks of ekphrastic description, accompanied by intricate photorealistic illustrations. Much of this treatment is done to facilitate the rich variety of perspectives and subjective experiences that Hoppin hopes to achieve through visual storytelling. The piece certainly contains the simple transitions of the earlier works in which an American traveler can be tracked from scene to scene, following their internal growth at witnessing various exotic sites. However, it also features layouts that experiment with a variety of different perspectives. In some cases, this means dynamic action-based sequences that illustrate the antics of the travelers as they struggle with the unfamiliar customs, such as entering a Turkish Bath. In others, the layouts align the reader's vision with that of the Orientalist gaze of the traveler whose vision might scan from subject to subject within a single locale or find a sense of sublime communion at a well-known tourist destination. Most often, Hoppin adopts a style that incorporates multiple overlapping visual modalities. In doing so, he achieves a kind of dual subjectivity: *On the Nile* both initiates a process of looking *at* the traveler as an external subject while simultaneously looking *through* the traveler's eyes to experience the sublime and rejuvenating effects that Hoppin imagines as part of a journey to the Middle East.

FIGURE 4.13. Augustus Hoppin, *On the Nile* (Boston: J. R. Osgood & Company, 1874), 23. Courtesy of the American Antiquarian Society.

In introducing his readers to these multiple perspectives, Hoppin interrogates the tensions and complexities of the tourist's gaze. In particular, he invites his readers to question the extent to which the gaze of the tourist is determined by consumerist ideology. Such moments of self-reflection cast *On the Nile* as a book preoccupied with tutoring its audience on how (and how not) to comprehend the picturesque imagery of the travel genre.

We notice this type of questioning in the plate entitled "Way Scenes on the Voyage to Cairo" (fig. 4.13). Hoppin's elaborate layout depicts different aspects of the traveling group's experiences near Cairo. Mostly, the illustration portrays idyllic tourist scenes of Egyptian life and terrain. Several Egyptian men crouch in a circle talking and eating bread; another man demonstrates his hookah; two of the Anglo travelers sit on a bluff admiring the camels and palm trees. However, Hoppin's caption calls these idyllic images into question by cautioning that an uncritical gaze may lead viewers astray. His prose description warns that the carefully curated route of the pleasure trip structures the tourists' gaze in potentially destructive ways. He writes, "Of course we are supposed to ignore for the moment the distress, and poverty, and general wretchedness of the people, and to

form our judgment simply from the picture before us," a carefully mani-
cured image that presents only "romantic clusters of white villages" and
"the general appearance of peacefulness and tranquility."[63] The effect is to
invite readers to reflect on and revise their viewing practices. Rather than
adopting the uncritical gaze of the tourist, Hoppin implores his audience
to examine how the search for the picturesque distracts from underlying
material realities. Hoppin's critique of the viewing practices associated with
the tourism industry reframes the whole project of travel literature itself.
The writer of the travel narrative and the travel comic, Hoppin suggests,
must attend not only to sights and experiences but to the complexities
of the very act of viewing. Although this sequence retains some elements
of a colonizing gaze (particularly in Hoppin's self-congratulatory gesture
of acting as savior to Egyptians), his self-awareness nevertheless reflects
a distinct shift away from the uncomplicated expressions of racism that
characterized his and others' earlier travel comics.

As much as Hoppin seems to maintain an earnest tone, readers can
occasionally spot small reminders that he is working in a genre that finds
its origins in humor and wit, maintaining the hallmarks of Töpffer's *Monsieur Vieux Bois* and Hoppin's own earlier humorous works. Thus, among
the whirling dervishes and other exotic sights are moments of comic relief
and even occasional pratfalls. One sequence provides a funny diagram of
how the uninitiated might mount a camel. Elsewhere, there are minor
flourishes in the artwork that subtly depart from his realist techniques.
This departure is especially evident in Hoppin's animal illustrations, which
often feature the slightest hint of cartoonish exaggeration. For example,
a distressed donkey named "Tobey No. 1" furrows his brow with a suspi-
ciously human facial expression as his trainer prepares him for cargo (fig.
4.14). Later on, when the tourists sample mocha coffee for the first time,
Hoppin comments on the "mild eyes and patient expression" of a camel
who seems enamored with the custom.[64]

This momentary turn to cartoonish humor in the otherwise realistic
world of *On the Nile* brings up an important point about Hoppin's larger
project: readers can view Töpffer's picture stories and the humorous picture
story in the United States as a potential foundation for participation in
a distinctively "literary" genre. In the early 1870s, Hoppin, his publishers,
and his reviewers all seem to envision a future in which comics participate

63. Hoppin, *On the Nile*, 23.
64. Hoppin, *On the Nile*, 30.

FIGURE 4.14. Augustus Hoppin, *On the Nile* (Boston: J. R. Osgood & Company, 1874), 30. Courtesy of the American Antiquarian Society.

directly in the respectable and lucrative market of travel writing alongside the likes of Taylor, Twain, and others. The medium of comics was understood as capable of containing the complex mix of autobiography, journalism, and cultural commentary that went into literary travel writing. They did not view comics as relegated to the literary ghettos of cheap entertainment, children's books, or the funnies page, and pursuing these heightened ambitions did not entail disavowing the conventions of comics. Elements that dated back to Hogarth and Töpffer—sketchy and cartoonish illustration style, melodramatic themes, and humor—all remain intact. Moreover, neither he nor his reviewers seem to deem this type of move as particularly ambitious or revolutionary.

The culture of comic sketchbooks in which Hoppin participated appears to have disappeared with little fanfare. Few, if any, artists identify themselves as direct successors influenced by Hoppin, Doyle, or others. Nevertheless, a bevy of twentieth- and twenty-first century works, independent of Hoppin's influence, adapted the humorous comic strip to extended travelogues with autobiographical, educational, and journalistic undertones. The most well-known of these is almost certainly Hergé's famed *Tintin* series with its protagonist's globetrotting adventures. Hergé's changing approach through the various iterations of *Tintin* is reminiscent of Hoppin's, evolving from early humorous works like *Tintin in the Land of the Soviets* (1929) in the children's magazine *Le Petit Vingtième* to subtle, introspective albums like *Tintin in Tibet* (1960). Indeed, the blend of unadorned illustration, light humor, and thematic complexity in the travel stories of *Tintin* regularly receive credit as the basis for the *ligne claire* style that would come to dominate the look and feel of Franco-Belgian *bandes desinées*. One can observe a similar dialogue between humorous comics and travel works in a host of twenty-first century graphic novels in America, whether it be autobiographical travelogues and sketchbooks like Craig Thompson's *Carnet de Voyage* (2004), Peter Kuper's *Diario de Mexico* (2009), and Eleanor Davis's *You & a Bike & a Road* (2016) or the ambitious travel journalism of Joe Sacco in works such as *Palestine* (2001) and *Days of Destruction, Days of Revolt* (2014).

The fact that these later artists would arrive at virtually the same conclusion as Hoppin did hardly seems like a mere accident of history. Rather, it suggests the rediscovery of latent potential within the medium of comics. This surprising image of twentieth- and twenty-first-century comic artists as unwitting excavators of older norms and conventions points back to the central theme of this book: The idea that so-called proto-comics were always headed toward the Sunday Funnies or superhero comics overlooks the sense of possibility that an artist like Hoppin could attach to his experiments with travel comics and other subgenres. In other words, all roads did not lead to "Rome" (or the Hearst newspapers or Marvel, as the case may be). For artists like Hoppin, comic strips were poised to make major contributions to the literary genre of "travel writing"—and possibly other areas of literary culture well. The fact that this move toward diversification would take hold in a consistent way only much later on is largely a matter of hindsight. Unfortunately, this genre of travel comics poses another example of lost literacies.

After the First Wave of US Comic Strips

The last decades of the nineteenth century marked a turning point for comic strips and picture stories in the United States. The wave that began with *Obadiah Oldbuck* and T. W. Strong's *Yankee Notions* was running out of momentum, displaced first by color magazines and then the extraordinarily successful Sunday newspaper comics. By the turn of the twentieth century, the artists, publishers, and publications who first brought comic strips to the United States had become virtually unknown to the public. Even so, this transition hardly signaled the end of the earlier comics' influence over comic strips in the United States. The eclectic repertoire and playful experimentation of the first wave of US comic strips (1842–83) remained as important guiding principles at the dawn of the Sunday newspaper comics.

Of course, the medium of the comic strip *did* eventually coalesce into the consistent visual language and conventions that would characterize twentieth-century comics. Throughout the twentieth century, a standard suite of elements like speech balloons, panel grids, fluid movement, recurring characters, and serialization became synonymous with the comics medium, extending from the funnies to the superheroes. As demonstrated in these final pages, the triumph of this standardized approach over the older experimental approach was startlingly abrupt, though it was also a transition that was never wholly completed.

By the 1870s, the format of the graphic album, which first brought Töpffer's work to the United States, had not been popular for nearly a decade. Travel albums like those of Hoppin, Doyle, and Carleton were a minor presence in the illustrated publishing market and the last gasp of a format in decline. If albums of that kind appeared in the 1880s, they have left few traces in the archive. Publications resembling the size and shape of the older graphic albums were popular in the first two decades of the twentieth century in the form of reprints of newspaper comics. Yet, these resemblances were largely coincidental as publishers appeared to have adopted the oblong format for reasons unconnected to the popularity of the Töpffer bootlegs or other graphic albums.[1]

The magazines that first featured comic strips were also fading. Strong left the business in 1865, selling *Yankee Notions* to writer Cornelius Mathews and moving to New Jersey, where he shifted his energies to real estate investments and printing show cards for other businesses. *Yankee Notions* continued for ten years after Strong's exit, but Mathews put far less emphasis on sequential comics.[2] The prestigious *Harper's New Monthly*, which had once dedicated two full pages to comic strips, stopped publishing comic strips entirely with the notable exception of occasional entries by Arthur Burdett Frost in the late 1870s and early 1880s. Several other monthlies survived into the 1870s, but they too struggled to maintain their financial prowess and artistic standards. *Nick Nax* ceased publication in 1872, followed by *Phunny Phellow* in 1873. *Comic Monthly* and *Leslie's Budget of Fun* endured through much of the 1870s, but like *Yankee Notions* were not producing the dynamic, sequential comic art that had once characterized those publications. *Wild Oats* was probably the most successful US humor publication through the mid-1870s, but it also fell on hard times in 1877 when editor George Small (a.k.a. "Bricktop") resigned, setting off an exodus of artistic talent. Between 1877 and its dissolution in 1883, *Wild Oats* relied primarily on secondhand engravings, few of which could be described as picture stories or comic strips.[3]

The forces driving this retreat were reminiscent of the developments of fifty years earlier when a convergence of technological and social changes initiated the experimental period I have described in this book. Technologies like color lithography and photoengraving rendered the time-consuming process of wood engraving obsolete almost overnight. The appearance of the earlier publications would seem antiquated to audiences after the 1880s. The cultural and artistic sensibilities, which seemed so

---

1. Smolderen, "Comics before Comics," 10.
2. West, *T. W. Strong*, 12.
3. West, "Wild Oats."

subversive when they emerged in midcentury New York, did not fare much better. The older comics appeared to many like relics of a print culture that dabbled in obscenity and failed to reflect the social diversity or values of the modern US. Frederick Burr Opper, creator of the famous newspaper comic *Happy Hooligan* (1900–1932), would thus reflect that when he started his career at *Wild Oats* in the 1870s, the comics catered to "the prevalent coarseness of public taste," a culture whose entertainment included "prize fighters [who] had not yet adopted boxing gloves" and the crude humor of "'Amateur Nights' at a Bowery theatre."[4] Needless to say, the earlier comics seemed out of step with what Opper and others saw as the broad appeal and family-friendly reputation of early twentieth-century comics.

The most immediate successors to the graphic albums and early humor magazines were color magazines like *Puck* and *Judge. Puck,* the most successful of these, began in 1876 and ran for about forty years, nearly double the time of the longest-lived magazines of the first wave of comic monthlies. Founded by Austrian immigrant Joseph Keppler, *Puck* attracted readers with beautiful full-page color political cartoons and enjoyed levels of readership and political influence that the earlier magazines could only have dreamed of. *Puck*'s circulation peaked at 125,000 copies amid growing interest in that year's presidential campaign. In many ways *Puck*'s cartoons were throwbacks to the elaborate political broadsides of the 1830s and '40s. Like these earlier works, the cartoons in *Puck* emphasized visual grandeur and complexity, crowding a single panel illustration with caricatures, allusions, and jokes that collided with forceful irony.[5] As a sign of how thoroughly the earlier humor magazines had been forgotten, Keppler's cover illustration for the first issue implied that *Puck* was the first and only humor magazine published in the United States. That illustration, titled "A Stir in the Roost: What Another Chicken?," depicted a brood of chickens, identified as major US publications including the *Tribune, Herald, Graphic, Leslie's Weekly,* and *Harper's Weekly.* The chicken labeled "*Puck*" was the oddball of the group and the only magazine title identified with humor.[6]

From the perspective of readership and distribution, color magazines like *Puck* and *Judge* were mere warm-up acts for the Sunday newspaper comics. Starting in the mid-1890s, comic strips began appearing in the

---

4. Opper, "Comics and Cartoons of Earlier Days."
5. West and Kahn, *Puck,* 11–14.
6. Gordon, *Comic Strips and Consumer Culture,* 15.

color supplements of many Sunday newspapers, signifying something new in the industry (if not the creation of a medium). In this new world of print culture, comic strips like R. F. Outcault's *Hogan's Alley* (1895), Rudolph Dirks's *The Katzenjammer Kids* (1897), Opper's *Happy Hooligan* (1900), and Jimmy Swinnerton's *The Little Tigers* (1903) were produced on an industrial scale and distributed to cities nationwide. The buying up of multiple papers by tycoons like William Randolph Hearst and Joseph Pulitzer meant that a given comic no longer appeared in a single publication but was made available to all of the papers that shared a common owner or were members of a particular newspaper syndicate.

By 1908 newspapers featuring comics boasted circulations of nearly eight million with at least eighty-three newspapers in fifty locations across the country.[7] Americans in every corner of the country were now reading what we understand today as comic strips. As a point of comparison, the graphic albums and humor magazines at the height of the first wave of comic strips enjoyed circulation in the tens of thousands and were mostly confined to the Northeast.[8] Audiences and artists for newspaper comic strips reflected the increasingly multiethnic and multiracial character of the United States. In 1890 over 30 percent of New York's population were immigrants or directly descended from an immigrant of a Central or Eastern European country. These waves of immigrants brought a new sensibility among artists and a wider audience for comics. As Jean Lee Cole puts it, "The desire to create mass appeal in an era when the audience for mass culture was increasingly multiethnic and multiracial meant that comic artists and writers had to make 'the Other Half' laugh" through comics that "displayed a breezy, urban (if not necessarily urbane) irreverence, full of ethnic dialect and comic caricature, and were packaged in eye-catching typography, vibrant color, and dynamic page design." Artists like Dirks and George Luks and the powerful editor Rudolph Block themselves all came from immigrant and working-class backgrounds and were likely recruited by newspapers for their ability to cultivate readership among these rapidly growing populations.[9]

---

7. On circulation figures and geographic distribution see Gordon, *Comic Strips and Consumer Culture*, 35–43, 161–68. See also Meyer, *Producing Mass Entertainment*, 19–26.

8. A notable exception to the regional limitations were graphic albums, especially *Obadiah Oldbuck*. See chapter 1 of this book.

9. Cole, *How the Other Half Laughs*, 7–8.

The elevated visibility of the newspapers meant that the circumstances of the artists themselves were quite different as comic strips transitioned from magazines to newspapers. In the "boisterously Bohemian" world of mid-nineteenth century comic strips, magazine artists depended on meager commissions for individual submissions and were, with only a few exceptions, anonymous to the public. Even Frank Bellew—the most prolific and successful comic strip artist of the 1850s, '60s, and '70s—received what could at best be described as middle-class earnings.[10] Years later, the final newspaper accounts to mention Bellew prior to his death were gossip pieces that ridiculed him for his frugality and preference for "cheap suits."[11] By contrast, later newspaper comic artists like Outcault and Opper were celebrities who enjoyed national name recognition, commanded hefty salaries, and even inspired bidding wars between newspaper tycoons.

Despite the vast gulf in circulation and circumstances, the approach to comics that had been pioneered by Bellew and his contemporaries in the 1850s clearly influenced the first newspaper comics when they appeared in the 1890s. The early Sunday comics sections more resembled pages from old humor magazines than the form the section would take in the decades to follow. Readers continued to encounter a cluttered assortment of multipanel strips, caricatures, and single-panel cartoons alongside jokes, anecdotes, and miscellany. The format of the actual comic strips also remained a free-for-all. There were few recurring series, and artists relied on a broad repertoire of narrative and visual techniques that could shift from week to week. Almost none of the elements that characterized the twentieth-century comic strip (e.g., recurring characters, speech balloons, standardized grids) were followed with any consistency.[12]

Oddly enough, Outcault's famous comics featuring the Yellow Kid character are among the best examples of how the newspaper comics sections of the 1890s confound the expectations that twentieth-century readers would associate with the medium. Outcault's comics in the 1890s have consistently been described by comics historians as the first comic strips in the United States. Yet a close inspection reveals that Outcault's Yellow Kid comics did not hew to a recognizably "modern" set of conventions but instead deployed an ever-shifting repertoire of techniques and

---

10. In 1867 Bellew earnings were reported as somewhere between $2,100 and $2,800 per year. "Income of Editors."

11. "Frank Bellew's Cheap Clothes"; and "One More Chance for American Art."

12. See Cole, *How the Other Half Laughs*, 70–72; and Maresca, *Society Is Nix*.

themes, reminiscent of humor magazine comics. Elements from the earlier humor magazines are demonstrated on the 1896 page pictured in figure 5.1. Alongside the cartoon, the editor inserts jokes, anecdotes, and a parody of "Bluebeard's Castle," illustrated by George Luks. A comparison with other Yellow Kid installments also reveals significant shifts in storytelling style from week to week. Some installments (like the one pictured) are cluttered single-panel cartoons, reminiscent of the satirical broadsides of the 1820s; others use sequential panel grids; still others use free-floating vignettes. Outcault mingles captions and speech balloons with incidental text appearing on street signs, placards, and clothing. His themes and plotlines vary in ways reminiscent of the subgenres I have discussed in this book. There were Yellow Kid comics based on public spectacles like horse racing and baseball, sketches of everyday life in tenements, installments presented as vaudeville performances, and travel comics inviting readers to go "Around the World with the Yellow Kid."[13] In short, the comics of Outcault and his contemporaries in the 1890s are very much the work of artists for whom experimentation and inconsistency seemed like deliberate choices.

The continued experimentation with form by Outcault and his cohorts of the 1890s invites a question: How did US comic strips evolve from a culture that embraced the multitudinous forms, genres, and methods to the now-familiar twentieth-century conventions for comic strips? As it turns out, this shift happened relatively quickly. Less than a decade after the appearance of the Yellow Kid, a reader would be hard-pressed to find a comic in a Sunday newspaper that did *not* hew to the familiar twentieth-century formula for comic strips.

If this consolidation had a smoking gun moment, it probably came sometime in the spring of 1901 when the comic strips appearing in the Hearst-owned newspapers suddenly began using speech balloons. Historian Ian Gordon notes that within a six-month period, nearly every artist who drew for Hearst—a group including Opper, Dirks, and Swinnerton—abruptly shifted from scant use of speech balloons to inclusion of that device in every installment of their weekly strips. Through 1902, speech balloons became the norm in the comics of the Joseph Pulitzer–owned newspapers and those of the McClure newspaper syndicate, effectively extending the change to every comic strip in the country. The prevalence of the speech balloon was followed by a suite of other conventions that

---

13. Even the Yellow Kid was conceived by Outcault as a social type rather than a recurring character. Outcault noted that the recurring appearances only occurred after audiences demanded them. See Gordon, *Comic Strips and Consumer Culture*, 29.

FIGURE 5.1. Richard F. Outcault, "Hogan's Alley Folk Have a Trolley Party in Brooklyn," *New York World—Colored Supplement,* August 9, 1896, 3. Courtesy of the San Francisco Academy of Comic Art Collection, Billy Ireland Cartoon Library and Museum, The Ohio State University.

would, by turns, become standard in newspaper comics. Panel grids, fluid movement, recurring characters, and serialization all became widespread conventions during the first three years of the 1900s.

Here again, Outcault's comics offer an instructive example. The release of Outcault's phenomenally successful *Buster Brown* series in 1902 offered a powerful demonstration of how quickly a standardized set of conventions had taken hold. *Buster Brown* featured few signs of the playful experimentation with form that had been a hallmark of the earlier comics featuring the Yellow Kid. Instead, *Buster Brown* maintained a consistent and predictable format, making use of speech balloons, fluid motion, recurring characters, and the same repetitive gag (fig. 5.2). Each week, Buster spent the first few frames of the comic getting into minor mischief amid a simple activity like going to the zoo, visiting the dentist, or having a birthday party. The comic then predictably concluded with a pratfall followed by Buster writing a humorous "resolution" about lessons he had learned over the course of that week's strip. In fact, the conventions of *Buster Brown* were so consistent and predictable that a reader could conceivably skip right to the slapstick punchline and humorous resolution simply by directing their attention to the last two frames. With only occasional exceptions, Outcault would follow these conventions closely over the course of *Buster Brown*'s twenty-year run.

While the precise reasons for the sudden exercise of editorial control in newspaper comics are unclear, it seems likely that publishers demanded a more predictable reading experience in response to comics' new status as a form of serialized mass entertainment. As Gordon notes, the new, more consistent comic sections were "better able to enter into a contract with readers by giving them what they wanted without too many surprises" and thus were copacetic with the culture industry's efforts to habituate the public to a routine of buying newspapers and comics.[14] Readers returning to *Buster Brown* or later installments of *The Katzenjammer Kids* did not need to cultivate literacy in the broad repertoire of techniques that characterized the earlier comics. The spring of 1901 was, in essence, the moment when the comic strip increasingly became what Scott McCloud terms "an invisible art"—a style of storytelling and visual communication in which readers could absorb action and dialogue with near subconscious efficiency.[15]

The new consistency in comics conventions paved the way for a host of innovations that allowed the medium to adapt to a new media landscape. Many critics have noted the affinities between the speech balloon and emerging forms of mechanized audiovisual technology at the turn of the twentieth century. Where technologies like the phonograph helped

14. Gordon, "Comic Strips" in *Comics Studies*, 18. See also Gordon, *Comic Strips and Consumer Culture*, 34–36.

15. McCloud, *Understanding Comics*, 60–69. See also Petersen, "Ineffable Image."

FIGURE 5.2. Richard F. Outcault, "Buster Brown Has a Birthday Party," *New York Herald—Comic Section*, October 19, 1902, 4. Courtesy of the San Francisco Academy of Comic Art Collection, Billy Ireland Cartoon Library and Museum, The Ohio State University.

audiences become accustomed to the instant gratification of sound delivered automatically to a passive listener, the speech balloon offered a parallel suggestion that sound could be assimilated directly into the flow of a strip's progressive action.[16] Equally important to the creation of a new sort of audiovisual stage were the robust forms of continuity in character and plot. Consistent storytelling methods paired with serialization laid the foundation for the development of more consistent characters and serialized storylines. The routine of encountering the same characters and settings in a common visual language imbued those figures with a powerful sense of coherence. Rather than relying on social types for context, readers now followed along with the continuing and often repetitive adventures of "mass

16. Exner, "Creation of the Comic Strip"; and Smolderen, *Origins of Comics*, 143.

mediated personalities" with whom readers developed a relationship as time progressed.[17] And the consistent use of panel grids and sequences depicting fluid movement created sensations of motion that presented themselves to the reader with stunning efficiency. This new approach to movement reached its apogee with the minimalism of Ernie Bushmiller's classic strip *Nancy* (1938). Bushmiller's instantly legible visual signs and tightly managed panel transitions produced a viewing experience so seamless that it bore a closer resemblance to the experience of watching a film than reading lines of text.[18] As one observer put it, it was "harder to *not* read *Nancy*" than to read it.[19] The same could be said for many of the comics appearing in newspapers and comic books throughout the twentieth century.

Yet, the transition to a uniform, streamlined visual language was never truly completed. Even as the editorial policies of the Sunday supplement embraced the concise vigor of an immediately legible approach, the artists themselves continued to find ways to experiment with form. Almost from the moment that stable conventions were established in newspaper comics, a new generation of rulebreakers emerged. Artists like Winsor McCay, George Herriman, and Lyonel Feininger all treated the newly established conventions as mere points of departure for new creative improvisations— rules that were meant to be broken. In the shifting dream landscapes and broken frames of McCay's *Little Nemo in Slumberland* (1905) readers thus encountered what critic Scott Bukatman describes as "a space of play and plasmatic possibility in which the stable site of reading or viewing yields to an onslaught of imaginative fantasy."[20] Parallel disruptions of convention occurred in the ever-shifting layouts and absurdist dialogues of Herriman's *Krazy Kat* (1913) and in Feininger's infusion of expressionist art into *The Kinder Kids* (1905) and *Wee Willie Winkie's World* (1906).[21]

What is more, those instances where the façade of stable conventions broke down are also among the most widely celebrated comics of the twentieth and twenty-first centuries. The "plasmatic possibilities" that Bukatman identifies in McCay are echoed across a range of modern comics' most widely lauded works, whether it be the imaginative improvisations of Bill

17. Gardner, *Projections*, 13.

18. Experiments with eye-tracking tests showed that viewers' absorption of movement in Bushmiller's *Nancy* typically precedes semantic comprehension of plot or dialogue. Newgarden and Karasik, *How to Read Nancy*, 73.

19. Qtd. in Newgarden and Karasik, *How to Read Nancy*, 23.

20. Bukatman, *Poetics of Slumberland*, 1.

21. Chute and DeKoven, "Comic Books and Graphic Novels," 178–80.

Watterson's *Calvin & Hobbes*, alternative comics' treatment of the medium as an "acutely personal means of artistic expression and self-expression" through the work of figures like Art Spiegelman and Lynda Barry, or in the technologically driven innovations of webcomic artists like Andrew Hussie and Kate Beaton. These artists are all rightly admired for innovative approaches that, in calling attention to new and experimental ways of reading comics, also introduce the possibility of new realms of visual and verbal perception. And while few can doubt the accomplishments of these figures, the history of nineteenth-century US comics helps us reframe them as members of a continuous tradition—throwbacks of sorts. Like their nineteenth-century counterparts, these latter-day rulebreakers excel at encouraging their readers to cultivate literacy in novel forms of visual and verbal perception. If the history of nineteenth-century US comics tells us anything, it is that deliberate attempts at formal innovation and play with perception were, from the start, some of the most exciting elements of the medium of the comic strip.

BIBLIOGRAPHY

Archives

American Antiquarian Society.

American Antiquarian Society Digital Collections, https://www.americanantiquarian. org/digital-collections.

American Broadsides and Ephemera, https://www.readex.com/products/american-broadsides-and-ephemera1749-1900.

America's Historical Newspapers from Readex, https://www.readex.com/products/americas-historical-newspapers.

American Historical Periodicals from the American Antiquarian Society, https://www. gale.com/primary-sources/american-historical-periodicals/.

Beinecke Rare Book and Manuscript Library Digital Resources at Yale University, https:// beinecke.library.yale.edu/digital-collections/digital-collections-beinecke-library.

Billy Ireland Cartoon Library and Museum, The Ohio State University.

Billy Ireland Cartoon Library and Museum Digital Collections, The Ohio State University, https://cartoons.osu.edu/collections/.

Google Books, https://books.google.com.

Harvard Digital Collection, https://library.harvard.edu/digital-collections.

Hathitrust, www.hathitrust.org.

Internet Archive, https://archive.org.

New York Public Library Digital Collections, https://digitalcollections.nypl.org.

Project Gutenberg, https://www.gutenberg.org.

San Francisco Academy of Comic Art Collection, The Ohio State University, Billy Ireland Cartoon Library and Museum.

Thomas Butler Gunn Diaries, Missouri Historical Society, https://mohistory.org/collections/item/A0632.

Online Resources for Periodicals and Graphic Albums

Most of the periodicals and graphic albums described in this book can be found online, often on open access sites. The directory below was accurate as of this writing (2023). Please refer to the Archives section for URLs.

Periodicals

American Comics Magazine (1834)
    American Historical Periodicals

American Pictorial (1848)
    American Historical Periodicals

Brother Jonathan (1842)
    American Historical Periodicals; Beinecke Library; Internet Archive

Comic Monthly (1859)
    American Historical Periodicals

Comic World (1855)
    American Historical Periodicals

Daily Graphic (1873)
    American Broadsides and Ephemera

Diogenes, Hys Lantern (1852)
    American Historical Periodicals; Hathitrust; Google Books

Elephant (1848)
    No known online access

Galaxy of Comicalities (1833)
    American Historical Periodicals

Genius of Comedy, or Life in New York (1831)
    American Historical Periodicals

Giglampz (1874)
    American Historical Periodicals; Hathitrust

Harper's Monthly (1850)
    American Historical Periodicals; Google Books; Hathitrust; Internet Archive

Harper's Weekly (1857)
    American Historical Periodicals; Google Books; Hathitrust; Internet Archive

John Donkey (1848)
American Historical Periodicals; Google Books; Hathitrust; Internet Archive

Jolly Joker (1862)
No known online access

Jubilee Days (1872)
American Historical Periodicals; Google Books; Hathitrust

Judge (1881)
Hathitrust

Judy (1846)
Hathitrust; Google Books

Leslie's Budget of Fun (1859)
American Historical Periodicals

Life (1883)
Hathitrust; Internet Archive

L'illustration: Journal Unversel
Internet Archive

Little Joker (1864)
American Historical Periodicals

Magpie (1868)
American Historical Periodicals; Hathitrust

Merryman's Monthly (1864?)
American Historical Periodicals; Hathitrust; Google Books

Mrs. Grundy (1865)
American Historical Periodicals; Hathitrust; Google Books

Nick Nax for All Creation (1852)
American Historical Periodicals

Old Soldier (1852)
American Historical Periodicals

Penny Yankee Doodle (1850)
American Historical Periodicals

Picayune (1851)
American Historical Periodicals

Pictorial John Donkey (1848)
American Historical Periodicals

Puck (1877)
American Historical Periodicals; Hathitrust; Google Books

Punchinello (1870)
American Historical Periodicals; Hathitrust; Google Books

Scraps (1829)
    American Antiquarian Society Digital

Vanity Fair (1860)
    American Historical Periodicals; Hathitrust; Google Books

Wild Oats (1872)
    American Historical Periodicals

Yankee Doodle (1846)
    American Historical Periodicals; Hathitrust; Google Books

Yankee Notions (1852)
    Hathitrust; American Historical Periodicals; Google Books

Young America (1856)
    American Historical Periodicals; Hathitrust; Google Books

Graphic Albums

The Adventures of Mr. Tom Plump (1850).
    Beinecke; Internet Archive

A.L.C. (pseud.). *The Wonderful! And Soul Thrilling Adventures by Land and Sea of Oscar Shanghai* (1855).
    Beinecke

Attwood, Francis Gilbert. *Manners and Customs of Ye Harvard Studente* (1877).
    Hathitrust; Internet Archive

Avery, Samuel Putnam. *My Friend Wriggles* (1850).
    No known online access

Bisbee. *Look before You Leap* (1872).
    No known online access

Carleton, George Washington. *Our Artist in Cuba* (1865).
    Google Books; Internet Archive; Hathitrust; Project Gutenberg

———. *Our Artist in Peru* (1866).
    Google Books; Internet Archive; Hathitrust

Cope, Horace. *The Reverend Mr. Sourball's European Tour* (1867).
    Google Books; Hathitrust

Cruikshank, George. *The Bachelor's Own Book* (Carey & Hart edition, 1845).
    Internet Archive

Delano, Alonzo. *The Miner's Progress* (1853).
    No known online access

Doyle, Richard. *The Laughable Adventures of Messrs. Brown, Jones, and Robinson!* (Dick & Fitzgerald edition, 1855).
    Beinecke

The Fortunes of Ferdinand Flipper (1855).
Beinecke

Gunn, Thomas Butler. *Mose among the Britishers* (1850).
New York Public Library Digital

Hayward, Nathan. *College Scenes* (1850).
No known online access

Hoppin, Augustus. *Crossing the Atlantic* (1872).
Google Books; Hathitrust; Internet Archive

———. *Hay Fever* (1873).
Google Books; Hathitrust; Internet Archive

———. *On the Nile* (1874).
Harvard Digital

———. *Ups and Downs on Land and Water* (1871).
Google Books; Hathitrust; Internet Archive

The Hunting Adventures and Exploits of Peter Piper in Bengal (1856).
No known online access

McLenan, John. *The Sad Tale of the Courtship of Chevalier Slyfox-Wikof* (1855).
Beinecke

Perk, Abner. *Merry Maple Leaves* (1872).
Google Books; Hathitrust; Internet Archive

Peters, William Thompson, et al., *The College Experience of Ichabod Academicus* (1849).
Beinecke; Google Books; Hathitrust

Read, James Alexander, and Donald Read. *Journey to the Gold Diggins* (1849).
Beinecke; Internet Archive

Schmitz, Matthew S. *The Sure Water Cure* (1840).
No known online access

Töpffer, Rodolphe. *The Adventures of Mr. Obadiah Oldbuck* (Wilson & Co. edition, 1844).
Beinecke; Internet Archive

———. *The Strange Adventures of Bachelor Butterfly* (1846).
Internet Archive; Hathitrust

XOX (pseud.). *Outline of an Expedition to California* (1849).
Beinecke

Sources

Adcock, John. Email to the author. June 25, 2021.

"An Adventure with a New-Jersey Mosquito." *Wild Oats,* October 16, 1873.

"The Adventures of Jeremiah Oldpot." *Yankee Notions,* March 1852.

"The Adventures of Jeremiah Oldpot." *Yankee Notions,* April 1852.

"Adventures of McTiffin at Long Branch." *Frank Leslie's Budget of Fun,* October 1866.

"The Adventures of Mr. Tom Plump." In *The Picture Book.* New York: Huestis & Cozans, 1850.

"The Adventures of Noahdiah Nobbs." *Brother Jonathan,* July 4, 1850.

"Advertising for a Wife." *Nick Nax for All Creation,* November 1856.

Agassiz, Louis. "A Letter from Professor Agassiz—Rodolph Toppfer, and Swiss and American Literature (from the *New York Evening Post*)." *Sacramento Daily Union,* December 5, 1865.

A.L.C. (pseud.). *The Wonderful! And Soul Thrilling Adventures by Land and Sea of Oscar Shanghai.* New York: Dick & Fitzgerald, 1855.

Alcott, Louisa May. *Kitty's Class Day.* Boston: Loring, 1876.

Allen, Robert Clyde. *Horrible Prettiness: Burlesque and American Culture.* Chapel Hill: University of North Carolina Press, 1991.

American Bibliopolist. Vol. 7. New York: J. Sabin & Sons, 1875.

"Archaelogical Intelligence." *Yankee Notions,* April 1858.

The Art of Landscape Painting in Water Colours. New York: T. W. Strong and G. W. Cottrell, 1850.

"At the Springs." *Nick Nax for All Creation,* September 1863.

Attwood, Francis Gilbert. *Manners and Customs of Ye Harvard Studente.* Boston: J. R. Osgood & Co., 1877.

"Au Bal Masque." *Le Charivari,* March 8, 1862.

"Au Bal Masque." *Le Charivari,* March 15, 1862.

"Au Bal Masque." *Le Charivari,* March 18, 1862.

Austin, Gilbert, Lester Thonssen, and Mary Margaret Robb. *Chironomia; or, A Treatise on Rhetorical Delivery.* Carbondale: Southern Illinois University Press, 1966.

Avery, Samuel Putnam. *My Friend Wriggles.* New York: Stearns & Company, 1850.

Avery, Samuel Putnam, Felix Octavius Carr Darley, Augustus Hoppin, William John Hennessy, and John McLenan. *The Harp of a Thousand Strings, or, Laughter for a Lifetime.* New York: Dick & Fitzgerald, 1858.

Bank, Rosemary. *Theatre Culture in America: 1825–1860.* New York: Cambridge University Press, 1997.

Barnes, James. *Authors, Publishers, and Politicians: The Quest for an Anglo-American Copyright Agreement.* Columbus: The Ohio State University Press, 1974.

Beard, Frank. "Old Time Art and Artists: Something About the Early Newspaper Illustrators in America and Samples of Their Work." *Our Day,* February 1896.

Beerbohm, Robert Lee. "Platinum Era Comic Books and Periodicals." Accessed January 18, 2023. https://www.facebook.com/groups/platinumperiodicals.

Bellew, Frank. *Art of Amusing Being a Collection of Graceful Arts, Merry Games, Odd Tricks, Curious Puzzles, and New Charades, Together with Suggestions for Private Theatricals, Tableaux, and All Sorts of Parlor and Family Amusements.* New York: G. W. Carleton & Co., 1867.

———. *A Bad Boy's First Reader.* New York: G. W. Carleton & Co., 1881.

———. "Brigham Blake, the Mormon Prophet, 'The Triangle' Visits Wallack's Theatre." *The Picayune,* June 2, 1858.

———. "The Fight for the Championship." *Comic Monthly,* May 1860.

———. "The 'Fourth' and the Pig." *Nick Nax for All Creation,* July 1856.

———. "Fourth of July." *Comic Monthly,* July 1861.

———. "Hot!: A Letter from Our Artist" *The Picayune,* July 12, 1856.

———. *Jeff Petticoats.* New York: American News Company, 1866.

———. "Life of Jeff Davis in Five Expressive Tableaux." *Comic Monthly,* September 1861.

———. "Master Charley in the Snow." *Harper's New Monthly Magazine,* February 1860.

———. "Master Charley's First Pantaloons." *Harper's New Monthly Magazine,* April 1860.

———. "Master Charley's Fourth of July." *Harper's New Monthly Magazine,* August 1859.

———. "Master Charlie's Sidewalk Acquaintances." *Harper's New Monthly Magazine,* November 1857, 861–62.

———. "Master Peter's Pranks with the Paint Pot." *Comic Monthly,* April 1861.

———. "More about Dog Days." *The Picayune,* August 2, 1856.

———. "Mr. Bulbear's Dream." *Diogenes Hys Lantern,* April 24, 1852.

———. "Mr. Bulbear's Dream—Continued." *Diogenes Hys Lantern,* May 15, 1852.

———. "Pictures by Our Dog Worryin' Artist." *The Picayune,* July 26, 1856.

———. "Recollections of Ralph Waldo Emerson." *Lippincott's Magazine of Popular Literature and Science,* July 1884.

———. "Samson Shanghai's Three Days on a Farm." *Harper's New Monthly Magazine,* June 1856.

———. "The Skirt Movement." *Yankee Notions,* January 1856.

———. "Tricks upon Canines." *Nick Nax for All Creation,* August 1857.

Blackbeard, Bill. "The Yellow Kid, the Yellow Decade." In *R. F. Outcault's The Yellow Kid: A Centenial Celebration of the Kid Who Started the Comics,* edited by Bill Blackbeard, 16–136. Northampton: Kitchen Sink Press, 1995.

Blackbeard, Bill, and Martin Williams, eds. *The Smithsonian Collection of Newspaper Comics.* 7th print. Washington, DC: Smithsonian Institution Press, 1988.

Bohan, Ruth. "Vanity Fair, Whitman, and the Counter Jumper." *Word & Image* 33, no. 1 (March 15, 2017): 57–69.

"Bohemian Days at Pfaff's." *New York Herald,* April 26, 1890.

"Books Just Rec'd." *Plain Dealer,* March 12, 1846.

Booth, Michael. "Comedy and Farce." In *The Cambridge Companion to Victorian and Edwardian Theatre,* edited by Kerry Powell, 129–44. Cambridge: Cambridge University Press, 2004.

Bricker, Andrew Benjamin. *Libel and Lampoon: Satire in the Courts, 1670–1792.* Oxford: Oxford University Press, 2022.

Brooks, Peter. *The Melodramatic Imagination: Balzac, Henry James, Melodrama, and the Mode of Excess.* New York: Columbia University Press, 1985.

"Brother Jonathan." *The Sun,* September 15, 1842.

Browder, Laura. *Slippery Characters: Ethnic Impersonators and American Identities.* Chapel Hill: University of North Carolina Press, 2000.

Brown, Dona. *Inventing New England: Regional Tourism in the Nineteenth Century.* Washington, DC: Smithsonian Books, 2014.

Brown, Jane E., and Richard Samuel West. *William Newman: A Victorian Cartoonist in London and New York.* Northampton: Periodyssey Press, 2008.

Brown, Joshua. *Beyond the Lines: Pictorial Reporting, Everyday Life, and the Crisis of Gilded-Age America.* Berkeley: University of California Press, 2002.

Brown, T. Allston. *A History of the New York Stage from the First Performance in 1732 to 1901.* Vol. 1. New York: Dodd, Mead, and Company, 1902.

Buckley, Peter George. "To the Opera House: Culture and Society in New York City." Dissertation, State University of New York at Stony Brook, 1984.

"The Budget's Review." *Bedford Street Budget,* July 9, 1845.

Bukatman, Scott. *The Poetics of Slumberland: Animated Spirits and the Animating Spirit.* Berkeley: University of California Press, 2012.

Burrows, Edwin G., and Mike Wallace. *Gotham: A History of New York City to 1898.* Oxford: Oxford University Press, 1999.

Butler, Judith. *Gender Trouble: Feminism and the Subversion of Identity.* New York: Routledge, 2007.

Butsch, Richard. *The Making of American Audiences: From Stage to Television, 1750–1990.* Cambridge: Cambridge University Press, 2000.

"The California Volunteer." *Yankee Doodle,* October 17, 1846.

Carbonell, John. Email to the author, April 14, 2020.

"Caricature in America." *Art Union,* November 1885.

Carleton, George Washington. *Our Artist in Cuba: Leaves from the Sketch-Book of a Traveller during the Winter of 1864–5.* New York: G. W. Carleton & Co., 1865.

———. *Our Artist in Peru: Leaves from the Sketch-Book of a Traveller during the Winter of 1865–6.* New York: G. W. Carleton & Co., 1866.

———. "Tale of an Umbrella." *Yankee Notions,* January 1857.

Carpenter, Frank G. "American Cartoons: Interview with Frank Beard, Illustrated by Himself." *Sunday Oregonian,* September 15, 1895.

———. "Taught by Pictures." *Evening Star,* September 14, 1895. Library of Congress.

Carracci, Annibale. *Diverse Figure al Numero Di Ottanta.* Marlborough, Wiltshire: Adam Matthew Digital, 2010. https://www.londonlowlife.amdigital.co.uk/documents/detail/diverse-figure-al-numero-di-ottanta-disegnate-di-penna-nellhore-di-ricreatione-da-annibale-carracci-intagliate-in-rame-e-cavate-dagli-originali-da-simone-gvilino-parigino-per-utile-di-tvtti-li-virtvosi-et-intendenti-della-professione-della-pittura-e-del-disegno./572004.

Carroll, A. L. "Four Experiences in Waltzing." *Harper's New Monthly Magazine,* July 1863.

"The Celebrated Racer de Meyer." *Yankee Doodle,* September 1846.

Cham (Amédée de Noé). "Aventures Anciennes et Nouvelles d'un Chasseur Connu." *L'illustration: Journal Unversel,* September 20, 1845.

Chaney, Michael A. *Reading Lessons in Seeing: Mirrors, Masks, and Mazes in the Autobiographical Graphic Novel.* Jackson: University Press of Mississippi, 2016.

Childs, Elizabeth. "Big Trouble: Daumier, Gargantua, and the Censorship of Political Caricature." *Art Journal* 51, no. 1 (Spring 1992): 26–37.

Chute, Hillary, and Marianne Dekoven. "Comic Books and Graphic Novels." In *Cambridge Companion to Popular Fiction,* edited by Scott McCracken and David Glover, 175–92. Cambridge: Cambridge University Press, 2012.

Chute, Hillary L., and Patrick Jagoda. *Comics & Media: A Special Issue of Critical Inquiry.* Chicago: University of Chicago, 2014.

Cliff, Nigel. *The Shakespeare Riots: Revenge, Drama, and Death in Nineteenth-Century America.* First edition. New York: Random House, 2007.

Clytus, Radiclani. "Visualizing in Black Print: The Brooklyn Correspondence of William J. Wilson Aka 'Ethiop.'" *J19: The Journal of Nineteenth Century Americanists* 6, no. 1 (Spring 2018): 29–66.

Cockrell, Dale. *Demons of Disorder: Early Blackface Minstrels and Their World.* Cambridge: Cambridge University Press, 1997.

Cole, Jean Lee. *How the Other Half Laughs: The Comic Sensibility in American Culture, 1895–1920.* Jackson: University Press of Mississippi, 2020.

Colletta, Lisa. "Introduction." In *The Legacy of the Grand Tour: New Essays on Travel, Literature, and Culture,* edited by Lisa Colletta, ix–xx. Madison, WI: Fairleigh Dickinson University Press, 2015.

Cope, Horace. *The Reverend Mr. Sourball's European Tour: The Recreations of a City Parson.* Philadelphia: Duffield Ashmead, 1867.

Couperie, Pierre, and Maurice C. Horn. *A History of the Comic Strip.* New York: Crown, 1968.

"Courting." *Yankee Notions,* 1860.

Crary, Jonathan. *Techniques of the Observer: On Vision and Modernity in the Nineteenth Century.* Cambridge, MA: MIT Press, 1990.

Crayon, Porte. "Artists' Excursion over the Baltimore & Ohio Railroad." *Harper's New Monthly Magazine,* June 1858.

"Crossing the Atlantic Illustrated by Augustus Hoppin." *New York Tribune,* June 14, 1872.

Cruikshank, George. *The Bachelor's Own Book.* Philadelphia: Carey & Hart, 1845.

———. "The Toothache." *Brother Jonathan,* June 17, 1854.

Cvetkovich, Ann. "Drawing the Archive in Alison Bechdel's Fun Home." *Women's Studies Quarterly* 36, no. 1 & 2 (Spring/Summer 2008): 111–28.

"Daily Bulletin of New and Cheap Publications." *American and Commercial Daily Advertiser,* March 3, 1846.

Darley, Felix Octavius Carr. "Cover Page." *The John-Donkey,* January 14, 1848.

———. "The Modern Drama." *Pictorial John Donkey,* April 1848.

———. "Shakespeare Illustrated." *The John-Donkey,* April 15, 1848.

———. "Shakespeare Illustrated." *The John-Donkey,* May 13, 1848.

Dauber, Jeremy Asher. *American Comics: A History.* New York: Norton, 2022.

Davenport, M. "The Doleful History of an Omnibus Horse." *Harper's New Monthly Magazine,* August 1860.

Davis, Eleanor. *You & a Bike & a Road.* Toronto: Koyama Press, 2017.

"Death of Frank Bellew." *Boston Herald,* June 30, 1888.

Delano, Alonzo. *The Miner's Progress, or, Scenes in the Life of a California Miner.* Sacramento: Daily Union Office, 1853.

Detsi-Diamanti, Zoe. "Staging Working-Class Culture: George A. Baker's 'A Glance at New York' (1848)." *Hungarian Journal of English and American Studies (HJEAS)* 15, no. 1 (2009): 11–26.

DiGirolamo, Vincent. *Crying the News: A History of America's Newsboys.* Oxford: Oxford University Press, 2016.

Doesticks, Q. K. Philander. "Doesticks Goes Trout-Fishing." *The Picayune,* August 29, 1857.

———. *Doesticks' Letters and What He Says.* Philadelphia: T. B. Peterson, 1855.

Doesticks, Q. K. Philander, and John McLenan. *Pluribustah, a Song with No Author.* New York: Livermore & Rudd, 1856.

Doyle, Richard. *The Laughable Adventures of Messrs. Brown, Jones, and Robinson!* New York: Dick & Fitzgerald, 1855.

DuComb, Christian. *Haunted City: Three Centuries of Racial Impersonation in Philadelphia*. Ann Arbor: University of Michigan Press, 2017.

Eisner, Will. *Comics and Sequential Art*. Tamarac, FL: Poorhouse Press, 1985.

"Englishmen's First Night in America." *Yankee Notions*, November 1865.

"Frank Bellew's Cheap Clothes." *Evening Star*, July 16, 1887.

"An Every-Day Adventure." *Leslie's Budget of Fun*, July 1860.

Exner, Eike. "The Creation of the Comic Strip as an Audiovisual Stage in the New York Journal 1896–1900." *ImageTexT: Interdisciplinary Comics Studies* 10, no. 1 (2018). https://imagetextjournal.com/the-creation-of-the-comic-strip-as-an-audiovisual-stage-in-the-new-york-journal-1896-1900/.

Eytinge, Solomon. "Recruiting for the War, in the City Hall, New York." *New York Illustrated News*, October 21, 1861.

"Famous as an Artist." *Boston Herald*, April 3, 1896.

Faflik, David. *Boarding Out: Inhabiting the American Urban Literary Imagination, 1840–1860*. Evanston, IL: Northwestern University Press, 2012.

"Fashions for 1867." *Nick Nax for All Creation*, February 1867.

"Fatal Case of Destitution and Infatuation." *Yankee Doodle*, February 20, 1847.

"The First Cigar." *Merryman's Monthly*, September 1864.

Fletcher, H. M. "Rodolphe Töpffer, The Genevese Caricaturist." *The Atlantic*, November 1865.

The Fortunes of Ferdinand Flipper. New York: Brother Jonathan, 1855.

"Frank Bellew, the Artist Who Died on Long Island." *Springfield Republican*, July 2, 1888.

"Frank Leslie to His Beloved Budgeteers." *Leslie's Budget of Fun*, September 1, 1860.

"Frank Leslie to the Budgetonians." *Leslie's Budget of Fun*, May 1, 1859.

"Frank Leslie to the Budgetonians." *Leslie's Budget of Fun*, September 15, 1860.

"From the Seat of War by Our Own Correspondent." *Comic Monthly*, May 1862.

"Fun for the Million." *Nick Nax for All Creation*, April 1858.

Gardner, Jared. "Antebellum Popular Serialities and the Transatlantic Birth of 'American' Comics." In *Media of Serial Narrative*, edited by Frank Kelleter, 37–52. Columbus: The Ohio State University Press, 2019.

———. *Projections: Comics and the History of Twenty-First-Century Storytelling*. Stanford, CA: Stanford University Press, 2012.

Gombrich, Ernst. *Art and Illusion: A Study in the Psychology of Pictorial Representation*. Princeton, NJ: Princeton University Press. Accessed December 27, 2022. https://archive.org/details/artillusionstud0000gomb/page/n9/mode/2up.

Gordon, Ian. "Comic Strips." In *Comics Studies: A Guidebook*, edited by Charles Hatfield and Bart Beaty, 13–24. New Brunswick, New Jersey: Rutgers University Press, 2020.

———. *Comic Strips and Consumer Culture, 1890–1945.* Washington, DC: Smithsonian Institution Press, 1998.

Graeme, Davison. "Little Boy from Manly." In *The Oxford Companion to Australian History,* edited by Davison Graeme, John Hirst, and Stuart Macintyre. Oxford: Oxford University Press, 2001. https://www.oxfordreference.com/view/10.1093/acref/9780195515039.001.0001/acref-9780195515039-e-891.

Graeme, Everitt. *English Caricaturists and Graphic Humourists of the Nineteenth Century: How They Illustrated and Interpreted Their Time.* London: Swan Sonnenschein, Le Bas & Lowery, 1886. https://archive.org/details/englishcaricaturoo_0/.

Grennan, Simon, Roger Sabin, and Julian Waite. *Marie Duval: Maverick Victorian Cartoonist.* Manchester: Manchester University Press, 2020.

Groensteen, Thierry. *M. Töpffer invente la bande dessinée.* Bruxelles: Les Impressions Nouvelles, 2014.

———. *The System of Comics.* Translated by Bart Beaty and Nick Nguyen. Jackson: University Press of Mississippi, 2007.

Gunn, Thomas Butler. *Mose among the Britishers.* Philadelphia: A. Hart, 1850. https://digitalcollections.nypl.org/items/f0ac6720-c864-012f-233b-58d385a7b928.

———. *The Physiology of New York Boarding-Houses.* Edited by David Faflik. New Brunswick, NJ: Rutgers University Press, 2009.

———. "The Restaurants of New York: House of Lords." *New York Picayune,* March 26, 1859.

———. *Thomas Butler Gunn Diaries Volume 5.* Diary. St. Louis, MO, 1852–53. Missouri Historical Society.

———. *Thomas Butler Gunn Diaries Volume 9.* Diary. St. Louis, MO, 1857–58. Missouri Historical Society.

———. *Thomas Butler Gunn Diaries Volume 11.* Diary. St. Louis, MO, 1859. Missouri Historical Society.

———. *Thomas Butler Gunn Diaries Volume 12.* Diary. St. Louis, MO, 1860. Missouri Historical Society.

———. *Thomas Butler Gunn Diaries Volume 14.* Diary. St. Louis, MO, 1860. Missouri Historical Society.

———. *Thomas Butler Gunn Diaries Volume 18.* Diary. St. Louis, MO, 1861–62. Missouri Historical Society.

Gunning, Tom. "The Art of Succession: Reading, Writing, and Watching Comics." *Critical Inquiry* 40, no. 3 (Spring 2014): 36–51.

———. "The Cinema of Attractions: Early Film, Its Spectator and the Avant-Garde." In *Early Film: Space, Frame, Narrative,* edited by Thomas Elsaesser and Adam Barker, 56–63. London: British Film Institute, 1990.

———. "Hand and Eye: Excavating a New Technology of the Image in the Victorian Era." *Victorian Studies* 54, no. 3 (March 22, 2012): 495.

Guth, Christine. *Art of Edo Japan: The Artist and the City 1615–1868.* New Haven, CT: Yale University Press, 2010.

Halttunen, Karen. *Confidence Men and Painted Women: A Study of Middle-Class Culture in America 1830–1870.* New Haven, CT: Yale University Press, 1982.

Hamilton, Sinclair. *Early American Book Illustrators and Wood Engravers.* Vol. 1. 2 vols. Princeton: Princeton University Press, 1968.

Hancock, La Touche. "American Caricature and Comic Art Part I." *The Bookman* 16 (October 1902): 120–31.

Hart, Merriam. *A Review of the Birds of Connecticut.* New Haven, CT: Tuttle, Morehouse, and Taylor, 1877.

Hartford Daily Courant, December 22, 1874.

Harvey, Robert C. *The Art of the Funnies: An Aesthetic History.* Jackson: University Press of Mississippi, 1994.

Hatfield, Charles. *Alternative Comics: An Emerging Literature.* Jackson: University Press of Mississippi, 2005.

Hayward, Nathan. *College Scenes.* Cambridge, MA: N. Hayward, 1850.

"He Licks Her (Elixir) of Life." In *Ellton's Comic All-My-Nack 1839.* New York: Ellton, 1838.

"The Heart-Rending Calamity Which Befel Mr. Dewdrop While Dressing for a Ball." *Yankee Notions,* March 1860.

Hedges, Chris, and Joe Sacco. *Days of Destruction, Days of Revolt.* New York: Nation Books, 2012.

Heidegger, Martin. "The Origin of the Work of Art." In *Martin Heidegger, Basic Writings,* edited by David Farrell, 139–206. San Francisco: HarperSanFrancisco, 1993.

"Here Is a Curious Thing!!" *Brother Jonathan,* September 17, 1842.

Higginson, Thomas Wentworth. *The Writings of Thomas Wentworth Higginson.* Vol. 3. Cambridge: Riverside Press, 1900.

Hodge, Francis. *Yankee Theatre: The Image of America on the Stage, 1825–1850.* Austin: University of Texas Press, 1964.

Hogarth, William. *Southwark Fair.* 1734. Print, 16 1/4 × 21 7/16 in. Metropolitan Museum of Art. https://www.metmuseum.org/art/collection/search/400729.

Holmes, Oliver Wendell. *The Autocrat of the Breakfast Table.* Boston: Phillips, Sampson and Company, 1858.

"Hoops Convenient Sometimes." *Comic Monthly,* May 1, 1859.

Hopkins, Livingston. "The First Cigar." *Wild Oats,* June 6, 1872.

———. "Out of the Frying Pan and into the Fire: Or an Adventure with a Jersey Mosquito." *Wild Oats,* August 29, 1872.

———. "Professor Tigwissil's Trip up the Nile." *Jolly Joker,* September 1876.

———. "A Romance As Is a Romance, or a Story without Words." *Wild Oats,* March 14, 1872.

———. "Shakespeare Illustrated." *Wild Oats,* October 24, 1872.

———. "Shakespeare Illustrated." *Wild Oats,* November 7, 1872.

———. "Shakespeare Illustrated." *Wild Oats,* December 5, 1872.

———. "Shakespeare Illustrated." *Wild Oats,* December 19, 1872.

Hoppin, Augustus. *Crossing the Atlantic.* Boston: J. R. Osgood & Company, 1872.

———. *Hay Fever.* Boston: J. R. Osgood & Company, 1873.

———. "Jonathan Abroad." *Yankee Notions,* September 1854.

———. "Jonathan Abroad." *Yankee Notions,* December 1854.

———. *On the Nile.* Boston: J. R. Osgood & Company, 1874.

———. "To Be Let." *Manufacturers' and Farmers' Journal,* August 9, 1852.

———. "Travel Sketches." American Antiquarian Society, Worcester, Massachusetts, ca. 1854. American Antiquarian Society Drawings Collection Box 39. Drawings Collection.

———. "A Trip to Niagara Falls." *Harper's Weekly Magazine,* October 2, 1858.

———. "A Trip to the White Mountains." *Harper's Weekly Magazine,* August 22, 1857.

———. *Ups and Downs on Land and Water.* Boston: James R. Osgood & Company, 1871.

"How Our Artists Travel." *Leslie's Budget of Fun,* May 1872.

Howard, Justin H. "A Dark Suspicion." *Yankee Notions,* December 1855.

———. "Miss Wiggins' Physiognomic Experiments." *Yankee Notions,* August 1865.

———. *Naughty Girl's & Boy's Magic Transformations.* New York: McLoughlin Brothers, 1882.

Howells, William Dean. *Their Wedding Journey.* Boston: James R. Osgood and Company, 1872.

Hughes, Bethany. "The Indispensable Indian: Edwin Forrest, Pushmataha, and Metamora." *Theatre Survey* 59, no. 1 (January 2018): 23–44.

"Humorous Police Reports." *Brother Jonathan,* January 1, 1857.

The Hunting Adventures and Exploits of Peter Piper in Bengal. New York: Brother Jonathan Press, 1856.

"In and Out-Door Sights about New York." *Brother Jonathan Pictorial.* January 1, 1857.

"Income of Editors." *Examiner,* June 12, 1867.

Inge, Thomas M. "Origins of Early Comics and Proto-Comics." In *Routledge Companion to Comics,* edited by Frank Bramlett, Roy T. Cook, and Aaron Meskin. New York: Routledge, 2016.

Irving, Washington. *The Sketchbook of Geoffrey Crayon.* Oxford; New York: Oxford University Press, 2009.

"It Is So Easy to Overdo a Good Thing." *Sacramento Daily Union,* December 2, 1871.

Johnston, David Claypoole. "The Johnstonian System." *Nantuckett Inquirer,* December 17, 1836.

Jones, Douglas A. "American; or, The Emergence of Audiences and Their Blackface Salve." *J19: The Journal of Nineteenth Century Americanists* 6, no. 2 (Fall 2018): 403–9.

———. *The Captive Stage: Performance and the Proslavery Imagination of the Antebellum North.* Ann Arbor: University of Michigan Press, 2014.

"Jones (to himself)." *Nick Nax for All Creation,* March 1869.

King, Ethel M. *Darley, the Most Popular Illustrator of His Time.* Brooklyn: T. Gaus' Sons, 1964.

Kunzle, David, ed. *Cham: The Best Comic Strips and Graphic Novelettes, 1839–1862.* Jackson: University Press of Mississippi, 2019.

———. *Father of the Comic Strip: Rodolphe Töpffer.* Jackson: University of Mississippi Press, 2007.

———, ed. *Gustave Doré: Twelve Comic Strips.* Jackson: University Press of Mississippi, 2015.

———. *The History of the Comic Strip, Volume 1: The Early Comic Strip; Narrative Strips and Picture Stories in the European Broadsheet from c.1450 to 1825.* Berkeley: University of California Press, 1973.

———. *The History of the Comic Strip, Volume 2: The Nineteenth Century.* Berkeley: University of California Press, 1990.

———. "Precursors in American Weeklies to the American Newspaper Comic Strip: A Long Gestation and a Transoceanic Cross-Breeding." In *Forging a New Medium: The Comic Strip in the Nineteenth Century,* edited by Pascal Lefevre and Charles Dierick, 159–85. Brussels: VUB University Press, 1998.

———, ed. *Rebirth of the English Comic Strip: A Kaleidoscope, 1847–1870.* Jackson: University Press of Mississippi, 2021.

———, ed. *Rodolphe Töpffer: The Complete Comic Strips.* Jackson: University of Mississippi Press, 2007.

Kuper, Peter. *Diario de Oaxaca Mexico.* Oakland, CA: PM Press, 2017.

Larkin, Jack. "What He Did for Love: David Claypoole Johnston and the Boston Irish, 1825–1865." *Commonplace: The Journal of Early American Life* 13, no. 3 (Spring 2013). http://commonplace.online/article/what-he-did-for-love/.

Lauster, Martina. *Sketches of the Nineteenth Century: European Journalism and Its Physiologies 1830–50.* New York: Palgrave Macmillan, 2014.

Lefevre, Pascal, and Charles Dierick, eds. *Forging a New Medium: The Comic Strip in the Nineteenth Century.* Brussels: VUB University Press, 1998.

Lehuu, Isabelle. *Carnival on the Page: Popular Print Media in Antebellum America.* Chapel Hill: University of North Carolina Press, 2000.

Leitch, Stephanie. "Visual Images in Travel Writing." In *The Cambridge History of Travel Writing,* edited by Nandini Das and Tim Youngs, 456–73. Cambridge: Cambridge University Press, 2019.

Leslie, Frank. "Frank Leslie to His Readers." *Leslie's Budget of Fun,* May 1859.

Levin, Joanna. *Bohemia in America.* Stanford: Stanford University Press, 2009.

Levine, Lawrence. *Highbrow/Lowbrow: The Emergence of Cultural Hierarchy in America.* Cambridge, MA: Harvard University Press, 1990.

"A Little Too Much." *Daily Inter Ocean,* December 5, 1871.

"Local Items—Turning Over a New Leaf." *Philadelphia Inquirer,* August 27, 1856.

"Local Matters—Whipple's Dissolving Views." *Manchester Daily Mirror,* August 23, 1851.

Lossing, Benjamin. *History of New York Embracing an Outline Sketch of Events from 1609 to 1830, and a Full Account of Its Development from 1830 to 1884.* New York: Perine Engraving and Publishing Company, 1884.

Lott, Eric. *Love and Theft: Blackface Minstrelsy and the American Working Class.* Race and American Culture. Oxford: Oxford University Press, 2013.

"Madame Rallings, French Millinery." *Nick Nax for All Creation,* February 1867.

Maresca, Peter, ed. *Society Is Nix: Gleeful Anarchy at the Dawn of the American Comic Strip, 1895–1915.* Palo Alto, CA: Sunday Press Books, 2013.

Martin, Justin. *Rebel Souls: Walt Whitman and America's First Bohemians.* Cambridge, MA: Da Capo Press, 2015.

Marvin, Carolyn. *When Old Technologies Were New: Thinking about Electric Communication in the Late Nineteenth Century.* New York: Oxford University Press, 1988.

"Masquerading." *Nick Nax for All Creation,* April 1865.

"Masquerading." *Nick Nax for All Creation,* March 1869.

Mathews, Cornelius. *Pen and Ink Panorama of New York City.* New York: John S. Taylor, 1853.

Mayer, David. "Encountering Melodrama." In *The Cambridge Companion to Victorian and Edwardian Theatre,* edited by Kerry Powell. Cambridge Companions to Literature. Cambridge: Cambridge University Press, 2004.

McCloud, Scott. *Understanding Comics: The Invisible Art.* New York: Harper Perennial, 1993.

McLenan, John. "The First Segar." *Yankee Notions,* March 1856.

———. "A Hint to Ladies Who Wish to Combine Usefulness with Fashionable Elegance." *Young America,* December 1855.

———. "The Lonely Pollywog of the Mill Pond." *Yankee Notions,* January 1856.

———. "Mr. Elephant and Mrs. Potiphar's Grand Soiree." *Harper's New Monthly Magazine,* October 1858.

———. "Mr. Slim's Aquatic Experience." *Harper's New Monthly Magazine,* August 1855.

———. "Mr. Slim's Experience at Sea." *Harper's New Monthly Magazine,* September 1855.

———. "Mr. Slim's Piscatorial Experience." *Harper's New Monthly Magazine,* August 1855.

———. "Mr. Toodles' Adventures in the West." *Brother Jonathan Pictorial,* July 4, 1857.

———. "Mr. Toodles Goes to the East Indies in Search of Excitement." *Brother Jonathan Pictorial,* January 1, 1857.

———. "Our Artist, His Adventures in Pursuit of a Sketch of That Statue." *Yankee Notions,* September 1853.

———. *Sad Tale of the Courtship of Chevalier Slyfox-Wikof, Showing His Heart-Rending Astounding & Most Wonderful Love Adventures with Fanny Elssler and Miss Gambol.* New York: Garrett & Company, 1855.

———. "Study of the Stars: Police Astronomy." *Yankee Notions,* January 1, 1853.

———. "Three Tableaux in the Life of a Broadway Swell." *Yankee Notions,* July 1857.

McLenan, John, Frank Bellew, and C.S. "Comicalities Page." *Harper's Weekly Magazine,* October 16, 1858.

Mellier, Denis. "The Origins of Adult Graphic Narratives." In *The Cambridge History of the Graphic Novel,* edited by Jan Baetens, Hugo Frey, and Stephen Ely Tabachnick, 21–38. Cambridge: Cambridge University Press, 2018.

Melton, Jeffrey Alan. *Mark Twain, Travel Books, and Tourism: The Tide of a Great Popular Movement.* Tuscaloosa: University of Alabama Press, 2002.

Meyer, Christina. *Producing Mass Entertainment: The Serial Life of the Yellow Kid.* Columbus: The Ohio State University Press, 2019.

Michelson, Bruce. *Printer's Devil: Mark Twain and the American Publishing Revolution.* Berkeley: University of California Press, 2006.

Micklewright, Nancy. *A Victorian Traveler in the Middle East: The Photography and Travel Writing of Annie Lady Brassey.* London: Taylor and Francis, 2017.

Miller, Angela L. "The Panorama, the Cinema and the Emergence of the Spectacular." *Wide Angle* 18, no. 2 (1996): 34–59.

Mitman, Gregg. "Hay Fever Holiday: Health, Leisure, and Place in Gilded-Age America." *Bulletin of the History of Medicine* 77, no. 3 (2003): 600–635.

Molotiu, Andrei. "List of Terms for Comics Studies." *Comics Forum* (blog), July 26, 2013. https://comicsforum.org/2013/07/26/list-of-terms-for-comics-studies-by-andrei-molotiu/.

"The Mosquito Guard." *Frank Leslie's Budget of Fun,* September 1876.

Mowatt, Anna Cora. *Fashion; or Life in New York.* London: W. Newberry, 1850.

"Mr. Augustus Hoppin." *Boston Weekly Messenger,* April 27, 1859.

"Mr. Bear (Soliloquizing)." *Nick Nax for All Creation,* December 1863.

"Mr. Meek Concludes to Go to the Camp Meeting." *Yankee Notions,* 1860.

"Mr. Spinks' Adventures on the Trial Trip of the Steamer Earthquake." *Yankee Notions,* July 1855.

"Mr. Tourist's Experience of the Jersey Mosquitoes." *Yankee Notions,* October 1860.

"Mrs. C. Sinclair." *Old Soldier,* March 1, 1852.

My Own ABC of Quadrupeds. New York: T. W. Strong, 1842.

Ndalianis, Angela. "Why Comics Studies?" *Cinema Journal* 50, no. 3 (Spring 2011): 113–14.

Neal, Joseph C. *Charcoal Sketches; or, Scenes in a Metropolis.* Philadelphia: E. L. Carey and A. Hart, 1838.

"New Publications—The Wonderful and Amusing Doings by Sea and Land, of Oscar Shanghai." *Richmond Whig,* May 22, 1855.

"A New Sketch-Book by Augustus Hoppin." *Evening Post,* December 6, 1871.

Newgarden, Mark, and Paul Karasik. *How to Read Nancy: The Elements of Comics in Three Easy Panels.* Seattle, WA: Fantagraphics Books, 2017.

Ngai, Sianne. *Our Aesthetic Categories: Zany, Cute, Interesting.* Cambridge, MA: Harvard University Press, 2015.

Nickels, Cameron. "Yankee Notions." In *American Humor Magazines and Comic Periodicals,* edited by David E. E. Sloane, 324–25. Westport, CT: Greenwood Press, 1987.

"Nick-Nax." *Nick Nax for All Creation,* May 1857.

Noonan, Mark J. "Printscape." *American Periodicals* 30, no. 1 (2020): 9–11.

"Notice to Rebus Solvers." *Nick Nax for All Creation,* February 1867.

Nunes, Jadviga M. Da Costa. "The Naughty Child in Nineteenth-Century American Art." *Journal of American Studies* 21, no. 2 (1987): 225–47.

"Obadiah Oldbuck Again on Horseback." *Commercial Advertiser,* February 8, 1845.

"Omnibus Gymnastics." *Leslie's Budget of Fun,* October 1, 1859.

"One More Chance for American Art." *New York Tribune,* July 18, 1887.

Opper, Frederick Burr. "Comics and Cartoons of Earlier Days." Unpublished Manuscript, ca. 1933. Frederick Burr Opper Collect, box 1, folder 1. Howard Gotlieb Research Center at Boston University.

"Our Artist in Search of the Bald Mountain Volcano." *Daily Graphic,* March 27, 1874.

Outcault, Richard F. "Buster Brown Has a Birthday Party." *New York Herald—Comic Section,* October 19, 1902. San Francisco Academy of Comic Art Collection, The Ohio State University, Billy Ireland Cartoon Library and Museum.

———. "Hogan's Alley Folk Have a Trolley Party in Brooklyn." *New York World—Colored Supplement,* August 9, 1896. San Francisco Academy of Comic Art Collection, The Ohio State University, Billy Ireland Cartoon Library and Museum.

Paine, Alfred Bigelow. *Thomas Nast: His Period and His Pictures.* New York: Macmillan, 1904.

Pedri, Nancy. *A Concise Dictionary of Comics.* Jackson: University Press of Mississippi, 2022.

Peeters, Benoît. *La bande dessinée entre la presse et le livre: fragments d'une histoire.* Paris: Bibliothèque nationale de France, 2019.

Perk, Abner. *Merry Maple Leaves, or A Summer in the Country.* New York: E. P. Dutton and Company, 1872.

Peters, William Thompson, Hugh Florien Peters, Garrick Mallery, and James Morris Whiton. *The College Experience of Ichabod Academicus.* United States, 1849.

Petersen, Robert. "The Ineffable Image inside the Comics of Lynda Barry." *Comics Journal,* October 12, 2022. https://www.tcj.com/the-ineffable-image-inside-the-comics-of-lynda-barry/.

"Preface to Volume I." *Yankee Doodle,* January 1846.

Punch, August 1, 1841.

"A 'Rage' of the Day—Sale of Curious Cents." *Charleston Courier,* November 9, 1858.

Ramsay, Stephen. *Reading Machines: Toward an Algorithmic Criticism.* Urbana, Chicago, and Springfield: University of Illinois Press, 2011.

Read, James Alexander, and Donald F Read. *Journey to the Gold Diggins.* New York: Stringer & Townsend, 1849.

Rede, Leman Thomas. *The Road to the Stage.* London: Joseph Smith, 1827.

Reilly, Bernard. "Comic Drawing in New York in the 1850s." In *Prints and Printmakers of New York State, 1825–1940,* edited by David Tatham, 147–62. Syracuse: Syracuse University Press, 1986.

Reynolds, David. *Beneath the American Renaissance: The Subversive Imagination in the Age of Emerson and Melville.* New York: Alfred A. Knopf, 1988.

Rinear, David L. *Stage, Page, Scandals, and Vandals: William E. Burton and Nineteenth-Century American Theatre.* Carbondale: Southern Illinois University Press, 2004.

Robb, Jenny E. "Bill Blackbeard: The Collector Who Rescued the Comics." *Journal of American Culture* 32, no. 3 (2009): 244–56.

Rourke, Constance. *American Humor: A Study of the National Character.* New York: Harcourt, Brace, and Company, 1931.

Sacco, Joe. *Palestine.* Seattle: Fantagraphics Books, 2001.

Saguisag, Lara. *Incorrigibles and Innocents: Constructing Childhood and Citizenship in Progressive Era Comics.* New Brunswick, NJ: Rutgers University Press, 2019.

Salazar, James B. *Bodies of Reform: The Rhetoric of Character in Gilded Age America.* New York: New York University Press, 2010.

"Saratoga." *Nick Nax for All Creation,* September 1863.

Savoy, Eric. "The Subverted Gaze: Hawthorne, Howells, James and the Discourse of Travel." *Canadian Review of American Studies* 21, no. 3 (1990): 287.

Schiff, Judith Ann. "Ichabod's Progress." *Yale Alumni Magazine,* February 2005. http://archives.yalealumnimagazine.com/issues/2005_01/old_yale.html.

Schivelbusch, Wolfgang. *The Railway Journey: The Industrialization of Time and Space in the Nineteenth Century.* Berkeley: University of California Press, 1986.

Schmitz, Matthew S. *The Sure Water Cure.* Philadelphia: Carey & Hart, 1840.

"Scraps, No. 6, for 1835." *Boston Daily Advertiser,* December 18, 1834.

Sears, John F. *Sacred Places: American Tourist Attractions in the Nineteenth Century.* Amherst: University of Massachusetts Press, 1998.

Seymour, Bruce. *Lola Montez: A Life.* New Haven, CT: Yale University Press, 1998.

"Shadows over the Way." *Harper's New Monthly Magazine,* January 1860.

"Sketches of the Publishers." *The Round Table,* April 14, 1866.

Sloane, David, ed. *American Humor Magazines and Comic Periodicals.* Westport, CT: Greenwood Press, 1987.

Sloane, David E. E. "A Study in the Humor of the Old Northeast: Joseph C. Neal's Charcoal Sketches and the Comic Urban Frontier." *Studies in American Humor* 3, no. 2 (2017): 178–203.

Smith, Solomon. *The Theatrical Apprenticeship and Anecdotical Recollections of Sol. Smith.* Philadelphia: Carey and Hart, 1846.

Smolderen, Thierry. "Comics before Comics: Early Cartoons, Picture-Stories, and the International Roots of the American Comic Strip." In *Society Is Nix: Gleeful Anarchy of the Dawn of the American Comic Strip 1895–1915,* edited by Peter Maresca, 6–8. Palo Alto, CA: Sunday Press Books, 2013.

———. *The Origins of Comics from William Hogarth to Winsor McCay.* Translated by Bart Beaty and Nick Nguyen. Jackson: University of Mississippi Press, 2013.

Sousanis, Nick. "The Shape of Our Thoughts: A Meditation on & in Comics." *Visual Arts Research* 38, no. 1 (2012): 1.

Stafford, Barbara Maria. *Voyage into Substance: Art, Science, Nature, and the Illustrated Travel Account, 1760–1840.* Cambridge: MIT Press, 1984.

"The Steel Hoops." *Nick Nax for All Creation,* December 1856.

Stephens, Henry Louis. "How the Boys Take It." *Vanity Fair,* August 11, 1860.

———. "Incident for a Book of American Travel." *Vanity Fair,* August 11, 1860.

———. "Plenty of Room for One More." *Vanity Fair,* March 16, 1861.

———. *Punchinello,* April 2, 1870.

———. "What Else Could They Be." *Vanity Fair,* July 14, 1860.

"The Strange and Wonderful Adventures of Bachelor Butterfly." *The Sun,* February 26, 1846.

Stoeffel, Caroline. Interview with the author, May 2021.

Strong, Thomas W. "Beloved and Honored Reader." *Yankee Notions,* January 1852.

———. "Introduction." *Yankee Notions,* January 1855.

———. "Preface to Volume 10." *Yankee Notions,* January 1861.

———. "Preface to Volume 13." *Yankee Notions,* January 1864.

———. "Strong's Publishing Warehouse, 98 Nassau, between Ann & Fulton Streets." In *Strong's American Almanac for 1848.* New York: T. W. Strong, 1848.

Taylor, David Francis. *The Politics of Parody: A Literary History of Caricature, 1760–1830.* New Haven, CT: Yale University Press, 2018.

Teukolsky, Rachel. *Picture World: Image, Aesthetics, and Victorian New Media.* Oxford: Oxford University Press, 2020.

Thomas, Evan. "A Renaissance for Comics Studies: Early English Prints and the Comics Canon." *Partial Answers: Journal of Literature and the History of Ideas* 13, no. 2 (2015): 255–66.

Thompson, Carl. "Nineteenth-Century Travel Writing." In *The Cambridge History of Travel Writing,* edited by Nandini Das and Tim Youngs, 108–24. Cambridge: Cambridge University Press, 2019.

Thompson, Craig. *Carnet de Voyage.* Marietta, GA: Top Shelf Productions, 2006.

Thon, Jan-Noël. "Who's Telling the Tale? Authors and Narrators in Graphic Narrative." In *From Comic Strips to Graphic Novels: Contributions to the Theory and History of Graphic Narrative,* edited by Daniel Stein and Jan-Noël Thon, 67–99. Narratologia. Berlin: De Gruyter, 2013.

Thoreau, Henry David. "Journal of Henry David Thoreau." Concord, MA, October 19, 1855. https://thoreau.library.ucsb.edu/writings_journals_pdfs/TMS19newTR.pdf.

"Those Who Have Read the Adventures of Mr. Obadiah Oldbuck." *The Capital,* June 7, 1874.

Tomc, Sandra. *Fashion Nation: Picturing the United States in the Long Nineteenth Century.* Ann Arbor: University of Michigan Press, 2021.

Töpffer, Rodolphe. "The Adventures of Mr. Obadiah Oldbuck." *Brother Jonathan Extra,* January 1, 1842.

———. *The Adventures of Mr. Obadiah Oldbuck.* New York: Wilson & Company, 1844.

———. "Histoire de M. Cryptogame." *L'Illustration: Journal Universel,* February 15, 1845.

———. "Monsieur Jabot." In *Rodolphe Töpffer: The Complete Comic Strips,* edited by David Kunzle, 5–57. Jackson: University Press of Mississippi, 2007.

———. *The Strange Adventures of Bachelor Butterfly.* New York: Wilson & Company, 1846.

"Travels of Our Artist in England." *Comic Monthly,* June 1861.

"Trials of a Man with a Gold Watch." *Comic Monthly,* April 1859.

"Trials of a Man with a Gold Watch." *Nick Nax for All Creation,* June 1857.

"Trip to California." *Diogenes Hys Lantern,* February 12, 1853.

Twain, Mark. *The Innocents Abroad, or, The New Pilgrim's Progress.* Hartford, CT: American Pub. Co., 1869.

Twain, Mark, and Charles Dudley Warner. *The Gilded Age: A Tale of to-Day.* Hartford, CT: American Publishing Company, 1873.

Underhill, Edward Fitch, and Q. K. Philander Doesticks. *The History and Records of the Elephant Club.* Philadelphia: T. B. Peterson, 1856.

"An Unromantic View of Egypt." *Cincinnati Daily Gazette,* August 12, 1873.

"Untitled Comic about Mr. Brown's Travels." *New York Picayune,* 1853.

"View on the Sixth Avenue by Hinkedeinkyahahandohrowlybowly." *Comic Monthly,* February 1862.

Walkiewicz, Alice. "The Humor of Circumstance: Caricature and the Foreign Tour of the British Middle Class." In *Artistic Responses to Travel in the Western Tradition,* edited by Sarah Lippert, 29–47. London: Routledge, 2018.

Waugh, Coulton. *The Comics.* Jackson: University Press of Mississippi, 1991.

"The Wayes of the Singer." *Nick Nax for All Creation,* December 1856.

Wechsler, Judith. *A Human Comedy: Physiognomy and Caricature in 19th Century Paris.* Chicago: University of Chicago Press, 1982.

Weitenkampf, Frank. "Frank Henry Temple Bellew." In *Dictionary of American Biography,* edited by Al Johnson, 165–66. New York: Charles Scribner's Sons, 1929. http://galenet.galegroup.com/servlet/BioRC.

West, Richard Samuel. "A Britisher among the B'Hoys: Thomas Butler Gunn and His Forgotten Comic Gem." *Imprint Journal of the American Print Collectors Society* 35, no. 11 (Autumn 2010): 16–29.

———. *T. W. Strong: Pioneer Publisher of the Pictorial Paper.* Northampton: Periodyssey Press, 2009.

———. "Wild Oats (1870–81)—Edited by George Small, Aka Bricktop." *Yesterday's Papers,* June 29, 2012. http://john-adcock.blogspot.com/2012/06/wild-oats-1870-1881.html.

West, Richard Samuel, and Michael Alexander Kahn. *Puck: What Fools These Mortals Be!* San Diego: Idea & Design Works, 2014.

Whitman, Walt. "Preface 1855—Leaves of Grass." In *Leaves of Grass and Other Writings: Authoritative Texts, Other Poetry and Prose, Criticism,* edited by Michael Moon, Sculley Bradley, and Harold William Blodgett, 616–36. New York: Norton, 2002.

Willems, Philippe. "This Strangest of Narrative Forms: Rodolphe Töpffer's Sequential Art." *Mosaic* 41, no. 2 (2008): 127–38.

Winter, William. *Old Friends; Being Literary Recollections of Other Days.* New York: Moffat, Yard and Company, 1909.

"Witticisms of the Masquerade." *Nick Nax for All Creation,* March 1866.

Wolfe, Toler. *A Book of Odds and Ends.* Winchester: Toler Wolfe, Republican Official, 1852.

"The Wonderful! and Soul Thrilling Adventures of Anarcharsis H. Brown ESQ" (Part I). *New York Picayune,* August 13, 1853.

"The Wonderful! and Soul Thrilling Adventures of Anarcharsis H. Brown ESQ" (Part II). *New York Picayune,* October 22, 1853.

"The Wonderful Hunting Tour of Mr. Borridge after the Deer." *Leslie's Budget of Fun,* June 1859.

Worth, Thomas. "Female Freemasons—The Mysteries of the Eastern Star Exposed." *Wild Oats,* February 20, 1872.

———. "The Great National Game of Baseball." *Wild Oats,* August 1, 1872.

———. "Horse Racing—A Few Scenes in the Life of a Turf Man." *Wild Oats,* September 12, 1872.

———. "Mr. and Mrs. Thumper's Experience in a Sleeping Car." *Wild Oats,* November 21, 1872.

———. "Scenes and Incidents of the Life of a New York Yachtsman." *Wild Oats,* October 24, 1872.

———. "The Boating Mania, The Haps and Mishaps." *Wild Oats,* July 18, 1872.

Young, David, and Thomas W. Strong. *The Tragic Almanac.* New York: T. W. Strong, 1843.

INDEX

STUDIES IN COMICS AND CARTOONS
Jared Gardner, Charles Hatfield, and Rebecca Wanzo, Series Editors
Lucy Shelton Caswell, Founding Editor Emerita

Books published in Studies in Comics and Cartoons focus exclusively on comics and graphic literature, highlighting their relation to literary studies. The series includes monographs and edited collections that cover the history of comics and cartoons from the editorial cartoon and early sequential comics of the nineteenth century through webcomics of the twenty-first. Studies that focus on international comics are also considered.

Printed in the USA
CPSIA information can be obtained
at www.ICGtesting.com
LVHW060100170924
791250LV00005B/21

9 780814 258965